Comparative Literature: A Very Short Introduction

VERY SHORT INTRODUCTIONS are for anyone wanting a stimulating and accessible way into a new subject. They are written by experts, and have been translated into more than 45 different languages.

The series began in 1995, and now covers a wide variety of topics in every discipline. The VSI library currently contains over 550 volumes—a Very Short Introduction to everything from Psychology and Philosophy of Science to American History and Relativity—and continues to grow in every subject area.

Very Short Introductions available now:

ACCOUNTING Christopher Nobes
ADOLESCENCE Peter K. Smith
ADVERTISING Winston Fletcher
AFRICAN AMERICAN RELIGION Eddie S. Glaude Jr
AFRICAN HISTORY John Parker and Richard Rathbone
AFRICAN RELIGIONS Jacob K. Olupona
AGEING Nancy A. Pachana
AGNOSTICISM Robin Le Poidevin
AGRICULTURE Paul Brassley and Richard Soffe
ALEXANDER THE GREAT Hugh Bowden
ALGEBRA Peter M. Higgins
AMERICAN HISTORY Paul S. Boyer
AMERICAN IMMIGRATION David A. Gerber
AMERICAN LEGAL HISTORY G. Edward White
AMERICAN POLITICAL HISTORY Donald Critchlow
AMERICAN POLITICAL PARTIES AND ELECTIONS L. Sandy Maisel
AMERICAN POLITICS Richard M. Valelly
THE AMERICAN PRESIDENCY Charles O. Jones
THE AMERICAN REVOLUTION Robert J. Allison
AMERICAN SLAVERY Heather Andrea Williams
THE AMERICAN WEST Stephen Aron
AMERICAN WOMEN'S HISTORY Susan Ware
ANAESTHESIA Aidan O'Donnell
ANALYTIC PHILOSOPHY Michael Beaney
ANARCHISM Colin Ward
ANCIENT ASSYRIA Karen Radner
ANCIENT EGYPT Ian Shaw
ANCIENT EGYPTIAN ART AND ARCHITECTURE Christina Riggs
ANCIENT GREECE Paul Cartledge
THE ANCIENT NEAR EAST Amanda H. Podany
ANCIENT PHILOSOPHY Julia Annas
ANCIENT WARFARE Harry Sidebottom
ANGELS David Albert Jones
ANGLICANISM Mark Chapman
THE ANGLO-SAXON AGE John Blair
ANIMAL BEHAVIOUR Tristram D. Wyatt
THE ANIMAL KINGDOM Peter Holland
ANIMAL RIGHTS David DeGrazia
THE ANTARCTIC Klaus Dodds
ANTISEMITISM Steven Beller
ANXIETY Daniel Freeman and Jason Freeman
APPLIED MATHEMATICS Alain Goriely
THE APOCRYPHAL GOSPELS Paul Foster
ARCHAEOLOGY Paul Bahn
ARCHITECTURE Andrew Ballantyne

ONLINE CATALOGUE

A Very Short Introduction

Our online catalogue is designed to make it easy to find your ideal Very Short Introduction. View the entire collection by subject area, watch author videos, read sample chapters, and download reading guides.

http://fds.oup.com/www.oup.co.uk/general/vsi/index.html

FEMINISM Margaret Walters
FILM Michael Wood
FILM MUSIC Kathryn Kalinak
THE FIRST WORLD WAR
Michael Howard
FOLK MUSIC Mark Slobin
FOOD John Krebs
FORENSIC PSYCHOLOGY David Canter
FORENSIC SCIENCE Jim Fraser
FORESTS Jaboury Ghazoul
FOSSILS Keith Thomson
FOUCAULT Gary Gutting
THE FOUNDING FATHERS
R. B. Bernstein
FRACTALS Kenneth Falconer
FREE SPEECH Nigel Warburton
FREE WILL Thomas Pink
FREEMASONRY Andreas Önnerfors
FRENCH LITERATURE
John D. Lyons
THE FRENCH REVOLUTION
William Doyle
FREUD Anthony Storr
FUNDAMENTALISM Malise Ruthven
FUNGI Nicholas P. Money
THE FUTURE Jennifer M. Gidley
GALAXIES John Gribbin
GALILEO Stillman Drake
GAME THEORY Ken Binmore
GANDHI Bhikhu Parekh
GENES Jonathan Slack
GENIUS Andrew Robinson
GEOGRAPHY John Matthews and
David Herbert
GEOPOLITICS Klaus Dodds
GERMAN LITERATURE Nicholas Boyle
GERMAN PHILOSOPHY
Andrew Bowie
GLOBAL CATASTROPHES Bill McGuire
GLOBAL ECONOMIC HISTORY
Robert C. Allen
GLOBALIZATION Manfred Steger
GOD John Bowker
GOETHE Ritchie Robertson
THE GOTHIC Nick Groom
GOVERNANCE Mark Bevir
GRAVITY Timothy Clifton
THE GREAT DEPRESSION AND THE
NEW DEAL Eric Rauchway
HABERMAS James Gordon Finlayson
THE HABSBURG EMPIRE Martyn Rady
HAPPINESS Daniel M. Haybron
THE HARLEM RENAISSANCE
Cheryl A. Wall
THE HEBREW BIBLE AS LITERATURE
Tod Linafelt
HEGEL Peter Singer
HEIDEGGER Michael Inwood
THE HELLENISTIC AGE
Peter Thonemann
HEREDITY John Waller
HERMENEUTICS Jens Zimmermann
HERODOTUS Jennifer T. Roberts
HIEROGLYPHS Penelope Wilson
HINDUISM Kim Knott
HISTORY John H. Arnold
THE HISTORY OF
ASTRONOMY Michael Hoskin
THE HISTORY OF
CHEMISTRY William H. Brock
THE HISTORY OF CINEMA
Geoffrey Nowell-Smith
THE HISTORY OF LIFE Michael Benton
THE HISTORY OF
MATHEMATICS Jacqueline Stedall
THE HISTORY OF
MEDICINE William Bynum
THE HISTORY OF PHYSICS
J. L. Heilbron
THE HISTORY OF TIME
Leofranc Holford-Strevens
HIV AND AIDS Alan Whiteside
HOBBES Richard Tuck
HOLLYWOOD Peter Decherney
HOME Michael Allen Fox
HORMONES Martin Luck
HUMAN ANATOMY Leslie Klenerman
HUMAN EVOLUTION Bernard Wood
HUMAN RIGHTS Andrew Clapham
HUMANISM Stephen Law
HUME A. J. Ayer
HUMOUR Noël Carroll
THE ICE AGE Jamie Woodward
IDEOLOGY Michael Freeden
THE IMMUNE SYSTEM
Paul Klenerman
INDIAN CINEMA Ashish Rajadhyaksha
INDIAN PHILOSOPHY Sue Hamilton
THE INDUSTRIAL REVOLUTION
Robert C. Allen

INFECTIOUS DISEASE Marta L. Wayne and Benjamin M. Bolker
INFINITY Ian Stewart
INFORMATION Luciano Floridi
INNOVATION Mark Dodgson and David Gann
INTELLIGENCE Ian J. Deary
INTELLECTUAL PROPERTY Siva Vaidhyanathan
INTERNATIONAL LAW Vaughan Lowe
INTERNATIONAL MIGRATION Khalid Koser
INTERNATIONAL RELATIONS Paul Wilkinson
INTERNATIONAL SECURITY Christopher S. Browning
IRAN Ali M. Ansari
ISLAM Malise Ruthven
ISLAMIC HISTORY Adam Silverstein
ISOTOPES Rob Ellam
ITALIAN LITERATURE Peter Hainsworth and David Robey
JESUS Richard Bauckham
JEWISH HISTORY David N. Myers
JOURNALISM Ian Hargreaves
JUDAISM Norman Solomon
JUNG Anthony Stevens
KABBALAH Joseph Dan
KAFKA Ritchie Robertson
KANT Roger Scruton
KEYNES Robert Skidelsky
KIERKEGAARD Patrick Gardiner
KNOWLEDGE Jennifer Nagel
THE KORAN Michael Cook
LAKES Warwick F. Vincent
LANDSCAPE ARCHITECTURE Ian H. Thompson
LANDSCAPES AND GEOMORPHOLOGY Andrew Goudie and Heather Viles
LANGUAGES Stephen R. Anderson
LATE ANTIQUITY Gillian Clark
LAW Raymond Wacks
THE LAWS OF THERMODYNAMICS Peter Atkins
LEADERSHIP Keith Grint
LEARNING Mark Haselgrove
LEIBNIZ Maria Rosa Antognazza
LIBERALISM Michael Freeden
LIGHT Ian Walmsley
LINCOLN Allen C. Guelzo
LINGUISTICS Peter Matthews
LITERARY THEORY Jonathan Culler
LOCKE John Dunn
LOGIC Graham Priest
LOVE Ronald de Sousa
MACHIAVELLI Quentin Skinner
MADNESS Andrew Scull
MAGIC Owen Davies
MAGNA CARTA Nicholas Vincent
MAGNETISM Stephen Blundell
MALTHUS Donald Winch
MAMMALS T. S. Kemp
MANAGEMENT John Hendry
MAO Delia Davin
MARINE BIOLOGY Philip V. Mladenov
THE MARQUIS DE SADE John Phillips
MARTIN LUTHER Scott H. Hendrix
MARTYRDOM Jolyon Mitchell
MARX Peter Singer
MATERIALS Christopher Hall
MATHEMATICS Timothy Gowers
THE MEANING OF LIFE Terry Eagleton
MEASUREMENT David Hand
MEDICAL ETHICS Tony Hope
MEDICAL LAW Charles Foster
MEDIEVAL BRITAIN John Gillingham and Ralph A. Griffiths
MEDIEVAL LITERATURE Elaine Treharne
MEDIEVAL PHILOSOPHY John Marenbon
MEMORY Jonathan K. Foster
METAPHYSICS Stephen Mumford
THE MEXICAN REVOLUTION Alan Knight
MICHAEL FARADAY Frank A. J. L. James
MICROBIOLOGY Nicholas P. Money
MICROECONOMICS Avinash Dixit
MICROSCOPY Terence Allen
THE MIDDLE AGES Miri Rubin
MILITARY JUSTICE Eugene R. Fidell
MILITARY STRATEGY Antulio J. Echevarria II
MINERALS David Vaughan
MIRACLES Yujin Nagasawa
MODERN ART David Cottington
MODERN CHINA Rana Mitter

MODERN DRAMA
Kirsten E. Shepherd-Barr
MODERN FRANCE
Vanessa R. Schwartz
MODERN INDIA Craig Jeffrey
MODERN IRELAND Senia Pašeta
MODERN ITALY Anna Cento Bull
MODERN JAPAN
Christopher Goto-Jones
MODERN LATIN AMERICAN LITERATURE
Roberto González Echevarría
MODERN WAR Richard English
MODERNISM Christopher Butler
MOLECULAR BIOLOGY Aysha Divan and Janice A. Royds
MOLECULES Philip Ball
MONASTICISM Stephen J. Davis
THE MONGOLS Morris Rossabi
MOONS David A. Rothery
MORMONISM
Richard Lyman Bushman
MOUNTAINS Martin F. Price
MUHAMMAD Jonathan A. C. Brown
MULTICULTURALISM Ali Rattansi
MULTILINGUALISM John C. Maher
MUSIC Nicholas Cook
MYTH Robert A. Segal
THE NAPOLEONIC WARS
Mike Rapport
NATIONALISM Steven Grosby
NATIVE AMERICAN LITERATURE
Sean Teuton
NAVIGATION Jim Bennett
NELSON MANDELA Elleke Boehmer
NEOLIBERALISM Manfred Steger and Ravi Roy
NETWORKS Guido Caldarelli and Michele Catanzaro
THE NEW TESTAMENT
Luke Timothy Johnson
THE NEW TESTAMENT AS LITERATURE Kyle Keefer
NEWTON Robert Iliffe
NIETZSCHE Michael Tanner
NINETEENTH-CENTURY BRITAIN Christopher Harvie and H. C. G. Matthew
THE NORMAN CONQUEST
George Garnett
NORTH AMERICAN INDIANS
Theda Perdue and Michael D. Green
NORTHERN IRELAND
Marc Mulholland
NOTHING Frank Close
NUCLEAR PHYSICS Frank Close
NUCLEAR POWER Maxwell Irvine
NUCLEAR WEAPONS
Joseph M. Siracusa
NUMBERS Peter M. Higgins
NUTRITION David A. Bender
OBJECTIVITY Stephen Gaukroger
OCEANS Dorrik Stow
THE OLD TESTAMENT
Michael D. Coogan
THE ORCHESTRA D. Kern Holoman
ORGANIC CHEMISTRY
Graham Patrick
ORGANIZED CRIME
Georgios A. Antonopoulos and Georgios Papanicolaou
ORGANIZATIONS Mary Jo Hatch
PAGANISM Owen Davies
PAIN Rob Boddice
THE PALESTINIAN-ISRAELI CONFLICT Martin Bunton
PANDEMICS Christian W. McMillen
PARTICLE PHYSICS Frank Close
PAUL E. P. Sanders
PEACE Oliver P. Richmond
PENTECOSTALISM William K. Kay
PERCEPTION Brian Rogers
THE PERIODIC TABLE Eric R. Scerri
PHILOSOPHY Edward Craig
PHILOSOPHY IN THE ISLAMIC WORLD Peter Adamson
PHILOSOPHY OF LAW
Raymond Wacks
PHILOSOPHY OF SCIENCE
Samir Okasha
PHILOSOPHY OF RELIGION
Tim Bayne
PHOTOGRAPHY Steve Edwards
PHYSICAL CHEMISTRY Peter Atkins
PILGRIMAGE Ian Reader
PLAGUE Paul Slack
PLANETS David A. Rothery
PLANTS Timothy Walker
PLATE TECTONICS Peter Molnar
PLATO Julia Annas

POLITICAL PHILOSOPHY David Miller
POLITICS Kenneth Minogue
POPULISM Cas Mudde and Cristóbal Rovira Kaltwasser
POSTCOLONIALISM Robert Young
POSTMODERNISM Christopher Butler
POSTSTRUCTURALISM Catherine Belsey
PREHISTORY Chris Gosden
PRESOCRATIC PHILOSOPHY Catherine Osborne
PRIVACY Raymond Wacks
PROBABILITY John Haigh
PROGRESSIVISM Walter Nugent
PROJECTS Andrew Davies
PROTESTANTISM Mark A. Noll
PSYCHIATRY Tom Burns
PSYCHOANALYSIS Daniel Pick
PSYCHOLOGY Gillian Butler and Freda McManus
PSYCHOTHERAPY Tom Burns and Eva Burns-Lundgren
PUBLIC ADMINISTRATION Stella Z. Theodoulou and Ravi K. Roy
PUBLIC HEALTH Virginia Berridge
PURITANISM Francis J. Bremer
THE QUAKERS Pink Dandelion
QUANTUM THEORY John Polkinghorne
RACISM Ali Rattansi
RADIOACTIVITY Claudio Tuniz
RASTAFARI Ennis B. Edmonds
THE REAGAN REVOLUTION Gil Troy
REALITY Jan Westerhoff
THE REFORMATION Peter Marshall
RELATIVITY Russell Stannard
RELIGION IN AMERICA Timothy Beal
THE RENAISSANCE Jerry Brotton
RENAISSANCE ART Geraldine A. Johnson
REVOLUTIONS Jack A. Goldstone
RHETORIC Richard Toye
RISK Baruch Fischhoff and John Kadvany
RITUAL Barry Stephenson
RIVERS Nick Middleton
ROBOTICS Alan Winfield
ROCKS Jan Zalasiewicz
ROMAN BRITAIN Peter Salway
THE ROMAN EMPIRE Christopher Kelly
THE ROMAN REPUBLIC David M. Gwynn
ROMANTICISM Michael Ferber
ROUSSEAU Robert Wokler
RUSSELL A. C. Grayling
RUSSIAN HISTORY Geoffrey Hosking
RUSSIAN LITERATURE Catriona Kelly
THE RUSSIAN REVOLUTION S. A. Smith
SAVANNAS Peter A. Furley
SCHIZOPHRENIA Chris Frith and Eve Johnstone
SCHOPENHAUER Christopher Janaway
SCIENCE AND RELIGION Thomas Dixon
SCIENCE FICTION David Seed
THE SCIENTIFIC REVOLUTION Lawrence M. Principe
SCOTLAND Rab Houston
SEXUALITY Véronique Mottier
SHAKESPEARE'S COMEDIES Bart van Es
SHAKESPEARE'S SONNETS AND POEMS Jonathan F. S. Post
SHAKESPEARE'S TRAGEDIES Stanley Wells
SIKHISM Eleanor Nesbitt
THE SILK ROAD James A. Millward
SLANG Jonathon Green
SLEEP Steven W. Lockley and Russell G. Foster
SOCIAL AND CULTURAL ANTHROPOLOGY John Monaghan and Peter Just
SOCIAL PSYCHOLOGY Richard J. Crisp
SOCIAL WORK Sally Holland and Jonathan Scourfield
SOCIALISM Michael Newman
SOCIOLINGUISTICS John Edwards
SOCIOLOGY Steve Bruce
SOCRATES C. C. W. Taylor
SOUND Mike Goldsmith
THE SOVIET UNION Stephen Lovell
THE SPANISH CIVIL WAR Helen Graham

SPANISH LITERATURE Jo Labanyi
SPINOZA Roger Scruton
SPIRITUALITY Philip Sheldrake
SPORT Mike Cronin
STARS Andrew King
STATISTICS David J. Hand
STEM CELLS Jonathan Slack
STRUCTURAL ENGINEERING David Blockley
STUART BRITAIN John Morrill
SUPERCONDUCTIVITY Stephen Blundell
SYMMETRY Ian Stewart
TAXATION Stephen Smith
TEETH Peter S. Ungar
TELESCOPES Geoff Cottrell
TERRORISM Charles Townshend
THEATRE Marvin Carlson
THEOLOGY David F. Ford
THINKING AND REASONING Jonathan St B. T. Evans
THOMAS AQUINAS Fergus Kerr
THOUGHT Tim Bayne
TIBETAN BUDDHISM Matthew T. Kapstein
TOCQUEVILLE Harvey C. Mansfield
TRAGEDY Adrian Poole
TRANSLATION Matthew Reynolds
THE TROJAN WAR Eric H. Cline
TRUST Katherine Hawley
THE TUDORS John Guy
TWENTIETH-CENTURY BRITAIN Kenneth O. Morgan
THE UNITED NATIONS Jussi M. Hanhimäki
THE U.S. CONGRESS Donald A. Ritchie
THE U.S. SUPREME COURT Linda Greenhouse
UTILITARIANISM Katarzyna de Lazari-Radek and Peter Singer
UNIVERSITIES AND COLLEGES David Palfreyman and Paul Temple
UTOPIANISM Lyman Tower Sargent
VETERINARY SCIENCE James Yeates
THE VIKINGS Julian Richards
VIRUSES Dorothy H. Crawford
VOLTAIRE Nicholas Cronk
WAR AND TECHNOLOGY Alex Roland
WATER John Finney
WEATHER Storm Dunlop
THE WELFARE STATE David Garland
WILLIAM SHAKESPEARE Stanley Wells
WITCHCRAFT Malcolm Gaskill
WITTGENSTEIN A. C. Grayling
WORK Stephen Fineman
WORLD MUSIC Philip Bohlman
THE WORLD TRADE ORGANIZATION Amrita Narlikar
WORLD WAR II Gerhard L. Weinberg
WRITING AND SCRIPT Andrew Robinson
ZIONISM Michael Stanislawski

Available soon:

DEVELOPMENT Ian Goldin
GENOMICS John Archibald
CRIMINOLOGY Tim Newburn
DEMOGRAPHY Sarah Harper
GEOLOGY Jan Zalasiewicz

For more information visit our website

www.oup.com/vsi/

Ben Hutchinson

COMPARATIVE LITERATURE

A Very Short Introduction

OXFORD
UNIVERSITY PRESS

OXFORD
UNIVERSITY PRESS

Great Clarendon Street, Oxford, OX2 6DP,
United Kingdom

Oxford University Press is a department of the University of Oxford.
It furthers the University's objective of excellence in research, scholarship,
and education by publishing worldwide. Oxford is a registered trade mark of
Oxford University Press in the UK and in certain other countries

First edition published in 2018

Impression: 4

Published in the United States of America by Oxford University Press
198 Madison Avenue, New York, NY 10016, United States of America

British Library Cataloguing in Publication Data
Data available

Library of Congress Control Number: 2017958002

ISBN 978–0–19–880727–8

Printed in Great Britain by
Ashford Colour Press Ltd, Gosport, Hampshire

Contents

Acknowledgements

Comparative literature is nothing if not a collective endeavour. By its very nature, it encompasses perspectives that go well beyond one's own; the sources listed at the end of the book—to which many more could have been added—give a sense of just how ecumenical the whole enterprise necessarily is. In the first instance, then, my thanks must go to comparatists past and present, without whose work such an introduction would have been impossible.

Alongside such distant readings, the book has benefited immeasurably from the close readings of its first three interlocutors: Francesca Orsini, Ritchie Robertson, and Shane Weller. No doubt they would not agree with every last emphasis or argument, but their generosity with their time and energy, and their careful attention to matters both editorial and intellectual, exemplify the virtues of the comparative community. I am indebted to their exactitude.

Colleagues in the British Comparative Literature Association (BCLA) have been a recurring source of stimulation over the last few years, as have friends in Denmark (Mads Rosendahl Thomsen), France (Emmanuel Bouju), and Germany (Marcel Lepper). Like every other author in the VSI series, no doubt, I am fortunate to have found Andrea Keegan and Jenny Nugee so unfailingly encouraging. To them, and to the anonymous readers at OUP whose suggestions challenged and cheered me, much thanks.

It goes without saying—and must thus be said—that this book, like everything else, would not have been possible without Marie, Max, and Hugo. *Merci.*

List of illustrations

Chapter 1
Metaphors of reading

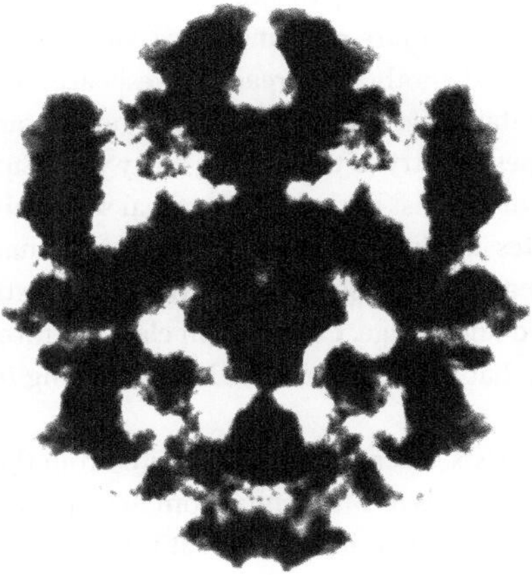

1. Reading into literature: the Rorschach test.

What do you see in the inkblot? Some see an abstract cloud; others discern a menacing mask. Some see the suggestive spaces; others focus on the lines that shape them. We can presumably all agree that the two sides of the image are symmetrical, but beyond that our brains process the information differently, projecting associations and prejudices—and hopes and fears—onto a shifting, undefined object. The image, in other words, is only as revealing as the observer (Figure 1).

Impressionistic as it is, Hermann Rorschach's inkblot test offers an instructive analogy for comparative literature. Understood as the reciprocal study of at least two forms of writing, comparative literature is both the most natural and the most constructed of intellectual activities. As we struggle to make sense out of one text or tradition, we instinctively compare it to another text or tradition. One side of the object mirrors and shapes the other (cover half of the image and it quickly loses any form of structure). Yet we also bring a whole set of political, historical, and cultural pre-dispositions to the comparison, a perceptual apparatus through which we conjure meaning as we compare it. To use one text to understand another—to read Shakespeare's *The Tempest* alongside Montaigne's essay 'On Cannibals', for instance, or to compare Chinese poetry of the Tang dynasty with European poetry of the modernist period—is to reveal something about one's own tastes and knowledge, if only the belief that there is something meaningful to be learned through contextualizing one's own tastes and knowledge. Comparison clarifies, through its very methodology, that reading literature is also reading *into* literature.

For literature exists, after all, comparatively. From the dramas of Antiquity to the novels of Modernity, from Eastern epics to Western classics, there is not a text in history that is truly self-sufficient. To read and to write is to work within an existing framework of characters, conventions, plots, and premises; how we understand one work of literature is contingent on how we understand another work of literature. The more we know, the more we contextualize; the more we learn, the more we compare. Knowledge itself is comparative. Beyond how we read, beyond how we write, comparison is hard-wired into the very ways that we think.

While this makes comparative literature among the most ambitious of intellectual disciplines, it also brings the whole undertaking into question. For if 'to read is to compare', in the pithy words of George Steiner, one of the most influential of contemporary comparatists, then fencing off a protected zone for its pursuit might, in fact, seem unnecessary, since we are constantly doing it anyway. What, to put it simply, is the force of *comparative* literature, as opposed to that of *literature*? To answer this question requires delving into the practice, the history, and the theory of the discipline.

Why, and indeed how, does one become a comparatist? In my case it began with a passion for languages, then for the literatures written in them, and then for how to join the dots between them. The moment the dots start to cohere into a pattern is the moment at which literature becomes truly comparative, and it is among the most exhilarating of intellectual experiences. To follow the evolution of the novel from Cervantes to Calvino, to study the history of the sonnet from Petrarch to Pushkin, is to navigate by new and larger constellations, drawn on by the delight of making cross-cultural connections. Anyone naturally inquisitive, whether with or without foreign language skills, can share this satisfaction. Curiosity, open-mindedness, intellectual ambition: these are the only prerequisites for making comparisons.

For there are few more fundamentally human instincts than the urge to compare. From the earliest inklings of self-consciousness, we tacitly understand ourselves in relation to others; as we grow older, we learn to gauge our development through constant reference to peers, developing finely tuned antennae for similarity and difference. Comparison can take many forms—empathy, envy, defensiveness, deference—but it always comes back to the perception of multiplicity, to the acknowledgement (whether grudging or grateful) that there is more than one way of being and more than one way of doing things. Looking beyond ourselves is how we learn.

Scholarly modes of comparison take this basic psychological drive and dignify it with disinterest. Yet the context of the observer continues to provide the crucial point of reference: comparative literature may aspire to the objectivity of a 'discipline', but in reality it is deeply complicit in the prejudices and positions that define it. Counter-intuitive though it may be to admit it in the opening pages of an introduction, there is in fact no such thing as a single, objective sense of comparative literature. However problematic the idea of 'literature' may be—and we will see that it is increasingly contested—the adjective 'comparative' indicates nothing so much as complete disagreement on how to approach it. Almost every comparatist has a different idea of how and what to compare; almost every comparatist has a different set of priorities. The only consensus is on the inherent instability of the term. Like governments in a democracy, we have the modes of comparison that we deserve.

This instability is the very essence of comparative literature. Both its meaning and its methodology depend on unsettling fixed canons, on forging fresh connections and mutually enriching links between disparate texts and traditions. Concepts such as 'world literature' or 'multilingualism' are merely the latest examples of the on-going attempt to confer stability on an inherently unstable concept; unlike the clearly demarcated fields of national literatures (English, French, Russian, etc.), comparative literature does not have a canon of texts so much as a canon of approaches to texts. Comparative literature, in short, constitutes an *in*discipline, a self-reflexive mode of reading rather than an object of study, or perhaps a self-reflexive mode of reading *in search of* an object of study. If this makes it akin to a Rorschach test, it also makes it a mirror for Modernity's intellectual anxieties regarding globalization.

International relations

But what *is* comparative literature? All comparatists will have heard this question at some point, if not at several, in the course of their working lives. Ambitious readers looking to stretch themselves are generally intrigued by the concept, but uncertain of its implications. And rightly so, in many ways; even the professionals cannot agree on a single term, calling it—to take just three examples—*compared* in French ('littérature comparée'), *comparing* in German ('vergleichende Literaturwissenschaft'), and *comparative* in English. Where the French past participle suggests that the comparing has already happened, and the German present participle that it is in the process of happening, the English adjective blurs the distinction between object and observer (is it literature that is comparative or the approach to it?). The very term itself, when considered comparatively, opens up a Pandora's box of cultural differences.

Yet this, in a nutshell, is the whole point. To look at literature comparatively is to realize just how much can be learned by looking over the horizon of one's own tradition; it is to discover more not only about other literatures, but also about one's own; and it is to participate in the great utopian dream of understanding the way cultures interact. In an age that is paradoxically defined by migration and border crossing on the one hand, and by a retreat into monolingualism and monoculturalism on the other, the cross-cultural agenda of comparative literature has become increasingly central to the future of the Humanities. We are all, in fact, comparatists, constantly making connections across languages, cultures, and genres as we read. The question is whether we realize it.

The aim of this *Very Short Introduction* is to render this comparative impulse conscious. From the point of view both of scholarship and of cultural history more generally, the book will consider the theory and the practice of comparative literature as expressions of changing intellectual climates, as well as of the colourful cast of exiles, émigrés, and explorers that has peopled these climates. The history and theory of comparative literature are the history and theory of how literary cultures have learned to view each other, of the understandings, misunderstandings, and privileged friendships that have emerged between differing modes of expression. The forces of Modernity that gave rise to the discipline—from colonialism and nationalism to exile and internationalism—are also the forces that shaped it, sculpting its project of analogy, antithesis, and cultural differentiation. Comparative literature, in short, constitutes something like the international relations of culture.

If such an understanding of comparative literature suggests that it is as much a political activity as it is a literary-critical one, it also points towards the changing ways in which it has been conceptualized. The history of comparative literature is not just the history of a discipline; it is also the history of the self-understanding of the discipline. Two categories have dominated this self-understanding: Modernity and Europe. This book duly traces the constitution of comparative literature in these terms—to do otherwise would be to distort the evolution of the discipline—but a counter-narrative could equally be constructed about pre-modernity and the world. As global historians are increasingly showing, there is no need to await the arrival of European Modernity—and indeed of the very idea of 'European Modernity'—to assert the possibility of a comparative perspective: long before the Renaissance, languages such as Sanskrit, Arabic, and Chinese rivalled Greek and Latin as cosmopolitan, supranational modes of expression. Multilingualism—between the vernacular and the *lingua franca*, for instance—was common in the Middle Ages. Comparative literature in this sense is also the interlinguistic relations of culture.

Within modern Europe, the development of comparative literature as a process of intellectual exchange between nations looks back, in geopolitical terms, to the post-1648 idea of national sovereignty enshrined in the Treaty of Westphalia. To be international, first one has to be national: the principle of the balance of power, along with that of religious (and by extension cultural) freedom, ensured that the various empires and 'dominions' began to pursue intercultural exchange in lieu of international war. By the 19th century—the era in which comparative literature would develop in earnest—this balance of power was reasserted, following the upheaval of the Napoleonic wars, by the Congress of Vienna in 1815, which fixed the European map for the next hundred years (see Figure 2).

The fact that the major empires (Prussia, Russia, Austria) had made major gains meant that numerous smaller states—and languages—were now subsumed within their purview. A range of differing cultures were housed within a handful of overarching groupings, the better to balance each other out at the supranational level; the conditions for comparison, one might say, were perfect. Yet for the emerging discipline of comparative literature, this imperial structure created a double bind, since it meant that attempts to overcome national divisions were tied precisely to those divisions, locked into a narrative of competing countries and colonies. Comparison developed, in short, within and between nations and empires—the Napoleonic, the Victorian, the Habsburg—as much as within and between languages and literatures. Understood in the geopolitical terms of the 19th century, comparative literature was also competitive literature.

Compare and contrast

Given such competing narratives, how can the process of comparing best be understood? Perhaps we might usefully begin by viewing it as the search for a master metaphor. The Belgian-born critic Paul de Man (1919–83) argued that modern literature constructs its own 'allegories of reading'; comparative literature, by extension, constructs metaphors of reading, models of how to interpret texts and cultures between languages and nations. Such metaphors may provisionally be broken down into two groups: those indicating connection or similarity, and those indicating disconnection or difference.

2. Europe at the Congress of Vienna.

Beginning with the former group, perhaps the most obvious metaphor for the comparative approach to literature is that of the 'crossroads'. Standing at the centre of any number of converging routes or spaces—the Silk Road, the Holy Roman Empire, the Republic of Letters—the comparatist, following this model, surveys and directs the passing traffic. Such a position confers numerous advantages: privileged access to a range of sources; exposure to competing perspectives; constant stimulation and (re-)negotiation. But it also risks being disorienting, placing the comparatist at the mercy of chance and circumstance, her head spinning furiously like the road runner in one of those cartoons where the traffic signs are all flipped around. More fundamentally, it also depends on a model of comparative literature that is not so much Eurocentric—the great fear of contemporary criticism in an age of postcolonial globalization—as 'centric-centric', since it implies that the comparatist must be at the centre of such debates as there are. In an age of 'Global South' and realigned 'peripheries', it is far from clear that such a centre can hold.

An alternative, increasingly important model of negotiation is that of the 'marketplace'. In an age in which successful authors write as much for an international as for a national audience, the cross-cultural 'marketability' of literature has become a significant criterion in determining what gets compared—and what gets written. The metaphor of the marketplace, that is to say, relates both to reader and to writer: comparative literature is all too often understood solely from the critical perspective, as a question of reception—yet it can also be seen from the authorial perspective, as an issue of creation. Already in the 1820s, Goethe, in launching the term 'world literature', used the metaphor of the marketplace—partly in the Enlightenment sense of a forum for trade and commerce, partly in order to encourage the dissemination of his own works. With one eye on possible foreign rights and editions, the author writes himself into the international marketplace of ideas just as much as the critic buys and sells these ideas; comparison requires having something to compare.

Monetized in this way, the metaphor of the marketplace points towards the socio-cultural framework in which comparative literature necessarily operates, towards the network of publishers, reviewers, translators, and professors who make it possible.

Metaphors such as 'crossroads' and 'marketplace'—as well as other, more overtly political, variations such as 'parliament' or 'united nations'—can be thought of as facilitating interaction between two or more perspectives. Indeed, one might go further and suggest that they mimic the very meaning of metaphor: just as the process of comparison functions as a simile—by saying that one thing is *like* another—so too it acts as a metaphor (from the Greek *meta-pherein*, to 'carry over' or 'transfer'), indicating as it does the ways in which we compare one idea to another. In the words of one of the earliest thinkers of the Western tradition, 'a good metaphor implies an intuitive perception of the similarity in dissimilars'. Aristotle's definition of genius might equally be applied to the way that comparatists approach literature, creating previously unsuspected links between two or more texts.

Yet metaphors can be misleading. Sometimes meaning is not so much 'carried over' as intercepted. The Danish critic Georg Brandes (1842–1927) described comparative literature as a telescope that both magnifies and reduces—since it sees further (e.g. across the whole of European modernism) by focusing on specific objects (e.g. texts by Ibsen, Strindberg, or Nietzsche)—and his image neatly captures the ambivalent nature both of comparison and of its attendant metaphors. How are we to understand those metaphors that call into question any easy sense of comparative literature as simply an intellectual import–export business? How are we to understand the mechanisms of difference, as well as of similarity? What, in short, of what one might term *contrastive* literature?

Contrastive literature forms the necessary counterpart to comparative literature: without difference, no similarity. In order to say that one thing is like another, one must implicitly say what it is *not* like; to compare presupposes the ability to contrast. Seen in this way, comparative literature is as much about reconfiguring comparisons as making them, and accordingly it attracts a corresponding group of metaphors centred on the creation of new perspectives and meanings. Perhaps the most prominent metaphor in this group is that of the 'melting pot'. Unlike the image of the crossroads, which suggests that texts and ideas may take different directions but will still keep moving in some previously recognizable form, the linguistic melting pot—in pre-modernity, Latin or Sanskrit; in postmodernity, 'world' literature in English or French—implies that local ideas undergo a fundamental *change* of form in order to find expression within (the many variations of) one 'global' recipient. Understood literally, this would imply that comparative literature reduces all writing to a single mould, out of which then emerges a range of new, reconstituted meanings.

Of course, comparison even within one language is not this straightforward; a single pot can contain a multitude of ingredients, ingredients that it is the role of the comparatist to taste and identify. Locating the border between one version of an idea and another—bringing them together, but also keeping them apart—is an essential aspect of comparative practice. If the model of the melting pot dissolves conflicting elements as much as it solves them, the idea of comparative literature as a 'border control point' invests the comparatist with greater powers still. For it suggests that she can just as well block the traffic of ideas as allow them safe passage, that she is authorized to rifle through texts in search of contraband content (vestigial attitudes of colonialism in modern European literature, for instance). The comparatist sits in judgement on the flow of ideas, with a more or less liberal, more or less *laissez faire* sensibility. That the assumption of such a position is ethically as well as aesthetically problematic is not the least of its provocations.

To study the history of the subject, however—and in particular the close relationship in the 20th century between the Jewish diaspora and the emerging academic discipline—is to realize that comparative literature is ultimately not so much about policing borders as crossing them. Comparatists choose to distance themselves from their own native cultures, to forgo their 'home' literatures in favour of a willed homelessness, the better to gain purchase on texts and tropes that transcend any single idiom. They choose not to belong to any one particular tradition—indeed, this 'unbelonging' is arguably their defining characteristic. As intellectual émigrés, comparatists make links between cultures, but in doing so they also, paradoxically, reinforce the distinctions between them. As such, the contrasts are as important as the comparisons, the disconnections as instructive as the connections.

Comparative literature in the 21st century

But why, one might ask, do such metaphors matter? Why should I—why should you—care about how comparative literature views itself? The answer lies not in specialist skirmishes, but in common sense. For in the case of comparative literature, the metaphors it lives by are arguably as important as the insights it makes possible. Unlike other disciplines, historically more secure in their intellectual and institutional status, comparative literature must constantly renew its sense of mission, constantly tell itself a new story about how and why literature(s) should be 'compared'. To be sure, this is not to claim that other areas of the Humanities are not equally restless and innovative in the ways that they view their work; but they are not defined by the same unceasing sense of insecurity as an approach that by definition works in the gaps *between* disciplines. It is the continuous need to justify itself, to itself, that marks out comparative literature as uniquely beholden to changing intellectual fashions, and thus to changing disciplinary metaphors. 'Comparative' literature, in other words, must be understood comparatively, which is to say as historically contingent and context-specific.

What we might provisionally take the adjective 'comparative' to convey, then, is that the *idea* of comparison—in conjunction with the idea of literature—is as important as its practice. The animating impulse of comparative literature is not just the urge to take a broad perspective across differing forms and languages of literary expression; it is also the—politically, ethically, and aesthetically charged—notion that this is a worthwhile undertaking in the first place. Comparative literature cannot get by, in other words, without a pinch of pathos, since it is the utopian dream of being in 'no place' (*u-topos*)—and thus in every place—that drives it.

More prosaically, comparative literature is also a question of themes and techniques. Often undertaken through the pursuit of overarching categories—such as sources, influences, motifs, genres, and myths—comparative literature constructs its arguments through as wide a range as possible of examples and counter-examples. The only orthodoxy is diversity, the attempt to incorporate other perspectives than one's own. Importantly, this is true not only of the critical perspective of the reader, but also of the creative perspective of the writer. For comparative literature is a technique as well as a theory: from Cervantes's claim that *Don Quixote*, the first modern novel, was written by an Arabic author, to the postmodern practice of constituting texts through references to other texts, modern literature could not exist without recourse to the comparative method. Comparison, that is to say, does not just occur after the event, in the mind of the reader, but also already during the process of composition, in the mind of the writer. What we have come to call intertextuality—T.S. Eliot incorporating Sanskrit into *The Waste Land*, Shakespeare echoing Montaigne—is simply another form of comparison, whereby meaning emerges out of the interaction between texts.

The relationship to intertextuality provides just one example of how comparative literature is defined by its strategic position between languages, literature, and culture. Literary theory, cultural studies, postcolonialism, world literature, translation studies, and reception studies: comparative literature in the 21st century draws on all these disciplines and more. Out of these points of intersection emerge a number of recurring debates—the changing notions of 'high' and 'popular' culture; the shifting hierarchy of 'original' and translated texts; concepts and criticisms of the 'canon'; the status and composition of the 'text'—debates that make comparative literature among the most dynamic of intellectual fields. Irrigated by any number of sources, it overflows with ideas as to how to conceive the role and purpose of the verbal arts in an ever more visual world.

For this, indeed, is perhaps the principal function of comparative literature in the 21st century. Comparatively speaking—a disciplinary necessity—the subject has emerged in surprisingly good health from the recent squeeze on the Humanities across much of the Western world, since it remains one of the diminishingly few disciplines open to those interested in foreign literatures and broader perspectives. For ambitious readers with an appetite for ranging beyond their own native traditions, comparative literature is the natural home. Yet it is also the natural home for all those 'big' questions about why literature—and by extension, culture—still matters. To compare literatures and cultures must be to do more than merely accrue the sum of their parts, it must be to ponder—and to protect—international and interlinguistic cultural relations. The surest way of moving beyond a purely subjective response to the Rorschach test, in short, is to study the practice, the history, and the theory of comparative literature.

Chapter 2
Practices and principles

What does it mean to 'do' comparative literature? If you have taken the time to pick up this book, you are presumably interested in reading as widely as possible. You may not yet be familiar, however, with all the ways in which this interest can be deepened through scrutiny and reflection. The newcomer to comparative literature could certainly be forgiven for feeling disoriented by the sheer volume of competing schools. Indeed, it sometimes feels as though that is all there is: methods, approaches, theories. To be a comparatist is to struggle, at times, to peel back the layers of accrued reflection on precisely what it is to be a comparatist. Yet there are a number of basic strategies for comparing literature, strategies that have continually recurred while developing with the discipline, and it is with such first principles that an introduction to the subject may best begin. Before considering the history and theory of comparative literature, we must first and most fundamentally consider the practice.

From the early 19th century to the early 21st, 'doing' comparative literature has meant doing something that is ultimately impossible—namely, mediating in an unprejudiced way between competing traditions, with full mastery of these traditions. If there is an implicit moral injunction inherent in comparative literature—read more widely! learn more languages!—it is an injunction that no one, in the final analysis, can live up to. In the words of Samuel Beckett, we can only fail better; the question is, how to fail best? Should we understand comparative literature as a kind of elite discipline, a Champions League for those who have already conquered at least one individual linguistic tradition? (This was Goethe's view: 'Only the proven connoisseur should compare', he claimed; 'the amateur should consider every achievement individually'.) Or should comparison begin even as we are still first encountering the individual languages and cultures in question? (This is the view implicitly taken by most undergraduate courses in comparative literature.) Should comparison come at the end, in other words, or at the beginning?

It is far from clear what it even means to read 'comparatively'. There are as many reasons to compare forms of literature as there are to interpret it: some critics compare for conservative reasons (defending 'European' culture, for instance), others for progressive ones (advocating international solidarity for minority groups); some critics prioritize textual, others prefer contextual modes of comparison. One person's literary comparatist is another person's cultural freedom fighter. With regard to the *technique* of comparative literature, however, we can identify a number of basic principles—considered, in the comparative spirit, as conceptual pairs—as constitutive of its disciplinary practice. Such categories of comparison underlie much of the work that is undertaken in the field; clarity on their advantages—and on their limits—is thus crucial for anyone wishing to understand the discipline.

Topics vs. methods

Perhaps the most basic question for the aspiring comparatist concerns the way in which to construct a 'comparative' argument. Is it the texts, or the approach to the texts, that determines the precise nature of a comparison? Comparing forms of writing can mean tracing variations in a particular theme across a range of contexts, but it can also mean comparing *the ways* in which one traces them. Comparative literature can be pursued, in short, through its topics or its methods.

Arguably the most common form of comparison involves identifying differing responses to a recurring question. This question may take the form of a motif or a myth (see Box 1), an issue or an idea, but it always presupposes a common topic that can be pursued across any number of variations.

The most straightforward version of this topical approach is simply to compare, across languages, a shared idea in two books or two authors: the dangerous effects of too much reading in *Don Quixote* and *Tristram Shandy*, for instance, or the image of the labyrinth in the work of Jorge Luis Borges and James Joyce. But one can also take the approach further and compare three or more related texts (say, the motif of adultery in *Anna Karenina*,

Box 1 Motifs and myths

One of the most widespread forms of comparative literature investigates the recurrence of key images or stories across a range of languages. Understood as a kind of recurring leitmotif or myth, these figures offer a readymade structure for comparison: examples might include the imagery of earthquakes in the Enlightenment, or depictions of the Wandering Jew in 19th-century literature. Such figures serve as helpful hooks for broader reflections on cultural memory and tradition—assuming, that is, that one asks not just what is being depicted and how, but also *why* (in our first example, the Lisbon earthquake of 1755 and the consequent loss of faith in God; in the second, paranoia about Jewish conspiracies behind international capitalism). Practised in this fashion, comparative literature can offer a window into how periods and places think, as well as into how they fit into the continuing conversation of cultural history.

The Scarlet Letter, and *Madame Bovary*) or even numerous texts by just one author—by Samuel Beckett, for instance, who wrote in two languages, or by the Portuguese poet Fernando Pessoa (1888–1935), who wrote in three languages and under three main 'heteronyms'. Alternatively, one might examine variant translations of a common source text (Shakespeare's sonnets, for example), or differing versions of the same story (J.M. Coetzee rewriting Defoe or Kafka, say, in the context of South African politics). As in chess, the number of moves in comparative literature is theoretically infinite.

Except, of course, that in practice it is not. The reality of the discipline is that a relatively small number of authors—such as the major ones cited earlier—tend to be compared again and again. This is equally true for the second category of comparison, driven by questions of method. If the topic-driven approach to comparative literature is determined by the (supposed) internal coherence of the objects under discussion, such coherence can also be ascribed to the texts by the observer's choice of method. In this model, the critic identifies an argument—the enduring importance of Latin to European literature, for instance, or the marginalization of female authors in the 19th century—and prosecutes it from a particular perspective (feminist, Marxist, postcolonial, etc.), assembling the evidence to reflect her ideology. The motif of adultery, to return to one of the examples cited earlier, can then be reconsidered from a feminist perspective: the point of comparison is no longer the topic itself so much as the methodological *approach* to the topic, which now becomes the determining factor.

An obvious problem with this model, however, is that the method may also become a *pre*determining factor. Deciding on a feminist (or Marxist or postcolonial) approach means that the textual evidence may be slanted to reflect the approach, like a Rorschach test that tells you what you already know. One can certainly compare *Anna Karenina*, *The Scarlet Letter*, and *Madame Bovary* as so many reflections of the oppression of women in the 19th century, but in doing so one is also implicitly comparing any number of other considerations (the consequences of capitalism, for instance, or the use of grammatical structures such as free indirect speech). One method, in other words, implies another. As is often the case with comparative literature, the trick is not to know where to *start* comparing but where to stop.

Underlying both the topical and the methodological approaches to comparison is the question of validity. The classic Franco-German model of comparative literature as elaborated in the 19th century (see Chapter 3) insisted on direct 'influence' as a precondition for comparison: without empirically identifiable proof, comparative claims were held to be invalid. This remains an important mode of comparison, but it has long since been supplemented by more supple forms of argument centred around what one might term, with Wittgenstein, 'family resemblances'. Looking *like* each other can reveal as much as deriving *from* each other, and comparisons based on this principle—about shared literary responses to the emergence of photography, for instance, or about the erotics of modernist style—have much to contribute.

By making possible associative, rather than merely additive, arguments, these looser models of exchange have helped open up intercontinental comparisons. No longer must one text or author share another's direct frame of reference; no longer must influence be verifiable solely through archives and manuscripts. Ancient Chinese and modern French writers can mutually elucidate one another through their exploration of common philosophical concepts; the Greek 'father of history' Herodotus can be compared across the centuries to Chinese and Arabic historians such as Sima Qian and Ibn Khaldun. Having licence to compare literatures beyond what can be empirically proven means that more wide-ranging, conceptual claims about the global circulation of issues and ideas become possible. The risks of such an approach—vagueness, over-determination—are obvious; the potential benefits, immense. Crucially, they depend on reconsidering the methods, as well as the topics, of comparative literature.

Periods vs. regions

Beyond the choice of topic or method, a great deal of comparative work, probably the majority, breaks down into two basic approaches: the historical and the geographical. Where the former looks longitudinally across time, the latter looks latitudinally across cultures. To compare these two categories of comparison is to consider the very basis of the discipline, torn between the literatures of the past and the languages of the present. If the richest work in practice constitutes a mixture of the two, it is because comparative literature looks both backwards and sideways.

Like much of the Humanities in the post-'theory' era (see Chapter 4), comparative literature has rediscovered its zest for the past. 'Historicize!' is among the more common pieces of advice given to aspiring comparatists, the subtext of which is often also 'contextualize!' To compare occurrences of a particular topic in different literary periods—the idea of walking in Romanticism and modernism, say, or responses to trauma after World War Two and the Indian partition—requires sensitivity not only to the relevant texts, but also to the changing contexts. There is truth in Benedetto Croce's complaint that comparative literature is essentially literary history, but only if one's sense of this history, like Walt Whitman's sense of himself, contains multitudes.

Another way of saying this is that the historical approach to comparison necessarily contains a geographical element, in as much as it implies a number of differing contexts within a particular period. Staying within just one culture would lend credence to Croce's reduction of comparison to literary history, since it is the kind of approach that can be practised perfectly well within single language traditions. To examine comparatively the idea of walking in Romanticism, to return to the example cited earlier, is to range across any number of European literatures, from Rousseau to Wordsworth, from Goethe to Leopardi. It is not, at least in the disciplinary sense of the term, to compare Wordsworth to Coleridge.

Obvious though this may seem, refining a sense of what comparative literature is *not* can be as helpful as defining what it is. There is a tendency at times for the discipline to serve as a catch-all for any approach to literature, indeed to culture, that does not immediately fit into existing disciplinary structures, as though the very term 'comparative' implied that anything goes. Perhaps the limits of its purview would be clearer if it were called comparative literature*s*, since the plural highlights the plurality of the discipline, its insistence on synthesizing at least two senses—or practices, or traditions—of literature. Thinking historically, across periods, is one way of foregrounding this plurality.

That said, the idea of periodization is far from uncontested. Although it has long been a prerequisite of university literature departments—from 'early modern' to 'postmodern', both appointments and courses are largely determined by period—the intellectual basis for such distinctions is far less solid than the institutional. Where does one draw the lines between periods, for one thing, and how does one arbitrate between overlapping categories such as 'post-Romantic' and 'Victorian'? How can one be sure that one is not retrospectively projecting a later sense of a certain period—which is to say, the accumulation of all the clichés about it—back onto it, thereby merely perpetuating a myth rather than challenging it? If fame, for the German poet Rainer Maria Rilke, is the sum of the misunderstandings that surround a new name, then so, arguably, is the idea of 'periods'.

Comparative literature can help with these misunderstandings, paradoxically, by adding to them. The notion of a period may correspond more to its aggregate of past and present rhetorical constructions than to any objective fact; precisely for this reason, however, the more rhetorical constructions are identified—and compared and contrasted—the more complete the picture of the period will be. One way of combatting what the literary theorist Franco Moretti calls the '*Zeitgeist* fallacy' is to take the fallacy seriously, as a manifestation of any number of national and international factors that offer insight on their own terms, as contextual evidence, into a period's self-understanding. To do full justice to Romanticism as a periodic category (to take this section's principal example), one must *de facto* be a comparatist, since its major works in France and Italy do not appear until the 1820s and 1830s—a full generation after its first flowering in England and Germany—and so in part constitute responses to the English and German precedents.

A related issue arises when one pursues periodization into an individual œuvre. We speak casually of 'early' or 'late' Shakespeare without pausing to reflect that these categories are themselves critical constructs: it was not until Edward Dowden's studies of the 1870s, for instance, that what we now consider the last plays—primarily the 'Romances' *The Tempest*, *The Winter's Tale*, and *Cymbeline*—were established as a separate group. Dowden's view of Shakespeare's late style as 'grave and glad, serene and beautiful' is only one possible model of lateness, however; equally plausible is the raging, rebarbative mode that Theodor Adorno identifies—to cite just one example—in the late works of Beethoven. A full appreciation of the category of late style, in other words, can only emerge through comparison of its many manifestations in differing forms of art and culture.

Such an approach to periodization suggests the comparatist's ever-broader horizons. Yet the pragmatic need for parameters has led, in recent decades, to an increasingly popular tendency to go the other way and zoom in on a specific year. 'On or about December 1910 human character changed', Virginia Woolf famously claimed; teasing out the reasons for, and manifestations of, such a momentous change is a prime task for the comparatist. Such a perspective can yield fascinating results (other years that have been approached in this fashion include 1913, 1922, and 1926), but it risks becoming blinkered as much as focused, restricting the critic to the artificial constraints of a calendar year. Some form of periodic division nonetheless remains indispensable, if only to regulate expectations. 'Literature's power to cultivate readers', writes Ted Underwood in the most sustained recent consideration of *Why Literary Periods Mattered* (2013), 'depends on vividly particularizing and differentiating vanished eras, contrasting them implicitly against the present as well as against each other'. *Comparative* literature's power depends on setting these eras not only against each other, but also against alternative versions of each other as they manifest themselves in differing national traditions.

This is another way of saying, then, that what I have termed the 'geographical' axis, across regions and languages, matters as much as the historical approach. Indeed, it arguably matters more, since it is possible to conceive a comparative approach that *only* looks across differing cultures -comparing Arabic, Indian, and European postmodernisms, for instance—without also considering their historical variations, while it is not really possible for comparative literature to be *only* historical (since this would fall within the remit of single language traditions). Comparison, in other words, has to look across before it looks back.

To be sure, the concept of a 'region' is no less contested than that of a 'period'. One of the great advantages of comparative literature—indeed, it is in many ways its mission statement—is that it can unsettle, through its broad, intercultural approach, preconceptions about particular countries or areas. Places, viewed comparatively, become spaces: 'transnational' area studies of regions such as Latin America or India have shown that the history and literature of these continents are just as rich—and just as comparable—as those of Europe. Yet such studies also show that the 'myth of continents', to cite an influential title, continues to provide our meta-geographical categories: for the sake of rhetorical argument, comparatists find it necessary to essentialize regions as homogenous cultural traditions, speaking of 'Europe', the 'West', the 'East', or 'Africa'. Of course, we all have a rough-and-ready idea of what such categories denote, but comparatists are caught in the double bind of needing to use them in order to pick them apart. 'Europeanists' or 'Orientalists' thus have an ambivalent relationship to the regional terminology with which they work, since it is both geographically legitimate and culturally questionable. Claims to a particular tradition, in other words, are also claims to the right to criticize this tradition.

It is obvious that such claims can only exist within specific political parameters. To take just the example of postwar Europe, the two major poles of West and East developed their own powers of attraction in ways that came to determine the major axes of comparison. In the West, the Franco-German dominance of comparative literature gave way, over the course of the century, to Anglo-American hegemony; that this reflects the broader reality of cultural and political power structures—not least, the increasing ubiquity of Global English—is, of course, not a coincidence. As Walter Cohen has shown in his magisterial *History of European Literature* (2017), Western Europe has been a victim of its own success since at least the Renaissance, with regional assumptions about form and content—the triumph of the vernacular over Latin, the increasing dominance of narrative fiction—foregrounding local preferences at the expense of global alternatives. To practise comparative literature in this context is to risk a colonial cringe in reverse.

In Eastern Europe, meanwhile, comparative literature was increasingly centralized around the USSR. Such a policy of centralization—with as many texts as possible translated into Russian, but almost none between the more 'minor' languages such as Bulgarian or Polish—was all the more striking in a region that is inherently comparative. Multilingual *Mitteleuropa*, as scholars such as Caryl Emerson and Galin Tihanov have shown, produced many of the leading theories of literary comparison. 'Slavic' culture—to cite another of the many transnational terms associated with the region—has always been a cradle of comparison, dominated by Russia but drawn to the Western prestige of France and Germany. That the 'fertile meta-capacities of the Central European mind' should have been harnessed to a single, state-sponsored agenda suggests the extent to which comparative literature is at the mercy of absolute power.

Beyond East and West, this regional consideration of comparative literature within Europe could equally be extended to North and South. In the former, the Nordic model of comparison understands Scandinavia as a continent unto itself, which means that much of its history has been devoted to comparing Danish, Swedish, and Norwegian literatures among themselves. In the latter, the Greco-Roman legacy has meant that the Mediterranean has long been viewed as the 'centre of the world'; modern historians such as Fernand Braudel, who drafted his monumental study of *The Mediterranean and the Mediterranean World in the Age of Philip II* (1949) while he was a prisoner of war in Germany, have merely reinforced this perception. Whatever point of the compass one follows, then, the overall point is clear: one regional category (Europe, the West) conceals another (Central Europe, Scandinavia). Comparatists, in short, spend their lives simultaneously constructing categories and taking them apart. If the richest comparative work mobilizes both history and geography, periods and regions, it is in full cognizance of this ambivalence.

Close vs. distant reading

How, though, does such ambivalence play itself out? How does comparative literature both construct and deconstruct its critical categories? The traditional basis of the discipline is the interpretation and juxtaposition of more than one literature in its original language. Having acquired the necessary linguistic skills, and having decided on her topic—a decision that is subject, inevitably, to changing fashions and power structures—the comparatist sets out to cross-refer any number of mutually enlightening texts, generally within some form of common framework (a period, a region, a motif, etc.). With slow philological rigour, she combs through one text for echoes of another; syntax, structure, argument, idiom—all these and more may offer up cues for comparison. Culturally curious and textually promiscuous, she is on the lookout for ways in which one work echoes, complements, or contradicts another, extending its effect beyond its ostensible confines. Similarity is good, but difference is better, in as much as it may point up some hitherto unsuspected aspect of the texts in question. Attention to detail, above all, offers a way of opening up broader arguments about time, manner, and place.

All of this is a way of saying that the traditional basis of comparative literature is close reading (see Box 2).

Box 2 Close reading

Associated with the 'Practical Criticism' that helped establish English literature as a discipline in the 1920s, and with the subsequent 'New Criticism' of the American 1940s, close reading focuses on syntax, sentence structure, semantic ambiguity, and imagery, as well as on the contextual resonance of specific words. Comparative close reading applies such techniques to more than one work from more than one tradition, examining the ways in which the micro-analysis of textual detail can open up the macro-analysis of contextual significance.

One might, for example, examine World War One through the prism of the national literatures that responded to it. Close reading in this context could involve comparing, say, poems by

Rupert Brooke, August Stramm, and Guillaume Apollinaire. Brooke's sonnet 'The Soldier' foregrounds Englishness—mentioned no less than six times in fourteen lines—as his salient quality; even in death there should be 'some corner of a foreign field / That is for ever England'. Given such sentiments, comparison with foreign literature seems especially important. Yet Brooke's very traditional sonnet structure contrasts violently with the expressionist 'scream' of Stramm's poetry. A poem of this title begins with neologisms and distorted syntax—'Days encoffining / Worlds cemeterying' (*Tage sargen/Welten gräbern*)—before proceeding through a series of one-word lines to conclude with the nihilistic crescendo of 'pains pains / pains / paining / notall' (*Wehe Wehe/Wehe/Wehen/Nichtall*). Such poetry can only be read closely, as an onomatapoeic response to the horror of the trenches. Apollinaire's 'Cotton in your Ears', finally, takes this a step further, recreating an explosion of artillery shells typographically, with the words of the poem shattering up the page (see Figure 3). Syntax, in short, enacts sentiment—such is the wager of close reading. While this approach can obviously also be taken to texts within a single language, it is only by comparing texts across several languages that a composite sense of differing responses to the war—sentimental in England, nihilistic in Germany, shattered in France—can be properly achieved.

Such a close, philological approach to literature remained more or less uncontested through much of the 19th and 20th centuries, deriving as it ultimately did from the prestige of Biblical exegesis. In the beginning was the Word; shortly thereafter came its interpretation. Authority, by definition, accrued to the author; the critic deferred to the text. The most orthodox models of comparison are intimately tied to this question of authority, cleaving closely to an 'original' and permitting comparison only where direct influence can be affirmed. 'There is no more urgent task today, for those who choose to account for the European

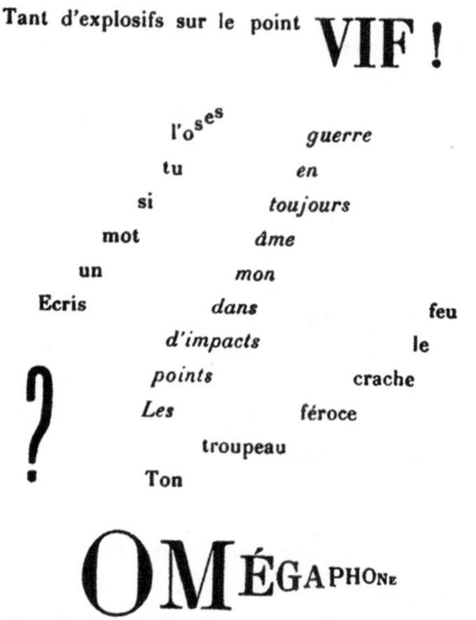

3. The shattering experience of war: Apollinaire's calligram 'Du cotton dans les oreilles' (1916).

literary movement, than to research as exactly as possible what the international relationships have been throughout the centuries': the French comparatist Joseph Texte's clarion call of 1898 exemplifies the then dominant Franco-German model of philological source-hunting as the proper preoccupation of comparative literature.

We are a long way from this today. Theoretical, technological, and not least cultural changes have profoundly altered the way we read. The theory wars of the 1970s and 1980s eroded authorial authority (see Chapter 4); even if Roland Barthes's claim for the 'death' of the author was overstated, there was no doubt that the critic, by making the meaning of texts contingent on the master theorist, was angling for primary status. Technological developments, meanwhile, have made it possible to compare vast numbers of texts through keyword searches and Internet databases. And there is no doubt that the postwar disappearance of deference—of class-based, unquestioning acceptance of authority—has changed the way we read. We are all authors now.

For comparative literature, these changes have led to the emergence of the idea of 'distant reading'. Coined by Franco Moretti in 2000, the term was originally meant to describe the inevitability of leaning on second-hand reports when dealing with a multinational corpus of world literature: pursued 'without a single direct textual reading', the power of such an approach was to be 'directly proportional to the distance from the text'. Rapidly, however, it morphed into a broader, catch-all term for the digital, data-driven approach to literature, one determined more by graphs, maps, and trees—to cite the title of Moretti's book of 2005—than by words, ideas, and texts. The established model of close reading gave way to an evolutionary model of distant reading that could trace, for instance, the rise of the novel in Britain, Japan, Italy, Spain, and Nigeria. Big data produced big patterns; metaphors—of the 'rise' and 'fall' of the novel—became materially visible.

From the point of view of comparative literature, Moretti's model has much to commend it. For one thing, it obviates the whole problem of translation; no more need one cringe at not working with the 'original' texts. In an era of ever-expanding conceptions of world literature, this is no little advantage. It also foregrounds, as honestly as possible, the critic's inevitable distance—geographical, cultural, linguistic—from so many of the texts that she studies; closeness is no longer the comparison devoutly to be wished for. Perhaps most importantly of all, distant reading makes possible—and legitimizes—large-scale studies of literature that would have been impossible in a previous age, certainly by any single scholar.

Seen from a distance, literary fortunes and fashions come into renewed focus—one has only to consider the rise of the term 'comparative literature' from 1800 to 2000 (see Figure 4).

However incomplete the Google corpus of books inevitably is (someone has to choose and classify them in the first place), this kind of graph offers a vivid—and, importantly, *verifiable*—sense of the rise of comparative literature as a discipline. Moretti has compared these tools to the invention of the telescope, and one can understand why; such graphs can be used to explore any number of comparative combinations, offering a long-distance lens through which to view changing trends and patterns. Even allowing for statistical variations and distortions, this is information worth having.

Why, then, do so many critics have a nagging feeling that something risks being lost in the transition from close to distant reading? The answer lies, perhaps, not so much in the specifics of distant reading as in what it represents. To say that distant reading makes close attention to textual detail redundant is too easy; if anything, computer searches and databases help facilitate studies of specific words and idioms. Proficiency in the interpretation of statistics and data is becoming an increasingly important skill for comparatists—there is no reason to think that celebrated close readers such as William Empson or Leo Spitzer, were they alive today, would not avail themselves of all available technologies in their analyses of literary style. The real transition, then, is not so much from one model of reading to another, as from one model of what reading *is for* to another. Close reading analyses the text as a work of art, invested with its own authority; close comparative reading inquires as to the relationship between competing modes of authority. Distant reading, on the other hand, treats the text as the expression of broader literary and cultural trends, mapping it onto the evolution of forms, genres, and ideas. Close reading, in short, is aesthetic, where distant reading is ultimately sociological.

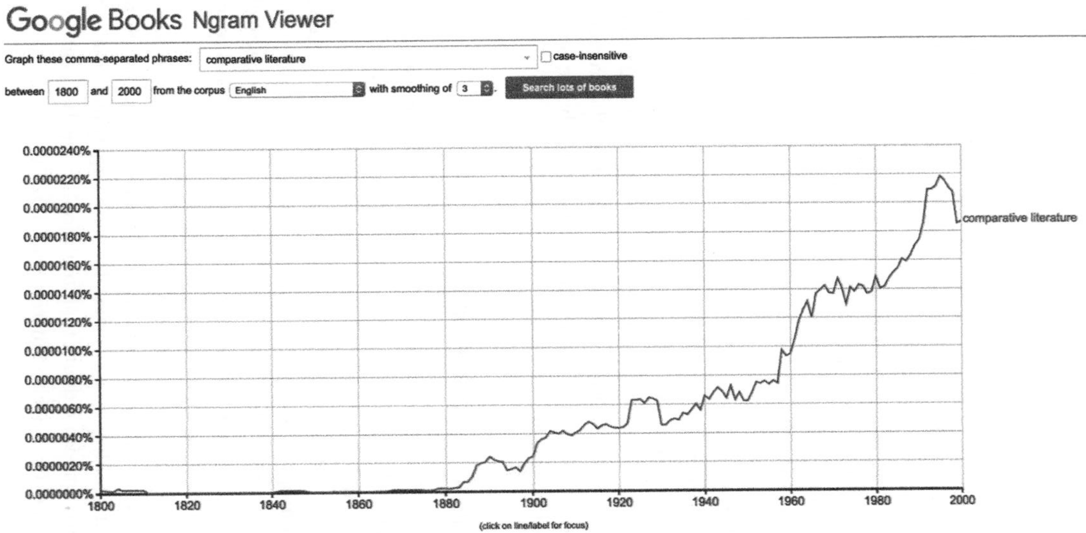

4. Citations of 'comparative literature' in English between 1800 and 2000.

Understood in these terms, it is no surprise that critics who are so heavily invested in the status of literature should seek to defend their 'closeness' to it. Partly, of course, this is a defensive expression of their privileged role as gatekeepers and interpreters of literary tradition. It is also, however, a profession of belief in this tradition, where the closeness of the reading is proportional to the authority—not only artistic, but also moral—ascribed to the texts under discussion. In extreme circumstances, stylistic analysis of major works can be a way of reaffirming the value of a tradition, forming a comparatist's version of inner exile: Erich Auerbach's *Mimesis* (1946) and Ernst Robert Curtius's *European Literature and the Latin Middle Ages* (1948), written against the backdrop of World War Two, provide perhaps the best-known examples of the phenomenon (see Chapter 3). Even in more normal circumstances, however, close reading implies intimacy not only with given texts, but also with the broader tradition and values of which these texts form a part. As such, it raises the crucial question of how comparatists understand and apply the very concept of 'tradition'.

Canon vs. counter-canon

In 1919, the young T.S. Eliot opened an essay with the startling claim that 'in English writing we seldom speak of tradition'. It is only a slight exaggeration to say that a century later, comparative critics seldom speak of anything else. Eliot argued that the European tradition was not set in stone once and for all, and that 'the individual talent' could even alter it retrospectively; the enduring influence of his own critical tastes—his preference for Dante over Milton, his championing of the Metaphysical poets—provides a case in point. Whatever his personal choices, however, there is no doubt that Eliot's literary heroes, like those of the Western tradition more generally, were largely pale, male, and stale—and there is no doubt that 'tradition', in the 21st century, can no longer be conceived merely traditionally.

Criticism of the Western tradition, of its biases and blind spots, has become one of the staple activities of comparative literature—indeed, over the last few decades this critical approach to ideas of tradition has arguably emerged as the discipline's *raison d'être*. Comparison has implicitly developed into compensation, into a way of redressing perceived literary and cultural injustices. To 'do' comparative literature means to assert specific areas of global literature as worthy of attention; in this regard, the discipline resembles nothing so much as a battlefield, a no-man's land of claims and counter-claims. For feminists, there are not enough women writers in the tradition; for postcolonialists, not enough 'ethnic minorities'; for translation scholars, not enough 'minor' languages; for Marxists, not enough representations of social realities. The one thing on which all parties seem able to agree is that Western European, middle-class men have taken up a disproportionate amount of space in the standard narratives of great literature. If history is written by the victors, literature has been underwritten by the oppressors.

The term that has come to encapsulate these disputes is the 'canon'. That this word derives from Biblical 'rules' or 'laws' is not the least of its provocations to secular Humanists of the 21st century; we no longer defer unthinkingly to religious modes of authority, so why should we defer to literary ones? As with religion, so with literature the term has polarized protagonists into two opposing camps. Conservative critics such as Harold Bloom or George Steiner defend the authority of the canon against what Bloom terms 'the school of resentment'; progressive critics—for want of a better term—attack it as hopelessly complicit in political and cultural oppression. Politics replaces aesthetics as the principal arbiter of validity.

Such quarrels, thankfully, are now mostly behind us. To practise comparative literature in the 21st century is to reap the benefits of these debates without being beholden to them; it is to work within an ever-expanding notion of the canon without feeling that one must constantly attack it. The canon certainly remains a key comparative battleground, but not in such a sterile, polarizing manner as in the closing decades of the 20th century. Instead, comparatists have been finding ways to reload the canon without firing it, to freshen up the bath water without throwing out the baby. If comparative literature got us into this mess, one might say, it is now doing its best to get us out of it.

The principal mode that has emerged for doing so is the capacious concept of world literature, the great advantage of which is that it extends the canon without losing too much energy contesting it. 'World' literature—at least in its 21st-century incarnations—simply repositions the Western tradition as part of a global whole, no more nor less important than any other area. To be sure, questions of canon occur not only in Europe and America; areas such as India and the Maghreb have their own traditions (and concomitant squabbles over them). Yet there is no doubt that the Western vision of the canon has vastly expanded over the last twenty years, as reflected in anthologies of world literature that now routinely include work from all corners of the globe and by all creators great and small. Comparative literature, in a very real sense, has won. Our quarrels now seem ended.

Yet we should be wary of crying victory too quickly. For one thing, aesthetic criteria will always remain subjective, whether from the point of view of individuals or from that of cultures. If a Chinese writer rises to worldwide prominence, is this because she is acclaimed by Chinese critics or by international (which in practice usually means English-language) critics? Institutions such as the Nobel Prize committee have an important role to play in canonizing international authors, particularly those who write in less prominent languages, but their decisions will always be partial, not to say political. Even those writers whose success arises through international rather than national reception—Susan Sontag's championing of the German writer W.G. Sebald's 'literary greatness' comes to mind as a recent example—arguably tell us more about one culture's preconceptions of another than anything else. To succeed internationally—and thus to be read, by extension, comparatively—it helps to correspond to the prevailing international image of your country, preferably in some critical, dissenting manner.

The problem, following this logic, is that the study of world literature, however one practises it, does not automatically imply a world perspective. Assessments of aesthetic quality will always be required, and they will always presuppose a given set of values. The canon may be modified by the introduction of the new (the really new) work of art, but who is to say what that work is? It is a truism that no cultural judgement is completely free of ideological baggage, and it will always remain true of the literary canon no matter how it is conceived, whether on a European, world, or planetary scale (see Chapter 4). With the Danish critic Mads Rosendahl Thomsen's notion of canonical 'constellations'—itself a useful term for understanding the gravitational pull of literary force fields—the imagery even goes interplanetary. But it still implies an observer, looking through a telescope from a given point on the Earth.

Perhaps the most striking aspect of the canon as it is currently discussed within comparative literature, then, is its sheer inflation. David Damrosch's terms for what he identifies as the three forms of the canon—'hypercanon' (the major authors), 'countercanon' (the previously marginalized, subaltern authors), and 'shadow canon' (the minor authors now pushed to the margins)—suggest the extent to which canonical theorization has proliferated in comparative literary studies. Indeed, in many ways what characterizes the discipline now is not so much a theory of the canon as a canon of theory; for certain followers, theoretical statements about comparison have assumed the authority of dogma. For all its anarchist energy, contemporary comparative literature seems to be in danger of replacing one canon with another.

Arguably more interesting at this point, then, are the practical implications of the canon debate, the ways it predetermines critical choices. Contemporary practice suggests that there is a risk of comparative literature emerging as a zero-sum game, whereby one author's critical gain is another's reputational loss. After all, there are only so many hours in the day; there are only so many books that can be read in a lifetime. Some version of a canon is a practical necessity, if only for working purposes. Interestingly, the real danger would seem to be not to Great White Males such as Shakespeare or Joyce, but to the smaller fry traditionally described as 'minor' authors. As Damrosch has shown—in an example of distant reading at one remove—statistical analysis of scholarly publications suggests that the major authors of the canon only stand to gain from being associated with comparative methodologies: transnational readings of *Heart of Darkness* or postcolonial readings of *The Tempest* are all too common. It is the lesser figures that have been squeezed out by the theoretical boom, since few careers are made on the back of comparative readings of minor poets. The irony, in other words, is that the assertion of one form of minority risks pushing out another.

Yet the implications of canon theory for *doing* comparative literature remain underexplored, not least in terms of establishing why one should choose to read comparatively in the first place. What does it mean for a Western critic to read an emerging African or Asian writer within an 'international', rather than a national, context? What does one gain from studying an established author such as Flaubert within a comparative canon of other international realists, as opposed to within the French tradition? However sensitive one is to the political prejudices behind the canon, there is always the risk of flattening out local differences by imposing universal perceptions. The scale, in short, requires careful calibration. One size does not fit all.

It is far from clear, then, that there is a single, correct strategy for constructing a comparative perspective on the canon. Should one concentrate, to take the examples just cited, on the 'great works' of European realism, or rather explore a counter-canon of lesser-known, possibly non-European texts? Should one accept the body of realist 'literature' as it has been passed down to us, or question the very concepts of realism and literature? Arguably it is only possible to construct a counter-canon after having first established a canon, but then this in turn would seem to give cultural priority to a predetermined 'tradition'. There is, in short, no single answer to such questions—but posing them remains a crucial aspect of comparative literature, both in theory and in practice.

Genres vs. styles

If criticizing the canon involves assessing the merits of one text or author in the light of another—and is thus an inherently comparative exercise—one of the principal ways of doing this is to explore the construction of genres and styles. To consider a genre or a style comparatively is to alter, however subtly, our view of it, since differing languages have differing generic and stylistic conventions. For the student of comparative literature, genres and styles not only offer hooks on which to hang an argument, but they also function as a way into both formal and historical conceptions of what literature is for.

Genre distinctions are as old as Antiquity. The three traditional categories—drama, lyric, epic—are the earliest avatars of what would become, in the modern era, the principal literary genres as we know them today: plays, poems, novels. Within these categories, a further basic distinction has traditionally obtained between comedy and tragedy, operating as what one might term modes of expression. Should one use literature to laugh at the world, like Democritus, or to weep over it, like Heraclitus? Montaigne may have sided with the former, but the higher status has traditionally accrued to the latter. In the hierarchy of emotions, tears have always trumped laughter, just as suffering has trumped pleasure.

Box 3 Genre theory

A significant body of thought has grown up around the idea of generic conventions. Understood as regulating a reader's expectations of a given text, such conventions can be confirmed, frustrated, or subverted, but for better or for worse they structure all literary interaction. In reading fiction, for instance, we 'suspend disbelief'; in reading autobiography, we expect truth (and are troubled when the pact is broken, as with fake memoirs of the Holocaust). The way that we interact with genres, often without even realizing it, relies on the comparative mechanisms of similarity and difference, since our expectations of a text are predetermined by our experiences of previous texts in the same genre. Both critical and commercial constructions of literature constantly locate themselves within such pre-existing genre distinctions, confirming or contorting them as the case may be. To say that one book is 'like' another is thus to make a comparison based on categories of genre.

From the point of view of comparative literature, the issue here is that such genre distinctions—whether or not they are truly universal—predetermine our aesthetic and affective responses (see Box 3).

To work within a given genre is to work with a whole set of precedents, prejudices, and presuppositions; one can neither write nor read a text without some knowledge of its conventions, even—perhaps especially—if the intention is to break these conventions. In the terms of the reception theorist Hans Robert Jauss, we read within a—stylistic, thematic, conceptual, even typographical—'horizon of expectation', without which meaningful engagement with literature is barely possible.

For the comparatist, defined by her broad horizons, this creates an intriguing quandary. To declare the 'death of tragedy', as

George Steiner did in one of his earliest books (1961), requires an extraordinarily wide range of reference—but it also requires regulating this range against its generic conventions (derived above all, in this case, from Ancient Greece). Marina Warner's comparisons of fairytales and enchanted stories from across Western and Eastern culture are only possible if the stories share certain stylistic or thematic similarities, such as frame narratives or wicked witches. Even Sir William Jones (1746–94), one of the first to treat 'lyrick' as a universal category, could do so only by imposing European standards onto Persian poems (he even translated classical Arabic poetry into Latin). Genres can mean different things in different times and places, in other words; practising comparative literature through the prism of a genre or mode amounts to a delicate balancing act, expanding the horizon of examples while constrained by the horizon of expectation.

More prosaically, genre categories are often used as a means of limiting or focusing an area of enquiry, in ways that may risk seeming arbitrary. If studies of naturalist drama or the Romantic lyric have more than practical coherence, however, it is precisely because they bring with them specific formal and emotional associations: the Scandinavian inflections of Ibsen and Strindberg in the first example, or the *Sturm und Drang* of angry young men in the second. Comparatists can work against such associations by giving them greater intercultural nuance, but they must also work *with* them to stake out their area of study. Comparative literature needs cliché as much as it negates it.

Stylistic conventions, meanwhile, can equally help or hinder the comparatist. Such conventions may operate at the level of periods (the Romantic lyric, the realist novel) or at that of rhetoric (the recurrence of organic imagery, the use of free indirect speech), but they always refer to *ways* of writing more than to the content itself; as such, they offer a model of comparative literature based primarily on aesthetic, rather than political grounds. This is not to say that stylistic choices cannot also be ideological choices—Dante's decision to write in the vernacular rather than in Latin, for instance, was nothing if not ideologically motivated—but their critical appreciation necessarily foregrounds the technical, aesthetic achievement. To understand *why* someone writes in a certain way one first has to understand *how* he writes.

The classic investigation of such stylistic choices remains Auerbach's *Mimesis*, which traces modes of realism all the way from Homer to Virginia Woolf by concentrating on differing levels of style (see Chapter 3). Ranging across classical, medieval, and modern literature, Auerbach reveals how changes in style drive the development of European writing. Significantly, he criticizes writers who stick too closely to the idea that certain stories or milieus require a certain style, from the 'low' register of comedy to the 'high' register of tragedy. Auerbach's argument is rather for a mixture of styles: both the humble and the sublime are necessary and valid responses to the human condition. Rhetoric must also be realistic.

From classical reception to colonial mimicry, from medieval liturgy to modernist literature, close readings of style form the bedrock of comparative literature. Such readings imply a common generic framework within which to compare; as Sheldon Pollock notes of Sanskrit literature, 'modes of literariness conceived of as regional styles within a cosmopolitan space' are a precondition of comparison. A given literary genre such as comedy or tragedy, that is to say, may contain any number of differing styles (such as high or low, courtly or vulgar), the comparison of which produces, in turn, thematic insights (about social and cultural status, for instance). Above all, for style not to be merely style—and for comparison not to be merely comparison, but to produce an argument that is more than the sum of its parts—it requires an organic, rather than an artificial relationship to that which it is describing. If textual meaning emerges from the shifting relationship between form and content, then so, in short, do the best comparisons.

Writers vs. readers

But who, finally, *are* the best comparatists? As a discipline, comparative literature has largely developed as the preserve of critics; as a practice, it is equally the privilege of authors. Comparison occurs not just after the event, in the mind of the reader, but also already during the process of composing a text, in the mind of the writer. Comparative literature is as much creative practice as critical theory: writers often anticipate and invite comparative approaches to their work—Eliot's notes to *The Waste Land* (1922) form an obvious instance—such that the reader is forced into taking a broad, multilingual perspective. Or they build the structure of comparison into their premises: Montesquieu's *Persian Letters* (1721) and Goethe's *West-Eastern Divan* (1819), to take just two examples, adopt a self-consciously 'Asian' perspective in order to gain critical purchase on contemporary Europe (and even these two examples must in turn be compared and contrasted, since Montesquieu was only using the Persian persona to defamiliarize France, whereas Goethe was genuinely interested in Islamic culture on its own terms). Pushed to an extreme, then, the very notion of literature can be seen as inherently comparative, in as much as it contains, potentially, a dizzying infinity of times and places. Literature, in short, is also a *site* of comparison.

Understood in this manner, 'doing' comparative literature takes on a new meaning. In its most fundamental sense, it simply means to write, to place oneself within an existing framework of references and relationships. Partly this is a function of the fact that many writers are also critics: for Eliot, for instance, no poet has complete meaning alone—'you must set him, for contrast and comparison, among the dead'. Yet even within the creative process itself, comparison plays a major role in assigning meaning, since new words and ideas derive, inevitably, from old words and ideas. As Ezra Pound noted, 'all ages are contemporaneous—and this is especially true of literature'.

If literature is thus inherently comparative, it is because it acts as a compressor, blending past, present, and future and conflating numerous, often conflicting cultural perspectives. Of course, it does not always do this to the same extent, and some styles and epochs seem to be more comparative than others. I have cited Eliot and Pound, for instance, as exemplars of modernism—now increasingly understood as *global* modernism—and certainly within the Anglo-American world the modernist manner was nothing if not obsessively intertextual, conceived as a way of foregrounding the internationalism of the postwar years. The exhausted European mind, ground down by the murderous attrition of the trenches, started looking further afield for inspiration: to India in the case of Eliot, to China in the case of Pound. Their poetry, with all its subsequent prestige and influence, is inconceivable without this intercontinental admixture.

Yet such comparative techniques were hardly new. The very first modern novel, for example, playfully foregrounds—or feigns—its hybridity. *Don Quixote* (1605–15), Cervantes claims, was translated from an Arabic version written by the historian Cide Hamete Benengeli (see Figure 5). No such person existed, of course—the name means something like Sir Hamid the Aubergine-Eater—but Cervantes uses him to insert the novel into contemporary debates about Spain's 'three cultures'. The Jews having been expelled in 1492, the Moors followed in 1609–14—which is to say, in the years between the two volumes of *Don Quixote*—leaving only Christians and 'new' Christians, forcibly converted from Judaism and Islam. Cervantes' authorial sleight-of-hand, then, forces attention onto the multicultural, interfaith tradition of Spain in the Golden Age, positioning his novel against the national decrees. By implying a comparative text constructed

5. The invention of translation: the supposed Arabic author of *Don Quixote*.

across two languages—and by giving it a comic twist—Cervantes was effectively speaking spoof to power.

It is no coincidence, then, that Jorge Luis Borges should have chosen Cervantes's masterpiece as the pretext, in both senses of the term, for his astonishing meditation on the nature of translation. The short story 'Pierre Menard, Author of the *Quixote*' (1939) is both satirical and salutary. Menard's inspired idea is to translate Cervantes *word for word* from Spanish into Spanish; with a straight face, Borges notes how revelatory it is to compare Menard's *Don Quixote* with that of Cervantes. When the latter, writing in the early 17th century, adduces 'truth, whose mother is history', Borges parses it as 'mere rhetorical praise of history'; when the former, in the 20th century, proposes exactly the same sentence, the idea is hailed as 'astounding'. Menard thus becomes the *author*, not the translator, of *Don Quixote*. As a commentary on translation, on reception, and on the contextual bias of comparative literature, the Argentinian author's story of a fictional Frenchman rewriting the Spanish classic is a stroke of genius. It is also, however, itself a work of comparative literature, conflating critical vision with creative verve.

Borges's story points to the increasing self-awareness that attends modern forms of comparison. Educated authors cannot but be aware of their modern, or postmodern, 'condition'; to write in the contemporary era is to situate oneself within the history not only of literature, but also of comparative approaches to literature. Postcolonial writing provides important examples of this: contemporary authors such as the Indian Amitav Ghosh or the Kenyan Ngũgĩ wa Thiong'o write in full knowledge of the leading theories of their condition, trained as they are to see through the imperial legacy (so much so, indeed, that Ngũgĩ now writes, once again, in his 'local' language Gikuyu). Just as much writing in the 21st century is 'born digital', so some texts are born 'hybrid' or born translated. 'Decolonising the Mind', to cite the title of Ngũgĩ's seminal study of 1986, is nothing if not a self-conscious process; *comparing* the minds of Europe and Africa—and not least, of the many different peoples within Africa—is heavily theorized from the start.

In considering comparative literature from the point of view of the writer, then, it may be useful to distinguish between differing degrees of self-consciousness. For there is an important difference between *consciously* encouraging the reader to compare and contrast (the modernist, postmodernist, or postcolonial model), and *unconsciously* writing oneself into situations that can then be read comparatively (one might call this the realist model, but it also applies to broad swathes of literary history more generally). In the former, the writer invites the comparison; in the latter, it is the reader who imposes it, albeit onto receptive ground.

Intertextuality may be the strongest mode of authorial comparison, but it is not the only one.

All this is a way of saying that writers are also readers, first and foremost of their own work. The more internationally minded among them—modernists, postcolonialists—are the most obviously comparative, but all writers work to compare and contrast themselves, implicitly or explicitly, with other forms of literature. The anxiety of influence, in Harold Bloom's famous phrase, is also the anxiety of comparison, the never-ending attempt to disambiguate one's own work from that of others, without whom one could not exist in the first place. Literature, whether consciously comparative or not, is a dance of similarity and difference, and it is writers, not readers, who set the tune.

When considering the practices and principles of comparative literature, then, we would do well to consider them from the perspective of both creators and critics. The increasing prominence of hybrid forms such as adaptation and 'inter-art' studies—where the emphasis is on the ways in which creation is inherently comparison—suggests, indeed, that this double perspective is emerging as a focal point for the discipline. Readers cannot compare without writers, and writers cannot compare without reading. On such first principles rest the many practices of comparative literature.

Chapter 3
History and heroes

Understood as a practice, comparative literature is—almost—as old as literature itself. The classical cultures of Antiquity contain their own comparative structure. Latin literature develops to a large extent by comparing itself, often unfavourably, with its Greek predecessor; the self-consciousness with which authors such as Virgil, Horace, and Ovid look back to their Hellenic sources provides perhaps the earliest example of comparative literature in action. The Greek mythology that would provide the material for so many comparative studies in subsequent centuries finds here its first foreign contextualization: exile, return, and metamorphosis emerge as both motifs of the texts and metaphors of the context, as ways of understanding how stories and ideas circulate. The history of European literature as a history of comparison begins.

If it is only in the modern period, however, that comparative literature emerges as a self-conscious discipline, then it is only in looking beyond Europe that the true force of this discipline becomes apparent. Seen from a Western perspective, one can plausibly divide the history of comparative literature into three categories: the history of how European literatures have been compared *inside* Europe; the history of how European literature has been compared with other cultures *outside* Europe; and the history of how literatures outside Europe—Egyptian, Persian,

Arabic, Chinese—have been compared among themselves. While this chapter largely concentrates on the Western, European story—since it is principally this story, for better or for worse, that has constituted comparative literature as a discipline—it is important to remember that non-Europeans have long been comparing, too. From Persian to Japanese, from pre- to postmodernity, comparison has never been a purely European privilege. As Karen Thornber has shown, Chinese, Korean, and Taiwanese readers were arguably more comparative than their European counterparts in the early 20th century, busy as they were comparing and contesting the Japanese literary empire. Asian critics have never needed Europeans to tell them how to compare.

Comparing the comparatists in this manner suggests a broader lesson for the discipline in the West, namely that it has been predetermined by its use of the nation as its building block. In response to the modern, post-Westphalian conception of the nation-state—to the idea of national sovereignty enshrined in 1648 and universalized over the course of the 19th century—comparative literature asserted itself as international. In doing so, however, it tied itself to the very idea that it sought to overcome, since comparison was now defined as international rather than interlinguistic. Intellectually speaking, there is no reason why this need be the case; the pre-modern practice of cosmopolitanism—as mediated through a *lingua franca* such as Latin or Arabic—shows that comparison can be conceived between languages just as easily as between nations. Politically speaking, however, the universalization of the European model enshrined the idea of international—and thus of national—comparison as the default setting of the discipline. As Sheldon Pollock has noted, the national narrative is a 'second-generation representation made possible only by the existence of a first-generation representation', namely language.

It is the particularity of the European conception of comparative literature, in other words, that it emerged, in its modern incarnation, at a time when the major European nations were competing internally to develop externally, pursuing an increasingly aggressive policy of expansionism towards other continents conceived as 'colonies'. As the influence worked its way backwards—with Asian, African, and American conceptions of literature helping to constitute the European model—so the discipline developed as an intercontinental enterprise. From the empire building of the 19th century, via the Jewish diaspora of the 20th century, to the postcolonial culture wars of the 21st century, the problems and prejudices of comparative literature have thus formed a cultural counterpart to the problems and prejudices of Modernity. To understand its history, in this spirit, is to understand why it matters.

Comparative philology

In 1872, an obscure, self-taught linguist working at the British Museum rewrote history. George Smith discovered—and, crucially, deciphered—a series of cuneiform tablets compiled sometime after 2500 BC, tablets that turned out to contain the story now generally viewed as the earliest extant work of literature (see Figure 6). Written in Akkadian, a version of Sumerian spoken in ancient Mesopotamia (modern Iraq), the epic of *Gilgamesh* caused a sensation, chiefly because it seemed to confirm the myth of the Flood as related in the book of Genesis. By comparing it to the Biblical version of the story, Smith claimed to have found independent corroboration of the Deluge; the Victorians now had a seemingly scientific way of justifying their Christian world-view. Previewed in *The Daily Telegraph* and announced to an audience including the Prime Minister William Gladstone, Smith's discovery—arriving in the wake of the geological and evolutionary revolutions—gave renewed impetus to the Creationism debate. The power of comparison had never seemed more evident.

The status of comparative literature in its early years—somewhere between archaeology, philology, literary scholarship, and cultural

6. The Flood, but not as we know it. *Gilgamesh*, British Museum.

history—emerges vividly from the unlikely story of Smith's *Gilgamesh*. On the one hand, the intellectual achievement is astonishing, the comparison of stylistic and thematic details insightful, if necessarily speculative: Smith distinguishes, for instance, between the 'inland' version of the Flood as given by the Bible and the 'maritime' version related by the tablets, and compares the hero of the epic to that great classical Greek hero, Hercules. Beyond the intellectual achievement, on the other hand, the Victorian reception of Smith's *Gilgamesh* also demonstrates the cognitive bias of the age, predisposed to view everything—even cultural artefacts from a distant time and place—through the classical, Christian prism of the British Empire. By 1872, in other words, comparative literature had become part of the broader project of cultural colonialism.

How had it got to this point? To answer this question, we need to go back to the roots of the discipline in the years around 1800. For the story of *Gilgamesh* suggests the extent to which comparative literature was born out of the spirit of comparative philology. Philology—the study of language in its historical texts and contexts (see Box 4)—boomed in the early 19th century, as colonialism opened up whole new continents for fieldwork. Comparisons between modern European and ancient Oriental languages became inevitable. Based on their experiences in British India, early Orientalists such as Sir William Jones argued that

Box 4 Philology

The study of language in its textual development, philology drove the development of the Humanities as we know them today. First mentioned by Plato, ancient philology comprised four main elements: language theory, rhetoric, textual criticism, and grammar. Over the centuries it evolved into a means of reconstructing historical contexts out of literary texts—extrapolating ancient ways of living, for instance, by reading Homer or Herodotus—and even helped define the periodization of European history into ancient, middle, and modern. As practised throughout the early modern era, philology represented a kind of (intimidatingly erudite) comparative literature before the fact: less a discipline than a set of critical practices, it relied on comparison as its principal technique, whether applied to classical, Biblical, or Oriental texts. As James Turner notes in his study *Philology: The Forgotten Origins of the Modern Humanities* (2014), 'the most numerous, obstinate, thoroughgoing practitioners of the comparative method in the West have been philologists'.

European and 'Asiatick' languages shared common roots in an original language that became known as 'Proto-Indo-European'. Unsurprisingly, Jones and his followers also attempted analogies between classical Asian languages—Persian, Arabic, Sanskrit—and the classical European languages of Latin and Greek. The colony of India was now to Britain what the colony of Britain had been to Rome, opening up a whole new front for comparative linguistics.

This colonial fieldwork became the basis for subsequent theorists of European Romanticism such as Friedrich Schlegel (1772–1829)—the man who introduced the concept of the 'Romantic' as a way of describing postclassical literature—to dream of finding 'the source of all languages, all thought, and all poetry of the human spirit' through 'comparative grammar'. Writing in 1820, Wilhelm von Humboldt described the aim of these early comparatists as being 'to establish on a better basis the comparative study of languages which heretofore has been highly superficial, unphilosophical, and wrongheaded'; the study of languages quickly shaded over into the study of cultures more broadly defined, particularly as these pioneering figures often undertook fieldwork in distant countries. A distinction began to emerge between what one might term 'explorers' on the one hand and 'armchair comparatists' on the other; between travellers and theorists.

It is not surprising, then, that problematic notions of 'West' and 'East' have haunted comparative literature since its inception. The Enlightenment belief in the progress of humankind privileged Western culture as the centre of the Republic of Letters. Following the French Revolution, the concept of 'Europe' surfed a wave of pathos, figuring in journal titles—*Europa* (1803), *Archives littéraires de l'Europe* (1804)—and any number of manifestos insisting, to cite one well-known tract of the time, on the common cultural heritage of *Christendom or Europe* (1802). Figures such as Madame de Staël worked hard to encourage international exchange within Europe, particularly along the all-important Franco-German axis, even introducing notably modern reflections on the role of women or on the North–South cultural division (for de Staël, for instance, Southern Europe functioned as a kind of internal Orient). The real Orient, however, remained a barely acknowledged presence at the edges of Christendom.

The rise of philology changed the nature of this comparison. Napoleon's 'savants' returned from the occupation of Egypt (1798–1801) with a new interest in Franco-Arabic intellectual relations; shortly afterwards the term 'comparative literature' even appeared, perhaps for the first time in Europe, when François-Joseph-Michel Noël and Guislain-François-Marie-Joseph de La Place advertised their *Leçons françaises de littérature et de morale* (1816) as a 'cours de literature comparée'. On the other side of the Rhine, meanwhile, enthusiasm for Schlegel's idea of comparative grammar—as expounded in his hugely influential study *On the Language and Wisdom of the Indians* (1808)—led to ever more heroic attempts at comparing languages. Figures such as Franz Bopp, with his almost comically learned *Comparative Grammar of the Sanscrit, Zend, Greek, Latin, Lithuanian, Gothic, German, and Slavonic Languages* (translated into English in 1845–53), took the intellectual craze for Indo-European languages to new heights; by 1842, a Philological Society had been founded in London, following the creation of similar institutions in France and Germany. In an age in which the study of languages and literatures was more closely entwined than today, Humboldt's stated ambition 'to compare the diverse languages of ancient and present times' encapsulated the general belief that comparison—both within Europe and without Europe—was at the cutting edge of scholarship.

Arguably the most influential figure behind the Romantic view of comparison was Johann Gottfried Herder (1744–1803). Herder's essay *On the Origin of Language* (1772) paved the way for subsequent developments in linguistics; his *Reflections on the*

Philosophy of the History of Mankind (1784–91), meanwhile, traced the seeming inevitability of progress and emancipation, leading Hegel and Schlegel, to name but two, to produce similar philosophies of history. If Herder's influence was equally important in the emergence of comparative literature, it was because of this signature blend of anthropology and philology. For Herder, international exchange has national consequences, since each nation is thereby reinforced in its own sense of cultural identity. Literature emerges as the expression of the organic unity of a nation, as what Herder terms the *Volksgeist*. To be sure, this is not an argument for an abstract concept so much as for concrete specifics: in his *Letters for the Advancement of Humanity* (1797), for instance, Herder produces one of the earliest critiques of the idea of comparative literature, criticizing the quarrel of the ancients and moderns—the French debate of the 1690s between those who claimed that the Classics remained unsurpassed and those who championed the supremacy of contemporary culture (see Chapter 4)—as ideologically rather than aesthetically driven. But the supposition that literature provides 'an expression of the highest ideal' remains constant.

It is worth dwelling for a moment on Herder's *Letters*, since they anticipate many of the issues surrounding comparative literature that would develop over the course of the 19th century. Herder argues that 'poetry is a Proteus', changing its forms according to its given context. He is both welcoming to, and wary of, the 'ocean of comparison' that this implies: welcoming, because literature provides a way of accessing national modes of thought from the inside out, rather than through the outside-in approach favoured by political history; wary, because nations invariably tend to prefer their own poets, or at the very least judge foreign poets against their own standards. After sketching out three main modes of comparison—genres and forms, sentiments, and historical specificity—Herder effectively argues for a version of the third mode, for what one might term contextual 'contingency': human nature may remain more or less unchanging, but cultural conditions vary, and must be appraised accordingly.

Herder's reflections on the methodology that this entails suggest, intriguingly, that comparative literature may be conceived as a version of what is known in philosophy as the Sorites paradox. This ancient paradox states that one can never quite pinpoint the difference between a grain of sand and a pile (*sorites* in Greek), since one can never be sure at what precise point the grains of sand becomes a pile. Herder implies a similar problem with the comparative method:

> No new category caused the great difference that has arisen between the Orient and the Occident, between the Greeks and us, but rather the mingling of peoples, of religions and languages, eventually the progress of customs, of innovations, of knowledge and experience—a difference hard to subsume beneath one word.

The Sorites paradox of comparative literature, then, is that one period or tradition shades into another at a point that can be very difficult to identify, despite ostensible differences of emphasis and idiom. Finding such a point—When does medieval literature end and that of the Renaissance begin? Where is the precise crossover point between Eastern and Western forms of poetry?—is the task of the comparatist.

That this point is to be sought not only between East and West, but also between Antiquity and Modernity, indicates one of the key axes of comparison in the 19th century. For European critics writing around 1800, the act of comparing notably extended across time as well as space. The principal reasons for this double emphasis—reasons that are respectively philological, cultural, and political—tell us much about the status and aims of comparative literature in its early years. Philologically speaking, the 19th century witnessed the emergence of anthropological linguistics, inspired by Herderian ideas, as a kind of interdisciplinary research field *avant la lettre*. Predominantly Germanic in its early years, this new science rapidly came to influence European notions of comparison more broadly. Indeed, it is one of the principal reasons why German became the language of scholarship in the 19th century; if Germany was not yet a national power in the early 1800s, it was certainly a cultural one.

Yet the crucial intellectual breakthrough of this period—a breakthrough that made possible the subsequent development of comparative literature as an autonomous mode of exegesis—was as much cultural as philological: namely, the move from a sacred to a profane model of criticism. The Bible, that is to say, began to be read critically, as a text like any other subject to exaggeration and historical variation; the 'life of Jesus'—to cite the title of David Friedrich Strauss's controversial study of 1835—became as historically questionable as any other event. Writing in 1848, the French critic Ernest Renan (1823–92) claimed that German philology had awoken 'the spirit of modernity' and that its critical methodology had made him renounce a career in the church, a career path emblematic of the growing importance of the Humanities in the 19th century. At the heart of the Humanities at this time—and at the heart of the comparative turn backwards to ancient languages and cultures—was the quest for 'origins'.

In the pre-Darwinian early 19th century, 'origin' was essentially a political concept. Imperialist ambition and competition drove the major European powers to seek legitimacy in ancient ancestors; the identification of cultural and linguistic precursors—for the Germans in Greece, for the French in Rome—was a sign of elective affinity as much as anything else, a kind of historically applied prejudice. Comparative literature was often little more than competitive literature, a thinly disguised attempt to dignify superiority through philology. This competition certainly took place inside Europe—with the dominant nations competing in a kind of cultural proxy war—but it also, to return to our starting point, took place outside Europe, with 'comparison' used as a stick with which to beat back the unenlightened savages beyond the pale. Lord Macaulay's notorious remark to parliament in 1835 that 'a single shelf of a good European library was worth the whole native literature of India and Arabia' exemplifies this prejudice, and points towards the limits of the comparative method as it emerged in these early years. With a few honourable exceptions, attempts at understanding European culture as part of a broader, global culture were predetermined—and thus, in the long run, undermined—by the assumption of unquestioned superiority. For better or for worse, the struggle to move beyond this assumption would come to define the discipline.

Towards world literature

There are, however, a number of alternative ways to formulate this assumption of prejudice, and their juxtaposition points towards the broader sense of comparative literature that emerged as the 19th century progressed. Two statements—one little known, the other perhaps too well-known for its own good—show the way. In his 1825 collection of aphorisms *Aids to Reflection*, Samuel Taylor Coleridge, the most internationally minded of the English Romantics, begins a long footnote in the following terms:

> The act of comparing supposes in the comparing faculty certain inherent forms, that is, modes of reflecting, not referable to the objects reflected on, but pre-determined by the constitution and mechanisms of the understanding itself. And under some one or other of these forms, resemblances and differences must be subsumed in order to be conceivable, and *a fortiori* therefore in order to be comparable.

Coleridge's passing comment constitutes the thinking man's counterpart to the unthinking prejudices of the 19th century. Yes, he concedes, the ways in which we compare are predetermined by the 'inherent forms' of our perceptual apparatus—but this need not be so much a cultural prejudice as a philosophical prerequisite: we cannot compare what we cannot conceive. Since 'resemblances and differences' can only be judged from a specific, limited point of view, it is better to be aware of this point of view than to be beholden to it. In the words of Dirty Harry, a man's gotta know his limitations.

Coleridge's philosophical formulation offers renewed purchase on what is probably the single most influential statement in the history of comparative literature. In 1827, the great national poet Goethe shared his views on the increasingly international nature of poetry; recorded for posterity by his conversation partner Johann Peter Eckermann, they marked the birth of *Weltliteratur*:

> I am more and more convinced [...] that poetry is the universal possession of mankind, revealing itself everywhere and at all times in hundreds and hundreds of men. [...] National literature is now rather an unmeaning term; the epoch of world literature is at hand, and everyone must strive to hasten its approach.

Two years after Coleridge's inquiry into the 'inherent forms' that underlie the act of comparing, Goethe seems to advocate the opposite conception. In the international market of Modernity, 'national' or local modes of literature are increasingly irrelevant; it is now world literature that we must pursue. Chinese novels, Goethe adds by way of example, have as much to say to us as their German or French counterparts; what counts is not the subject matter so much as its manner of treatment. Poets should not try to compete with the historian in recording events—a distant echo here of Aristotle's insistence on the superiority of the imaginative writer to the historian, since the former relates not how things were, but how they *might* be—but should rather 'make something of a simple subject by a masterly treatment'. For Goethe, then, comparison is essentially of style, not of content.

The poet's immediate response to his own clarion-call is as interesting, however, as the declaration itself. Despite his grand rhetorical gesture towards a sweepingly universal sense of world literature, Goethe is not unaware of the problem of prejudice:

> While we thus value what is foreign, we must not bind ourselves to some particular thing, and regard it as a model. We must not give this value to the Chinese, or the Serbian, or Calderon, or the *Nibelungen*; but, if we really want a pattern, we must always return to the ancient Greeks, in whose works the beauty of mankind is constantly represented.

Where Coleridge writes of 'modes of reflecting', Goethe reflects on the *models* for reflecting: how are we to assess world literature fairly, given that no external, impartial perspective is possible? Fittingly, Goethe's own words illustrate this problem, since his twists and turns—we should not ascribe value to any particular foreign tradition, he claims, yet we should, paradoxically, ascribe it to the Greeks—betray his own point of view as a typically Hellenophile German of the early 19th century.

Despite his universalist ambitions, then, Goethe's model of world literature implies a very European yardstick. In this, of course, he is hardly alone in the early decades of the 19th century. Where Goethe avers that 'there is being formed a universal world literature, in which an honourable role is reserved for us Germans', a French critic like Philarète Chasles (1798–1873) can claim, in announcing his 1835 study of *The Comparison of Foreign Literature*, that 'I will concern myself primarily with France, [...] the most sensitive of countries.' Tellingly, Chasles justifies his celebration of France as the most receptive—and thus 'comparative'—of nations by placing it within the broader context of European hegemony: 'What Europe is to the rest of the world, France is to Europe; everything reverberates toward her, everything ends with her.' Chasles can thus think of his comparative method as both patriotic and cosmopolitan; nationalism is sanctified as Europeanism.

Whatever the prejudices inherent in the term, Goethe's coinage of *Weltliteratur* marks a watershed in the history of comparative literature. It matters little that he was not, in fact, the first to use the word; that honour goes to his friend Christoph Martin Wieland (1733–1813), and for all we know to others before him. What matters is rather that Goethe was *perceived* as having coined the term, thereby conferring his Olympian prestige on it. With the publication of Eckermann's conversations with Goethe in 1836, 'World literature' as a concept was launched.

The extreme capaciousness of the term—its great strength but arguably also its greatest weakness—rapidly came to apply to 'literature' as well as to the 'world'. Just twenty years later, in 1848, it turned up in the most unlikely of places: *The Communist Manifesto*. With the colonization of trade and industry by the cosmopolitan middle-classes, claim Marx and Engels, 'national one-sidedness and narrow-mindedness become more and more impossible, and from the numerous national and local literatures there arises a world literature'. The authors suggest an implicit parallel between commodities and texts, both of which now circulate, in the mid-19th century, with complete disregard for national boundaries. This may seem a radical redeployment of the aesthetic idea of *Weltliteratur*, but in fact already in 1827 Goethe repeatedly reaches for the language of 'value' (both in his conversations with Eckermann and elsewhere), speculating on rising markets in China and Serbia before returning to the gold standard of Ancient Greece.

Understood in its historical context, this conflation of commercial and cultural modes of circulation is hardly surprising. Economic metaphors of value and circulation define the mid-19th century imagination: the great Realist novels of the 1850s and 1860s by Dickens, Flaubert, or Tolstoy import capitalist models of accumulation into the sphere of culture, with the hero of the *Bildungsroman* acquiring his stock of cultural capital in order to move up in society. Yet we need not necessarily interpret models of commerce in the pejorative sense that we might now attribute to the 'commercial' exploitation of culture. In the case of Goethe, for instance, one can understand the metaphor of the 'marketplace' positively, in the Enlightenment sense of a forum for international exchange, the currency of which is as much cultural as commercial. Here as elsewhere, then, the models of comparison must themselves be approached comparatively.

What metaphors of value also convey, however, is the sheer multiplicity of Modernity, the proliferation of meaning brought about by the industrial and technological revolution. 'There was never such a miscellany of facts', writes Emerson in an essay of 1850 on Goethe as a 'representative man'.

> The world extends itself like American trade. We conceive Greek or Roman life, life in the Middle Ages, to be a simple and comprehensible affair; but modern life to respect a multitude of things.

If comparison imposed itself as an inevitable consequence of this proliferation of perspectives, so, interestingly, did a conservative recursion to the canon. In a period threatened by such uncontrollable forces, the literary mind retreated to tried and tested values: at the precise mid-point of the 19th century, Emerson's list of 'representative men'—Plato, Swedenborg, Montaigne, Shakespeare, Napoleon, Goethe—carefully circumscribes the limits of the Western world. In place of the Pillars of Hercules (see Figure 7), Emerson erects the pillars of hermeneutics, as markers of the known, decidedly European world.

This is not to say that comparative literature was exclusively the province of White Anglo-Saxon Protestants. By the 1870s,

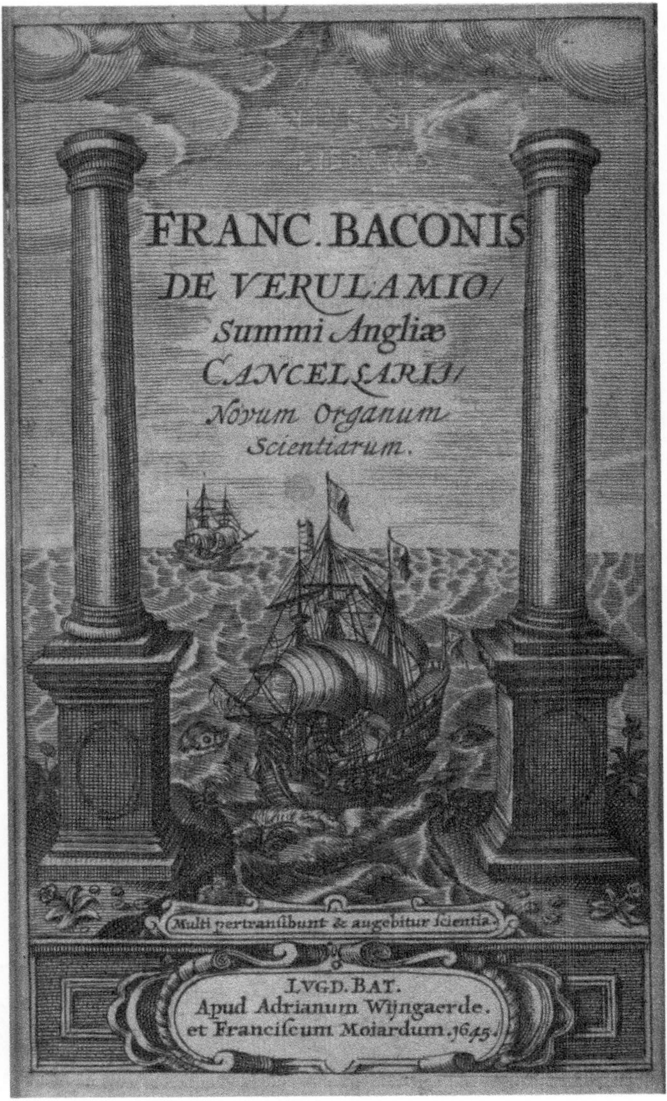

7. The Pillars of Hercules as depicted on the frontispiece to Francis Bacon's *Novum Organum* (1620).

comparative literary studies were beginning to emerge on the far eastern edge of Europe. In 1872—the same year in which George Smith published his version of *Gilgamesh*—the University of Moscow opened a Department of World Literature; in 1875, St Petersburg followed suit with a Neo-Philological Society. The presiding spirit behind this latter initiative was a literary historian by the name of Aleksandr Veselovsky (1838–1906), who would go on to become arguably the single most important figure in the development of comparative literature in Russia. Veselovsky pioneered the study of international patterns of influence as a way of understanding national modes of development. Interested in particular in folklore and fairytales, Veselovsky used comparative methods to explore the relationship between East (Russia) and West (Europe). His study of *The Western Influence in New Russian Literature* first appeared in 1881; by 1916 it had gone through an impressive five editions, indicating its wide reception.

Veselovsky's view of comparative literature as the study of sources and influences derives its importance from the historical context of late 19th-century Russia. For Veselovsky, as for many of his contemporaries and compatriots—the generation of the so-called Silver Age—Russia was a culturally backward continent that could only develop by looking to the West. The progress of Russian culture could be charted, he believed, by comparing it to that of Western Europe. Ultimately, this would be to Russia's advantage, since the very receptivity of Russian culture would ensure that it became ever richer and stronger. Through incorporating international influences, the national culture would emerge as a fuller version of itself. Here as elsewhere—the argument re-emerges in Oswald de Andrade's 'Manifesto Antropófago' (1928), for instance, which proposes that Brazil should 'cannibalize' Europe in order to absorb its cultural nutrients—comparative literature functions as an exercise in nation building.

It is worth pausing for a moment to reflect on what this implies. If comparative literature as it was practised in 19th-century Europe emerged as the continuation of international relations by other means, this took two principal forms: empire building and nation building. The former model applied to the nations that were politically and militarily dominant, above all England and France; the latter, to those that were struggling to articulate their own identity on the international stage—here one might think of Russia or Denmark. (Germany, the country from which so much of the impetus for comparative literature emerged, occupies a pivotal position between the two models, since although it only emerged as a nation in 1871, it had long occupied a leading position culturally.) In literature as in politics, the dominant nations were aggressively expanding their sphere of influence—often in the form of large, multilingual empires—while the emerging nations were engaged in more defensive attempts to establish the importance of their own cultures through comparing them to others. Literature, to return to the economic metaphors of currency and value that define *Weltliteratur*, was a version of cultural capital, to be acquired and invested through international exchange.

One of the more interesting consequences of this is that it is often cultures perceived as 'marginal' that are more genuinely comparative, for the simple reason that they have more to gain from international cooperation. Russian Symbolism at the end of the 19th century is a case in point, drawing as it does on Schopenhauer and Nietzsche in Germany, Mallarmé and Verlaine in France, Pater and Wilde in England, and Ibsen and Strindberg in Scandinavia. Writing in the preface to the 1896 edition of *The Western Influence in New Russian Literature*, Veselovsky notes that 'respect [...] for European culture has gradually arisen', and that the field of comparative literary studies has developed commensurately from 'isolated workers' to 'friendly collective labour'. By the early 20th century, then, it is no surprise that the poet Osip Mandelstam can diagnose a 'yearning for world culture' as a constituent element of his generation's poetry. For comparative virtue emerges from cultural necessity: the great advantage of coming from the perceived margins of international culture—an advantage that obtains to this day—is that it makes possible the synthesis of existing trends. Looked at from this perspective, comparison is the privilege of posterity.

Discipline and publish

The years 1870–80 saw the emergence of comparative literature as a discipline not only in Russia, but also elsewhere in Europe. In Denmark, the literary critic Georg Brandes sought to overcome the Scandinavian cultural cringe towards continental Europe by developing a comparative method that both appropriated and alienated foreign literature. Brandes' image of the telescope—'one end magnifies, the other reduces'—neatly captures the ambivalence of his relationship to the dominant European traditions: on the one hand, he admired major writers of the continent such as Anatole France or Friedrich Nietzsche, publishing prolifically on them; on the other hand, he dreamed of establishing Danish literary figures as their equal. His celebration of the 'Men of the Modern Breakthrough'—the phrase that has come to define the Danish modernists of the late 19th century—can be understood in this light, as an attempt to harness comparative literature to the defence of minority languages. For a critic as ambitious as Brandes, to bring together the Nordic and continental traditions was a natural aspiration; like so many of the leading theories of comparison, however, it was not without national self-interest.

The tendency for comparative literature to develop at the margins of dominant cultures—but also to be recuperated by them—is nowhere more vividly apparent than in the work of Hugó Meltzl (1846–1908). Meltzl's very name—he is variously given as Hugó Lomnitzi or Hugó Meltzl de Lomnitz—suggests the 'principle of polyglottism' with which he has become associated. Born in a part of Hungary that is now Romania, Meltzl grew up speaking German under the Austro-Hungarian empire—in an area, more specifically, that ever since Bram Stoker's *Dracula* indelibly evokes what one might term 'the internal Orient' of Europe: Transylvania. Having trained in Heidelberg, in 1872 Meltzl returned to Transylvania to a professorship in German, at the age of just 26. Five years later, in 1877, he would found the first journal of comparative literature anywhere in the world.

The story of this journal tells us much about the status of comparative literature in these seminal years of the discipline. Working with an older colleague, the professor of comparative philology Samuel Brassai, Meltzl conceived the idea of a truly cosmopolitan publication. The title itself—*Acta Comparationis Litterarum Universarum*—was originally given in three languages (Hungarian, German, and French) before settling into the transnational solution of Latin; contributions, the editors declared, could be submitted in no fewer than ten official languages. Perhaps inevitably, the practice did not quite live up to the theory, with over two-thirds of the essays being published in either Hungarian or German. Equally inevitable, no doubt, was the very limited success to which such an ambitious enterprise was fated, with no more than a hundred copies ever being circulated. Indeed it is in many ways amazing that the journal lasted as long as it did, running for eleven years before shutting down, under pressure from rival publications, in 1888.

From the disciplinary perspective, however, the founding and the closing of *Acta Comparationis* tell an eloquent story. Meltzl's manifesto for the journal, published in the first issues of 1877, calls for comparative literature—understood, in the manner of the 19th century, as touching upon 'philosophy, aesthetics, even ethnology and anthropology'—to become a fully established academic discipline. Meltzl defines this discipline in contrast to literary history, which has become little more, he argues, than a tool for cultural nationalism. His 'comparative principle', on the other hand, was to have two main poles of interest, namely translation and *Weltliteratur*—the latter understood not in the jingoistic sense of German literary historians, but in the true Goethean sense as 'nothing less than the emerging discipline of the future: Comparative Literature'.

This new discipline should be driven, Meltzl declares, by the 'principle of polyglottism' (see Box 5). Abjuring 'foggy, cosmopolitanizing theories' of comparative literature, the principle of polyglottism represents the direct commerce of texts between themselves, the hope that nations as disparate as Hungary, Portugal, Germany, and Iceland might talk to each other in their own languages. If this ambition seems hopelessly impractical, a Borgesian dream of universal communication, it was designed to protect the lesser languages and to ensure that more marginal literary traditions might also maintain a voice. The journal's aim,

Box 5 'Principle of Polyglottism'

In his manifesto of 1877, Meltzl defines the principle of polyglottism in contrast to the principle of translation: where the latter is confined to the *indirect* commerce of literature, the former insists on *direct* commerce between literatures. Meltzl thereby sketches out two basic modes of comparison, modes that would be foundational for the development of comparative literature over the subsequent century. If translation involves intermediaries, polyglottism seeks unmediated access to foreign cultures, bringing them together in a Babel of competing tongues. The utopian impracticality of such an ambition—how many comparatists can read more than even a handful of languages?—is only partially mitigated by Meltzl's concession that, in practice, his journal should limit itself to ten languages, namely those that have achieved 'classicism'. That all of these languages were European is typical of the late 19th-century view of comparison: when Asian literature finally accepts 'our' alphabet, declared Meltzl, it will be worthy of inclusion.

in short, was to form 'a small polyglot parliament on various problems of Comparative Literature'.

The reality of the discipline, however, soon punctured Meltzl's pathos. In 1887, the German scholar Max Koch announced a new journal in Berlin, with the suspiciously familiar title *Zeitschrift für vergleichende Literaturgeschichte*. That the German version of *Acta Comparationis* was *Zeitschrift für vergleichende Literatur* was no coincidence; Koch was muscling in on Meltzl's territory. Beyond the usual petty academic rivalries, the struggle between the two journals matters because it illustrates the power structures underlying the development of comparative literature: from the margins of the German-speaking world, Meltzl attempts to focus attention on more international, polyglot modes of comparison; but the empire soon strikes back, declaring, from the privileged vantage point of the world city Berlin, that 'German literature and the advancement of its historical self-understanding' will henceforth form the centre of comparative interests. From minor rebellion to major repression, comparative literature advances in zigzags between the peripheries and the centres.

After the first dedicated journal, the first full-length book on comparative literature did not take long to arrive. Once again the biographical details reinforce the sense of a discipline at the margins: the Dublin-based lawyer Hutcheson Macaulay Posnett (1855–1927) published his study in 1886, just as he was emigrating to New Zealand. The author's call, in his preface, for the establishment of Chairs in comparative literature 'at the leading universities of Great Britain, America, and the Australian Colonies' suggests both the pedagogical and political context within the English-speaking world; if the subject was as yet unestablished, its potential reach was vast, indeed imperial. The harvest, in Posnett's words, was 'plenteous'.

The history of this harvest goes back, Posnett holds, as far as Dante's *De Vulgari Eloquentia* (*c.*1302), a treatise on the importance of the vernacular ironically written in Latin. Dante's subsequent decision to write the *Divine Comedy* in contemporary Italian marks, for Posnett, the beginning of the 'modern comparative science'; the subsequent rise of the continental nation-states encouraged cultural competition within Europe, while the discovery of the New World sharpened the sense of contrasts lurking outside of it. All these developments, argues Posnett in the teleological manner of the day, culminated in the Victorian era; modern scholarship was crucially now *aware* of the need for comparison, rather than pursuing it unthinkingly. 'We may call *consciously* comparative thinking the great glory of our nineteenth century.'

Posnett's historicization of comparison aside, perhaps the most interesting aspect of his study from a disciplinary perspective is its attempt to establish comparative literature as a science. We are so used to thinking of it as part of the Humanities that this conception of the discipline comes as a surprise to the modern reader. Yet *Comparative Literature* was published as part of an 'International Science' series, and indeed Posnett's whole method constitutes an attempt to establish what amounts to a sociological approach to comparative literature. Tracing the development of literary culture from clan to city, from nation to 'cosmopolitan humanity', Posnett emphasizes what he terms 'the relativity of literature', the ways in which its inflections change as society changes. Out of this evolution emerges world literature, understood as a product of ever more universal social forces.

As the discipline started gathering pace in the 1890s, Posnett's historical, evolutionary model of comparative literature quickly found supporters. Ferdinand Brunetière (1849–1906), one of the most influential figures in the French school, took the idea of evolution literally, developing, in a study of lyric poetry, an explicitly Darwinian model of the growth and decay of literary genres. In a lecture of 1900, he applied this model to national literatures more broadly, claiming that comparison is as much successive as simultaneous, since nations take turns to dominate European culture: Italy from 1450 to 1600; Spain from 1600 to 1670; France from 1660 to 1750; England from 1720 to 1820; Germany from 1820 to 1870. Yet by the end of the 19th century, argues Brunetière in a manner that anticipates the debates of some hundred years later, the hegemony of Europe had to be put in a broader perspective: 'European literature is only a branch, or better yet a province, and maybe even a narrow province, in the almost infinite field of comparative literature.' The global ambition of the discipline was becoming increasingly apparent.

This ambition was also starting to manifest itself on the other side of the Atlantic. Over the course of the 1890s, the first Chairs of comparative literature were founded at the Ivy League universities; in a sign of the increasing self-confidence of the discipline, pioneers such as Charles Mills Gayley (1858–1932) started agitating for the creation of an American 'Society of Comparative Literature'. In an essay of 1903, Gayley argues for a largely historical, sequential understanding of comparison: 'first the history of each literature; then the historic relations between literatures. That in turn is followed by the synthesis in literature as a unit.' If the model is still recognizably that of the 19th century—emphasizing the importance of anthropology and concluding that comparative literature amounts to 'literary philology'—it is also recognizably European in the way it builds a process of development into literary history. At the dawn of the new century, that is to say, for better or for worse Europe was still the cultural centre of comparison.

The crisis of the 'European mind'

As the 'long nineteenth century' drew to a close in the years leading up to World War One, the colonial model of comparison—with intellectual fashions radiating out from Europe like spokes from a wheel—came to a head. The rise of modernism in the early decades of the 20th century heralded a renewed focus on internationalism in literature and literary criticism. Despite the vital impulses it received from American expatriates such as Ezra Pound and T.S. Eliot, modernism was in many ways the last great European movement, a swansong to the high culture of the continent. From Russian formalists to Italian futurists, from French surrealists to German expressionists, the avant-garde circulated—and collaborated—across Europe. Inevitably, comparative literature came to reflect this.

For all the internationalism of the modernist era, however, it is striking just how little the term 'comparative' is actually used at this time. Anthologies of the discipline struggle to find explicit statements of comparison from this period, for the simple reason that there are so few. Partly this relates, one may presume, to the black hole of the two world wars, which sucked in the more considered attempts at international exchange. Yet it also owes much to the fact that the comparative impulse came to express itself, in this period, in a number of alternative terms: avant-garde, international, European. Foremost among these terms was the notion of 'crisis'.

If the years 1914–45 represent the darkest period of modern European history, they also mark its most sustained period of conceptualization. This is not, in fact, a paradox: the sense of crisis that pervades the period produces a heightened sense of urgency, of rushing to save European culture against its own ruin. Last-ditch attempts at asserting a shared cultural legacy abound; despite—or perhaps because of—all evidence to the contrary, 'Europe' is mobilized, time and again, as the common basis for comparison between competing nations. The period from which this emerges most clearly are the years immediately following World War One. In the aftermath of such carnage, the idea of Europe as an overarching category assumed quasi-redemptive status, with figures of the stature of Romain Rolland, Stefan Zweig, and Benedetto Croce asserting its continuing relevance as the cultural precondition for comparison and reconciliation. The period represented the high-water mark, in other words, of attempts to establish what Count Richard von Coudenhove-Kalergi would call, in his manifesto of 1923, *Paneuropa*.

The prodigiously polyglot Coudenhove-Kalergi (1894–1972) was in many ways the founder of the European Union. In the course of a life dedicated to European unification, he fought tirelessly for greater political and cultural collaboration between the various continental countries, advocating a 'United States of Europe'. As the son of an Austro-Hungarian diplomat and a Japanese heiress, his own multinational heritage convinced him of the need for enhanced integration: 'the man of the future will be of mixed race', he wrote, somewhat misguidedly, in 1925. 'Today's races and classes will gradually disappear owing to the vanishing of space, time, and prejudice.' Here as elsewhere, Coudenhove-Kalergi's pan-Europeanism offered an antidote to the bubbling poison of fascism that was starting to corrode Europe.

Polyglot figures of this sort, switching effortlessly between a dizzying array of languages, embody the internationalist spirit behind comparative approaches to literature in the early 20th century. The cultural and intellectual ambition that drives such figures is quite staggering at times, but it also risks reinforcing a lingering sense of Europe as the controlling centre of the world. Europe may be only 'a little promontory on the continent of Asia', wrote the French poet Paul Valéry (1871–1945) in an influential essay of 1919, but it is also 'the brain of a vast body'. Valéry's essay 'The Crisis of the Mind' is perhaps the single most enduring document of the European mentality in this period. First published in English, the essay begins by acknowledging the death drive of Modernity—'We later civilizations... we too now know that we are mortal'—before proceeding to adumbrate the crisis of European culture in appropriately elegiac terms. The common cause of contemporary culture, the poet suggests, is its frailty.

From the point of view of comparative literature, Valéry's essay outlines what one might term a graveyard model of comparison.

Like an 'intellectual Hamlet', the modern European meditates on the skulls of fallen giants: Leonardo da Vinci, Kant, Hegel—they all oppress him with their tombstone gravity. One day, Valéry asserts, even the names France, England, and Russia may sound to future ears like Nineveh and Babylon do to ours, ghostly echoes of a distant past. The three enduring legacies that underlie the European mind—the Roman, the Christian, and the Greek—have driven the continent for thousands of years, but they are also what risks disappearing now that Europe looks like disintegrating. The military crisis may have passed, but economic crisis determines the present—and who knows how our intellectual crisis will dictate the future? At stake for cultural critics of the 1920s and 1930s was nothing less than the existence of European culture.

Of course, critics did not always agree on how best to serve this culture. Broadly speaking, one can divide approaches to comparative literature in this period into left-wing and right-wing methodologies, into progressive and conservative visions of the European literary legacy. The left-wing vision emerged principally from Eastern Europe, with its socialist arguments about the precise relationship between aesthetics and politics. Thinkers as disparate as the Russian and Czech formalists on the one hand, and genre theorists such as Georg Lukács or Mikhail Bakhtin on the other, all saw themselves as perpetuating, in their differing ways, the Marxist legacy of politically engaged criticism.

The debates between Lukács and Bertolt Brecht regarding the European tradition brought these differences to a head. In a version of comparative literature by another name, over the course of the 1930s Lukács and Brecht disputed the extent to which pre-Marxist literature—from the Greeks to the Renaissance, from Shakespeare to the Romantics—retained continuing relevance for the modern age. With the 'social mission' of art as the prize—and drawing on an extraordinarily broad range of reference, from English opera to Japanese Noh plays (to take just Brecht)—the two intellectual pugilists pursued a kind of Marxist quarrel of the ancients and moderns: in the red corner, the new aesthetics of committed literature; in the blue corner, the bourgeois Humanist inheritance. This was comparative literature with added ideological punch.

It wasn't only the left-wing critics who came out swinging, however. If many of the leading modernists came to hold conservative views, this was also true of the comparatists. Oswald Spengler's bestseller *The Decline of the West* (1918–22) set the tone for many a postwar jeremiad about the passing of the 'European mind'. Spengler's broad-brush approach to history, culture, and religion was nothing if not comparative; not only his tone, but also his methodology influenced authors of the stature of T.S. Eliot and Gottfried Benn. Yet equally there were subtler, less strident ways of seeking to 'conserve' the European legacy—and it was at this point that a golden generation of comparatists came to the fore.

Stamboul training

It is one of the more mordant ironies of modern intellectual history that the Nazi fetishization of 'national' culture should have given such decisive impetus to the development of international modes of criticism. The increasingly autocratic tenor of the 1930s led a generation of comparatists to take refuge in the international republic of letters; for German—and above all, for German-Jewish—cultural critics, comparative modes of thinking began to assume decisive, existential importance. Pushed into exile at first metaphorically, and then literally, such critics consoled themselves by taking the long view of European culture. Try as he might, Hitler could not efface history.

Following the cessation of hostilities in 1918, an ambitious group of German-language scholars had started turning their attention abroad. In the spirit of postwar reconciliation, these scholars of *Romanistik*—a discipline that is by definition comparative, working across Romance languages such as French, Spanish, and

Italian—adopted a consciously European mindset, emphasizing overarching categories such as Romance or Latin literatures as a way of resisting what they perceived as the narrow reductionism of national traditions. If the work of these critics represents the last great hurrah of the European model of comparative literature, it is because they had already gone into a kind of voluntary intellectual exile before some of them were forced into a compulsory geographical one. Among the various influential comparatists of this period—other significant figures in which included the Hungarian scholars Mihály Babits and Antal Szerb, who respectively wrote histories of 'European' (1935) and 'World' literature (1941) marked by the collapse of the Austro-Hungarian empire in 1918—three great names stand out: Ernst Robert Curtius (1886–1956), Leo Spitzer (1887–1960), and Erich Auerbach (1892–1957).

Often grouped together as a 'golden age' of comparative literature, the three critics in fact displayed considerable differences of talent and temperament. A deeply conservative figure, Curtius enjoyed the most conventional career of the three, obtaining a post in Bonn around the start of World War One and staying there throughout World War Two. Sometimes suspected, for this very reason, of implicit collaboration with the Nazi regime, Curtius in fact cast his net as widely as possible across the Humanist history of European culture, promoting Franco-German understanding and turning in particular to what he saw as the neglected pre-modern period. Throughout the years of the Third Reich, Curtius was working on what would emerge, in 1948, as one of the enduring masterpieces of the discipline: *European Literature and the Latin Middle Ages*.

The importance of Curtius's study can be measured not only by its geographical breadth, but also by its historical depth. Ranging from Antiquity to Modernity, from Homer to Goethe, Curtius traces the 'Europeanization' of literary history, focusing in particular on medieval literature in Latin as a pivotal period in which the presence of a *lingua franca* enabled modern European culture to emerge. In this, his approach was typical of the age: alongside a defiant insistence on international exchange, much of the best work of the 1940s is characterized by a return to the always already comparative Middle Ages. In a letter of 1944, Curtius outlined the appeal of the period in memorably pragmatic terms: 'It doesn't seem to have dawned on anyone how nonsensical the modern division of labour is between national languages, national literatures, and national philologies. What would one think of a medieval historian who only wrote about German events and who only made use of German-language sources?'

Curtius's historical approach to comparative literature can be set against the philological methodology favoured by Spitzer. The most mercurial of the three great *Romanisten*, the Viennese Spitzer was a polyglot in the best central European tradition. Ranging with equal facility over numerous languages, Spitzer was the comparatist's comparatist, combining philological and psychological analysis to incisive effect. Underpinning his prolific output was a recurring preoccupation with stylistics, with the ways in which linguistic detail reflects conceptual argument. Style, in Spitzer's hands, emerged as something like the body language of language, offering vital clues to its movements and meaning.

By the time of his essays on *Linguistics and Literary History*, published in the same year as Curtius's masterpiece in 1948, Spitzer had come to summarize his methodology under the concept of the 'philological circle'. In a manner typical of his approach to stylistics, Spitzer held that a single stylistic feature—Rabelais's use of neologisms, for instance—could be used to open up a broader understanding of a work as a whole; this whole then modifies and contextualizes, in turn, our view of the stylistic features. Something similar could be said to apply to Spitzer's view of the European tradition more generally: analysis of a single text opens up its linguistic details; but these details are then understood within the broader, comparative context of what the Germans term *Geistesgeschichte* (intellectual history), a context that alters, in turn, our perception of the individual work. Spitzer would no doubt have endorsed Nabokov's memorable advice to his students to 'fondle the details'.

It is striking, however, that there is one major context that these Romanists largely ignored, namely the biographical. The omission is all the more telling given their own circumstances: the decision to focus on the philological legacy of the Humanist tradition can be seen as an attempt to distance themselves from the swirling chaos of their times. In the cases of Spitzer and Auerbach, this metaphorical distance became literal as they fled into exile. In the fateful year of 1933, Spitzer left Nazi Germany for a position in Istanbul; three years later, he left Europe for a Chair at Johns Hopkins University in Baltimore. Auerbach would inherit Spitzer's position in Istanbul, fleeing Germany, for his part, in 1935. For a few short years, then, Istanbul became the training ground for comparative literature as it would emerge after the war.

The postwar development of the discipline arguably owes more to Erich Auerbach than to any other single thinker. Partly this is attributable to the glamour of exile: for a discipline as susceptible to symbolic capital as comparative literature, Auerbach's association with the city on the Bosphorus—poised between East and West, between Asia and Europe—is hard to resist. It is also, however, a function of his extraordinarily wide-ranging work, above all his masterpiece *Mimesis: The Representation of Reality in Western Literature* (1946). Written during the war years in Istanbul—Auerbach would move to the USA in 1947—*Mimesis* set the template for comparative literature in the second half of the 20th century. In a series of close readings ranging from Homer to Virginia Woolf, Auerbach extrapolates from what he terms 'points of departure' to recount the history of Western literature as a constant renegotiation between high and low styles, and between differing levels of realism. In the opening chapter, to take just one example, he contrasts the moment in which the former nursemaid

8. 'Odysseus and Eurycleia', Christian Gottlob Heyne.

Eurycleia recognizes the homecoming hero Odysseus by his scar (see Figure 8) with Abraham's sacrifice of Isaac in the Book of Genesis, before opening out into a broader discussion of modes of description in the *Odyssey* and the *Old Testament* more generally. Having established this comparative technique, Auerbach then pursues it all the way through the classical, medieval, and Modern periods.

Remarkably, Auerbach claimed that he did all this without reference to 'a rich and specialized library', stranded as he was in wartime Istanbul. This legend of the bookless, isolated scholar is no doubt overstated, but it is no less instructive for that. Some have even argued that it is the reason for the book's success, suggesting that Auerbach was forced to write a more original book than he might otherwise have done had he clung more slavishly to his sources. Yet his respect for the Western tradition is obvious, and for all its originality *Mimesis* is a conservative book in the best sense of the term, an attempt to conserve Humanist culture in the era of Auschwitz. The elegiac tone that this produces is part of its power: the great age of these major Germanic comparatists, working in heroic exile from the Nazis, was also the *late* age of European culture as defined by its distance from its Latinate, Christian roots. If Auerbach remains such a pivotal figure in the history of the discipline, it is because he both celebrated the past and anticipated the future.

Nowhere is this more evident than in an essay of 1952 entitled 'Philology of World Literature'. Auerbach acknowledges that the move beyond Europe is starting to gain purchase by this point, but he also shrewdly identifies the problem with *Weltliteratur* as it is developing in these postwar years: with the rapid spread of only two dominant models of culture—European-American and Russian-Bolshevik—differences in language and literature risk being flattened out and standardized, such that the dream of world literature may soon be 'at once realized and destroyed'. Auerbach's own experience of exile echoes into his plangent description of what one might term, with reference to Spitzer's philological circle, the 'comparative circle': the most valuable asset a critic has is his own culture—yet it is only when he moves away from this culture that he acquires true insight into it. By the end of World War Two, the same logic might be said to apply to Europe.

'Comp lit' goes global

In the footsteps of pioneering figures such as Spitzer and Auerbach, the discipline of comparative literature began gathering pace in the 1950s largely as a transatlantic affair. If Hitler helped develop the nuclear bomb in America by driving his Jewish scientists away from Europe, he did something similar with literary criticism. European émigrés took their expertise to the

East Coast universities, and their influence continued into the next generation of leading comparatists such as George Steiner or Jean Starobinski, Europeans with (at least partly) American training. Comparative literature had outgrown its continental origins.

Perhaps the most influential figure in the development of what soon came to be known as 'comp lit', in the USA, was René Wellek (1903–95). A Czech émigré at Yale, Wellek wrote numerous important literary studies, including *Theory of Literature* (co-authored with Austin Warren in 1949) and the eight-volume *A History of Modern Criticism*. His doctrine was the broadest of churches; rejecting the narrower, largely French focus on sources and influences, Wellek understood 'comparative' as indicating any approach 'transcending the limits of one national literature'. Ideally, he argued in an essay entitled 'The Crisis of Comparative Literature' (1959), one would simply do away with the adjective altogether, speaking of 'professors of literature' just as one does of professors of philosophy. Wellek's inclusive understanding of the discipline helped found what is sometimes known as the 'American School' of comparative literature, a theoretically inclined version of the discipline that is still thriving today.

That is not to say that he necessarily agreed with such theoretical developments. Wellek in fact came to criticize what he termed the 'new nihilism' of deconstruction and poststructuralism, concerned that its linguistic self-obsession would scare off students and deprive literature of its basic Humanist resonance. Whether this emphasis on rhetorical technicalities antagonized students or attracted them—certain kinds of graduate students will always be drawn to difficulty—there is no doubt that the comparative curriculum in the USA became increasingly theoretical, with figures like the 'Yale School' critics Geoffrey Hartman and Paul de Man advocating critical theory as an essential element of the discipline in the 1960s and 1970s. 'The emphasis', de Man wrote in one curriculum proposal of 1975, 'has increasingly moved toward literature as a language about language, or a metalinguistic discipline'. Given that Wellek himself never learned to speak this meta-language, it is ironic that so many of its native speakers should have given the prestigious lecture series in comparative literature named after him at the University of California.

Beyond the USA, the discipline began establishing itself worldwide in the postwar period. Broadly speaking, comparative literature evolved over the second half of the 20th century as an enduring reaction against the nationalist fervour of the first half. Jewish literary scholars took their 'European mind' with them as they fled the continent, but they also took with them a sense of being irrevocably unhoused, a kind of transcendental homelessness, to borrow a phrase from Lukács. The comparative perspective emerged as a means of making cultural virtue out of political necessity, as a way of establishing a permanent state of exile in the spaces between cultures. It is no surprise, then, that smugglers and spies should have become the metaphors of choice for comparatists—'lifelong, I have tried to act as a double or triple agent', writes Steiner in his autobiography, 'seeking to suggest to one great language and literature the necessary presence of the other'. It is equally unsurprising that many of the most original developments in the discipline should have emerged from the global margins.

The realignment of comparative literature as a global discipline—with its attendant reassessment of the language of 'centre' and 'peripheries'—began to take hold in earnest in the 1960s. Indian, Chinese, and African versions of the discipline had long existed, all with their own local emphases and inflections (the first department of comparative literature was opened in India in 1956, for instance), but they had struggled to gain attention in a literary marketplace dominated by the major Western languages. By the time of the social upheavals of the 1960s, however, established power structures and authorities were increasingly coming under fire, culturally as well as politically. The long march of postcolonialism through the intellectual institutions of the West began to gather pace after the Caribbean theorist Frantz Fanon published *The Wretched of the Earth* in 1961, and the subsequent student movements shared the sense of rising up in international solidarity against national strictures. The literary—and in particular, 'French'—theory that would come to shape comparative literary studies throughout the 1970s and 1980s developed out of this spirit of globalized thinking. It has often been noted that many of the leading thinkers of this period—Jacques Derrida with his doctrine of deconstruction, Julia Kristeva with her concept of 'intertextuality' (see Box 6)—emerged not from literary centres such as Paris, but from the cultural peripheries of Algeria or Bulgaria. In a famous phrase of the time, the empire was writing back.

Box 6 Intertextuality

First introduced by the Bulgarian-French critic Julia Kristeva in 1966, the term 'intertextuality' has enjoyed an astonishingly successful career across the Humanities. All texts, the original idea suggests, are constructed through 'the absorption and transformation' of other texts; every piece of writing is 'a mosaic of quotations'. Although this was almost literally true of modernist works such as *The Waste Land* or *Finnegans Wake*—with their mixture of allusion, quotation, pastiche, and translation—in the multimedia era of saturated knowledge intertextuality has developed into a more diffuse, metaphorical term encompassing any kind of reference by one text to another. As a model for comparative literature, intertextuality offers a significantly broader canvas than 'influence', since it highlights not only the relationship of one work to another, but also the ways in which we make sense of this relationship through pre-existing frameworks. Meaning itself, in short, is to be found in the spaces 'between' texts.

It is still writing back. The theories and debates that defined comparative literature as the 20th century drew to a close—translation studies, cultural studies, cosmopolitanism, feminism, Orientalism—remain with us today, albeit in altered form. They do not constitute the history so much as the continuing story of the discipline; as such, their proper place is in Chapter 4 of this book. Comparative literature has long since become a global enterprise (albeit one that has increasingly sought to question the very idea of globalization), and its present state reflects its—constantly contested—position as a literary United Nations. However problematic the historical emphasis on Europe remains, it has driven the discipline's development as lubricant, irritant, and secret agent of international relations. If comparative literature has become ever more politicized over the course of its history, it is only by understanding this history that its present state—and possible future status—can be fully appreciated.

Chapter 4
Disciplines and debates

Writing in 1993, the British scholar Susan Bassnett claimed that comparative literature was in decline; ten years later, the Indian critic Gayatri Chakravorty Spivak went one step further and declared the 'Death of a Discipline'. Barely a decade on, such obituaries have been proven emphatically wrong. Arguably more than any other discipline in the Humanities, comparative literature has experienced a surge of interest in recent years, driven by its strategic position between languages, literary criticism, and cultural studies. Indeed, it is in many ways defined by this position, by its porous relationship to neighbouring areas of scholarship; equal parts parasite and chameleon, comparative literature draws sustenance from other fields of enquiry just as it takes on their colours. If this makes it particularly vulnerable to changes in intellectual fashion—itself an important, if underexplored subject—it also makes it a placeholder for broader debates about the changing status and purpose of literary culture in the 21st century.

The very term 'comparative literature' is in many ways a category in search of a meaning. Perhaps the biggest lesson of recent years is that both parts of it are provisional. We have seen how the adjective 'comparative' alters its emphasis with changing political and linguistic circumstances; yet the noun 'literature', too, is far from the stable signifier of traditional assumption. With the rise of literary theory in the 1970s, and of cultural studies in the 1980s, the idea of the 'text' began to be contested. As the barriers between 'high' and 'popular' culture became increasingly blurred, as the concept of the 'canon' became increasingly problematic, the previously unquestioned legitimacy of literature as the ultimate form of verbal art came under fire. *Comparative* literature, already inherently contingent, was doubly destabilized. Now more than ever, it asserted itself as an *in*discipline.

Another way of saying this is that since the 1960s comparative literature has splintered into a range of competing disciplines. Perhaps the most accurate way to gauge its place within the Humanities today is thus to consider its various incarnations in neighbouring disciplines, including literary theory, cultural studies, postcolonialism, world literature, translation studies, and reception studies. Understood as a composite of these and other related fields, comparative literature always presupposes a *point* of comparison; in this sense, comparative practices are always also comparative prejudices (even if, following the argument of the philosopher Hans-Georg Gadamer, prejudices are not necessarily negative, since they make judgements possible in the first place). Given the emphasis that it places on the critic as well as on the creator, the indiscipline of comparative literature emerges from these debates as a mode of enquiry in which the observer's predilections—and presuppositions—are as important as those of the object under observation. Comparative literature is also, in short, comparatists' literature.

Literary theory

At the heart of contemporary conceptions of comparative literature is a paradox. In order to justify itself, it has become ever more theoretical; yet for this reason the ostensible object of this theory—literature—has become ever more marginalized. Theoretical discussions of the subject have proliferated, to such an extent that they sometimes seem to push out the actual work of comparing one text with another; within the academy, comparison is often more conceptualized than carried out, more theorized than practised. It is impossible to understand the growth of comparative literature, in short, without also understanding the growth of literary theory.

The astonishing success of literary theory across a broad range of the Humanities—as exemplified by such influential schools as structuralism, poststructuralism, feminism, and postcolonialism—has depended on necessarily comparative premises. Literary theory emerged, that is to say, out of comparative literature: its iconoclastic energy derives, among other sources, from a rejection of neat, national traditions, from an attempt to rethink traditional models of writing. Theory, unlike practice, travels readily between countries; in the international marketplace of ideas, theoretical models are easy to transfer, since they are, 'in theory', universally applicable. That this encourages a natural tendency for ambitious comparatists to theorize about their subject is hardly a surprise. Writing *about* comparing has always been as central to the discipline as comparing writing.

What has changed in the last fifty years is that literary theory has emerged as a discipline in its own right. If comparative literature was a key battlefield for the 'theory wars' of the 1970s and 1980s (see Box 7), its landscape bears the scars, perhaps the most significant of which is that the very concept of 'literature' became problematic. In his seminal *Course in General Linguistics* (first published posthumously in 1916), the Swiss thinker Ferdinand de Saussure had proposed a basic distinction between language understood as a collective phenomenon (*langue*) and speech understood as an individual intervention (*parole*). In calling attention to the social and linguistic codes implicit in how we understand 'works' of literature—to what one might term the relationship between text and context—Saussure's distinction effectively marked the starting point of modern literary theory.

Box 7 Theory wars

Modern literary theory—the roots of which go back to Saussure's linguistics at the start of the 20th century, and to the Romantics a century before him—took off in the 1960s. As higher education expanded in the postwar decades, scholars in the Humanities began focusing less on texts themselves and more on the 'structures' of language, and on the ways in which we write about (and indeed how we write about how we write about) texts: criticism became 'theory'. Throughout the 1970s and 1980s, so-called theory wars raged between opposing ideologies: structuralists decried Marxists, feminists attacked Freudians. However self-involved such spats may now seem—at times they recall Monty Python's People's Front of Judea squabbling with the Judean People's Front—at stake in such debates was an essentially political question: who has the right to say what literature means? Theorizing literature meant politicizing literature, whether understood as a local or a universal phenomenon.

This increased self-consciousness regarding the preconditions of writing had important consequences for comparative literature, placing an ever-greater premium on the ideological allegiances of the critic. Literary theory has had the paradoxical effect of constraining the autonomy of literature, depicting it as a product of the forces—economic, psychological, political, cultural, or sexual—acting upon it. *Hamlet*, seen through psychoanalytic eyes, emerges as a story of Oedipal conflicts; *The Tempest*, reread from a postcolonial perspective, reflects the early modern exploitation of the New World. The critic's role becomes to tease out what the text 'really' means, what it tells us despite its ostensible intentions; the comparative critic's role, by extension, becomes to compare what numerous texts really mean, and to establish what literature understood as an interlinguistic phenomenon tells us despite its ostensible intentions.

All of which raises the basic question of what the 'literary' really is. As René Wellek noted in 1959, 'we must face the problem of "literariness", the central issue of aesthetics'; translated into the terms of high theory (sometimes termed 'French theory'), Wellek's literariness re-emerges as Roland Barthes's *écriture*. From his first book, *Writing Degree Zero* (1953), through to later works such as *The Pleasure of the Text* (1973), Barthes developed an original perspective on the ways in which textual meaning is produced as 'writing'. Importantly from the point of view of comparative literature, Barthes effectively weaponizes literary style as an ideological phenomenon: in *Writing Degree Zero*, for instance, he opposes individual style to collective language (Saussure's *langue*), praising Albert Camus's *The Outsider* as an example of 'white writing' that resists, through its neutrality, ideological appropriation (unlike, say, 19th-century realism with its self-conscious claims to the status of 'Art'). To compare styles is thus to compare ideologies.

Barthes's notion of *écriture* was given a decisive twist in 1967, the year in which Jacques Derrida published three major books. Derrida's aim, famously, was to 'deconstruct' the Western tradition; the main way that he set out to achieve this was by picking apart the standard binary oppositions—presence vs. absence, speech vs. writing, nature vs. culture—that structured Western thought. Derrida's principal weapon in this undertaking was his notion of *différance*, a term that he coined to signify how meaning is produced through a simultaneous process of differing and deferring that renders that meaning at once plural and never quite present. Quite aside from the inherently comparative nature of Derrida's approach—he took his texts from a range of linguistic traditions—his startlingly incisive methodology had two major implications for comparative literature. First, the concept of *différance* entails a comparative approach to language itself: meaning only emerges in the interstices and 'differences' between one sign and another (for instance, between *différence* and *différance*). Second, the project of deconstruction could be—and was—extended to the relationship between national traditions, such that the 'canon' of Western literature itself began to be picked apart and re-examined. In an anti-authoritarian era, the consequences of Derrida's attack on the ideological premises of language were far-reaching.

One of these consequences was the rise of theoretically inflected feminism. The field of 'women's writing' (*écriture féminine*) was equally ripe for deconstruction, its premises and technique dictated for so long by patriarchal presuppositions. Over the course of the 1970s, theorists such as Hélène Cixous and Julia Kristeva came to focus on 'the madwoman in the attic'—the title of an influential reconsideration of Victorian literature by Sandra Gilbert and Susan Gubar—exploring how female writers struggled to develop their own voices under pressure from male conceptions of language and authorship (what became known as 'phallocentrism'). The laugh of the Medusa, to cite Cixous's influential essay of 1975, became a rallying cry for the feminist reconceptualization of approaches to literature, and emerged as a basis for reassessing the hierarchy of major and minor—understood as masculine and feminine—texts. To compare literatures was also, under this new dispensation, to compare the genders of literatures; the madwoman in the attic gave way to the comparatist in the cellar, laying the foundations for a gender-specific reading of literary tradition.

The rise of literary theory thus signalled a renewed attention to the rhetorical techniques of literature, as well as to the very concept of literature understood as a cultural construct. In truth there is no such thing as 'theory', only a proliferation of theories, each one foregrounding a particular *method*—from structuralism to deconstruction, from psychoanalysis to feminism—rather than a given *topic* (to return to the terms discussed in Chapter 2). But the underlying consequence for comparative literature is clear: namely, an increased self-consciousness regarding the notions of both 'comparison' and the 'literary'. If comparative literature remains a highly theoretical discipline, it is because of this basic tendency to question and contest its own premises.

Cultural studies

As literary theory was beginning to take hold in Paris in the 1950s and 1960s, on the other side of the Channel a different kind of intellectual movement was developing. With the increasingly mixed, postcolonial society of the postwar era came an increasingly broad, postmodern sense of culture. Previously taken to indicate the elite achievements of the human mind, the term now started to include within its purview a much wider range of reference, from minority sub-cultures to majority consumerism. Where literary theory engages almost exclusively with extremely complex works of art—Derrida's *Dissemination* (1972), for instance, discusses text such as Mallarmé's *A Throw of the Dice* or Philippe Sollers's *Numbers*—the new science was to be a much broader church, eclectic in its interests and ecumenical in its endeavours. In the spirit of postwar democratization, the undereducated as well as the overeducated were now afforded equal legitimacy in their customs and habits, the mandarins and the masses viewed as part of the same social fabric. With this panoramic perspective, a new discipline was born: *cultural studies*.

The study of culture, to take just the English-speaking world, goes back at least as far as major conservative thinkers such as Matthew Arnold in the 19th century and T.S. Eliot in the early 20th, with the former's *Culture and Anarchy* published in 1869 and the latter's *Notes Towards the Definition of Culture* in 1948. Cultural studies, however, was very much a postwar invention. Where the study of culture took as its focus a traditional understanding of 'high' art, cultural studies turned the idea on its head. As developed by pioneering figures such as Richard Hoggart and Stuart Hall—both associated with the Birmingham School—cultural studies was as much a sociological as an aesthetic theory. Hoggart's *The Uses of Literacy* (1957), echoed and expanded by like-minded thinkers including

Raymond Williams and E.P. Thompson, advocated the continuing vitality of working-class culture, in part as a means of resisting the increasing hegemony of what their German colleagues in the Frankfurt School would call the (largely American) 'culture industry'. Hall, a 'cultural comparativist' formed by his experiences growing up as a colonial subject in Jamaica, was equally at home discussing Henry James as a 'diasporic' novelist or the politics of race, class consciousness or contemporary cinema. For this postwar generation of critics, culture was to be found in the grass roots as much as in the Hollywood hills.

If both the Birmingham and the Frankfurt schools tended to left-wing, not to say Marxist analyses of prevailing orthodoxies and power structures, there were also important differences between them. Unlike their German counterparts, for instance, the British cultural theorists—whose tactics Hall pithily defined as 'talking culturally about politics and politically about culture'—were particularly interested in youth culture as an expression of identity and class-consciousness, as well as in the politics of immigrant and minority cultures such as those of West Indians or East Asians. Perhaps the defining difference between the two approaches, however, was the interest that the British cultural theorists developed not only in advanced art, but also in everyday artefacts: newspapers, cinema, television, advertisements. In the postwar era of flattened cultural hierarchies, a text could be anything designated as such; it is the way that we perceive the text that assigns it this status, not its inherent qualities. Textuality, it emerged, is in the eye of the beholder.

The implications for comparative literature were obvious. In the age of mass media, two basic courses were now available to the comparatist: either to cling to the 'canon' as the only legitimate source of culture; or to embrace the brave new world of the textual revolution. Roland Barthes's *Mythologies* (1957) provides an early expression of the rapidly blurring lines between the two courses.

Presented as a study of 'semiology' or the science of signs, the book is in many ways a primer in media studies as it was developing in the 1950s, suggesting the ways in which 'theory' and 'culture' were emerging as mutually informing concepts. Modernity, like Antiquity, has its mythologies, and Barthes's eagle eye finds them harnessed in the service of capitalism in the most improbable of places: wrestling, soap advertisements, Einstein's brain. In one essay, he decodes a photograph of a black boy in uniform saluting on the cover of *Paris Match* (see Figure 9) as a collection of signifiers intended to show that 'France is a great empire', capable of eliciting the devotion of all its citizens irrespective of race or colour.

We are all, Barthes thereby implies, complicit in the great brainwashing of the modern era, duped by big business and greedy government. With considerable ingenuity, he exposes the work of culture in the age of ideological manipulation, astutely identifying the ways in which linguistic signs signal more than they mean to.

What Barthes's seminal study also shows, however, is that the role of the critic was becoming increasingly politicized. Barthes adopts a pose that would become common over the next fifty years, namely that of high culture appropriating low culture. By taking the mass media seriously, while at the same time exposing its manipulative mechanisms, the critic is able to show not only that he lives in his era, but also that he is wise to its tricks. Cunningly, Barthes thereby implies his own, meta-mythological narrative: the goody is the critic, an intellectual superman with X-ray vision who can see through the ideological surfaces of contemporary culture; the baddy is the bourgeoisie, that recurring villain of the French intelligentsia, wedded to the false consciousness of consumerism. In effect, then, such an approach—one anticipated by an earlier generation of thinkers such as Walter Benjamin or Theodor Adorno—replaces one mythology with another, that of the critical hero undaunted by the overwhelming forces ranged against him.

9. 'A comparative order of facts, ideas, decisions': colonialism in a glossy magazine. Reproduced from Roland Barthes, *Mythologies* (1957).

This sleight-of-hand helps to explain the success of both literary theory and cultural studies as models of comparative literature. Both approaches—whether to elite art or to mass-market media—foreground the critic, raising his work from its traditional, secondary role to the status of a primary intervention in contemporary culture. The interpretive power of cultural studies, to be sure, is considerable: with its combination of aesthetics and sociology, and its focus on urgent contemporary issues, it represents a genuinely comparative undertaking, interdisciplinary *avant la lettre* in its gay science of mixed media and collapsed hierarchies. Yet it also places a particular burden of responsibility on the critic, who must now not merely analyse pre-existing texts—whether verbal, like literature, or visual, like skin colour—but also identify and politicize them. To adapt Marx: literary critics have only interpreted the world; the point, for cultural critics, is to see through it.

No longer beholden, then, to an already established set of canonical works, the cultural critic is given free licence to compare whatever catches her attention; it is the very act of analysis and comparison that dignifies the chosen artefacts with the status of 'text'. Whether the same level of subtlety and sophistication is present in an advertisement as in a poem or novel is irrelevant; it is the critic who brings this apparatus with her. The advent of cultural studies has thus simultaneously lowered and raised the stakes for comparative literature: lowered, because *everything* is now subject to comparison, not just 'literary' texts; raised, because the choice of texts to be compared inevitably implies a political position. Here more than ever, comparison emerges as an ideological as well as an aesthetic enterprise.

Postcolonialism

Nowhere is this ideological undertone more evident than in the context of postcolonial theory. Perhaps the single most influential theory to have emerged in the last fifty years, postcolonialism developed following the dissolution of the major European empires after World War Two. The British in Asia and the French in Africa provide the two most obvious examples of continents in which retreating powers left behind a contested cultural legacy, but elsewhere across the world, too—in Latin America, in the

Caribbean—imperial influences continued to be felt and fought. Independence, for many former colonies, was just the beginning.

The implications of postcolonialism for comparative literature are complex and controversial, but the principal issue at stake, in culture as in politics, is that of power. Who controls the production and interpretation of culture? Who determines the dominant modes of expression? The classic problem of postcolonialism is that of autonomy, in the moral and cultural as well as in the political sense. Politically speaking, a nation can become independent overnight; intellectually speaking, it can take generations. The withdrawal of an imperial power leaves behind an uneasy mixture of local custom and colonial mimicry, of defiance and deference—a situation that is compounded, of course, by the simple fact of having to write in an imported language. In order to be heard internationally, some Indian writers turn to English, some African writers to English or French (the fact that still more do not, preferring to write in their own native languages, is an inconvenient truth that complicates the standard critical emphasis on Anglophone and Francophone literature). As many a 'colonial' writer has asserted, the medium inevitably distorts the message, imposing modes of thought and expression that are not always best suited to conveying local experience. The result risks being a chimera, neither native fish nor foreign fowl.

From the point of view of comparative literature such a chimera is, of course, endlessly fascinating. The very in-betweenness of postcolonial culture, its provisional, politicized nature, its mixture of domestic and foreign influences, and its constantly shifting combination of local context and universal resonance: all this is the very essence of comparison. As with literary theory more generally, postcolonialism as applied to literature is inherently comparative, which explains why it has developed into such a powerful wing of the modern discipline—and into a way, to use the historian Dipesh Chakrabarty's term, of 'provincializing

Europe'. It is hardly surprising, then, that many of its best-known concepts reflect this, enacting what one might term the always already comparative nature of postcolonialism.

The wave of independence that swept over Africa in the 1960s—in 1960 alone, some seventeen sub-Saharan countries regained their sovereignty from France, Britain, and Belgium—was made possible by the new world order of the postwar era. Ideologically speaking, however, a groundswell of anti-colonial sentiment had already been building before the war, nowhere more forcefully than in the imperial capital, Paris. In the early 1930s, in the heart of the French establishment, three black students from the colonies—Aimé Césaire from Martinique, Léon-Gontran Damas from French Guiana, and Léopold Senghor from Senegal—coined the concept of *négritude*. As a provocation, as a way of reclaiming their supposedly 'inferior' racial position as a mark of strength, the term was a masterstroke. As a defining concept of the transition from colonialism to postcolonialism, it resonated into the subsequent careers of its three founders: Césaire and Damas represented their countries to the French parliament; Senghor became the founding president of Senegal. Rarely has theory been spoken so successfully to power.

Aesthetically speaking, *négritude* represented an attempt to assert African values against adopted European ones. The problem, of course, was that in an era of colonial control, in which native and imperial aesthetics were inevitably entangled, this was easier said than done. Theorists such as Césaire and Senghor fought hard to establish what they saw as authentically African art—as opposed to its fashionable imitation in *l'art primitif* of early 20th-century Europe—but the ways in which they did so, inevitably, were themselves informed by European as well as by African thought. Nietzsche's celebrated distinction, as elaborated in *The Birth of Tragedy* (1872), between 'Dionysian' and 'Apollonian' art—the former primal and untamed, the latter serene and controlled—emerged, to cite just one example, as an important intertext: African art was to form the organic, Dionysian counterpart to superficial, Apollonian Europe. In practice, however, the two were understood comparatively, the thought of the one informing the aesthetics of the other.

Alongside Africa, the other major continent to develop postcolonial models of literature was Asia. If reducing such vast continents to a handful of concepts is inevitably misleading—after all, India alone has twenty-two official languages—the single most influential concept to emerge out of postcolonial theory criticized precisely this reductivism. Published in 1978, Edward Said's study *Orientalism* (see Box 8) demonstrated the ways in which European literature has imposed a small number of clichés on—what it takes to be—the 'Orient'. The East emerges as the mirror image of the West: exotic, feminized, submissive. It exists only in the mind of the observer, whose supposed knowledge of

Box 8 *Orientalism*

Europeans have always romanticized Asia, but it took a critic of Edward Said's acumen to see that 'western conceptions of the Orient', to cite his book's subtitle, insinuate themselves even into the stylistic and philological presuppositions of literature. The Orient of writers such as Chateaubriand and Nerval, Said claims in the opening statement of his book, is essentially a European invention; the fact of (Middle) Eastern culture may be indisputable, but the fantasy requires external observers to conceive it as the exotic foil to their own, Christian culture. In the manner of Michel Foucault, Said discerns in this Orientalist fantasy the assertion of knowledge as power. In claiming knowledge of the Orient, Europeans implicitly assert their authority over it; in homogenizing it into one indiscriminate mass, they deny it autonomy. As a model of comparative literature, *Orientalism* thus criticizes the very idea of comparison as predicated upon an imbalance of power.

the Orient—based on little more than legend and myth—gives him power over it. It is the incarnation, in short, of the Other.

Said's groundbreaking model was quickly applied beyond the Orient to all areas of colonial interaction. It has certainly not been without its critics (particularly given the way in which Said appropriated the previously neutral descriptor 'Orientalist' as a pejorative): some have found his concept of Orientalism monolithic and self-undoing, others have criticized his readings of Western texts as unfair and inaccurate. The concept has nonetheless been enormously influential, and indeed it has been extended both backwards—as in Srinivas Aravamudan's study of *Enlightenment Orientalism* (2011)—and sideways, to cognate terms such as 'arcticism' in northern Norway. As a Palestinian, Said was acutely aware of the political and cultural sensitivities surrounding the Western image of the Middle East; as a literary critic schooled in the European tradition, he was alive to the ways in which comparing literatures often amounts to condemning one as inferior. Understood in the broadest sense as a critique of how the observer distorts the object—sometimes called the Wizard of Oz effect ('pay no attention to that man behind the curtain')—Orientalism created a school of comparative literature unto itself.

Influential concepts such as *négritude* and Orientalism suggest that beyond the imbalance of power inherent in colonial literature, the trick of much postcolonial literature has been to make a virtue out of its compound necessity. Although the problematic relationship between colonizer and colonized is nothing new in European literature—one need only think of Robinson Crusoe 'educating' Friday in Daniel Defoe's novel of 1719—it assumed new pertinence in the age of globalization and the imperial 'boomerang'. Writing in 1981, for instance, the Caribbean theorist Edouard Glissant proposed 'diversity' as the appropriate ambition for the postcolonial era, encouraging Western literatures to reflect on a 'new relationship with the world, by which they would signal no longer their preeminent place in the Same, but their shared task in the Diverse'. By 1994, the Indian critic Homi Bhabha had repurposed this into his influential concept of 'hybridity', a condition in which the colonial subject mimics the master and thereby gains a transnational perspective on the shifting balance of power between colonizer and colonized. More recently, 'autoexoticism'—the deliberate appropriation of imperialist misrepresentations in order to subvert them, such as the Irish exaggeration of their own marginality and strangeness—has emerged as a further way of foregrounding the productivity of the postcolonial condition. Comparison itself, in short, has developed into a hybrid.

If comparative literature thrives on the pathos of internationalism, however, it is worth noting that postcolonialism is driven largely by *nationalist* rhetoric. To be sure, it is not generally of the crude, far-right kind that disfigured Europe in the 20th century, but is akin rather to Schiller's image of the 'bent twig' (as picked up by Isaiah Berlin) that springs back against an allegedly superior force in assertion of its independence. Both Glissant and Bhabha, for instance, assert the primacy of native writing in these terms: Glissant defines national literature as 'the urgency for each group to name itself'; Bhabha claims that 'increasingly, "national" cultures are being produced from the perspective of disenfranchised minorities'. International models of postcolonialism, in other words, are predicated upon national self-assertion. Such, we have seen, is the history of comparative literature.

World literature

If there is one model of comparison that has come to the fore since the turn of the millennium, it is that of world literature. The term is hardly new, as we saw in the previous chapter: from Wieland and Goethe to Brandes and Posnett, it resonates across the 19th century as the *de facto* object of study for comparative literature.

Throughout this time its horizons remained decidedly European, however, adumbrating a quasi-colonial vision of the world controlled by an imperial centre. It is only with the advent of the 20th century that world literature took a global turn.

Instructive examples of this development can be found at either end of the century in the contribution to debates on world literature of Bengali. In 1907, the poet and polymath Rabindranath Tagore (1861–1941) was invited to give a lecture to the National Council of Education in Calcutta. Tagore insisted on discussing not comparative, but *world* literature: the Bengali term *Vishwa Sahitya*, he contended, does much greater justice to the diversity of the Indian sub-continent, in part because it does not correspond to the foreign, European notion of comparative literature. Tagore rejects what he sees as the problematic Western emphasis on the 'nation', emphasizing rather the dynamic, interdependent nature of literature, which he views not as 'the mere total of works composed by different hands' but as a 'part of man's universal creativity'. Most of us, admonishes Tagore, think of literature in the manner of a 'rustic', parcelling out patches of land piece by piece. To this provincialism he opposes his concept of *Vishwa Sahitya*, understood as the 'universal spirit' manifesting itself through the verbal arts.

Nearly a century later, another Bengali thinker proposed an alternative form of world literature. In her Wellek Lectures on the *Death of a Discipline* (2003), Gayatri Chakravorty Spivak, whose concept of the 'subaltern' helped open up a debate in the 1980s about how best to give voice to minority cultures, outlines what one might term a postcolonial form of world literature: 'planetarity'. The standard models of Anglophone, Francophone literature, etc., can no longer serve in the post-cold-war era, suggests Spivak; what is now required is a version of comparison that takes into account the non-Western traditions of comparative literature, and that thus allows the 'Global South'—which is to say the less developed, poorer countries previously designated by such terms as 'third world'—to speak for itself, in its own languages, rather than via a centralized, metropolitan elite. Spivak's opposition of the planet to the globe recalls Tagore's opposition of 'world' to 'comparative': globalization suggests corporate control and standardization; the planet, on the other hand, is what we inhabit, 'on loan'. She does not cite him, but Spivak seems to echo Tagore's ecological metaphors; in the era of global warming and climate change, we are all interconnected in ways that go well beyond cartographic distinctions. World literature must become planetary literature.

The example of these two Bengali thinkers—and one could add others, such as the writer and critic Buddhadeva Bose or the historian Dipesh Chakrabarty—suggests that world literature has been revivified by expanding beyond its European origins. Chakrabarty's criticism of the 'historicist' approach to world development—in which capitalist Modernity originates in Europe and then spreads inexorably elsewhere—extends even to the construction of time, tethered as 'Eurochronology' is to a Greenwich, rather than to a global meridian. Certainly the evolution of comparative literature can be criticized in these terms, however noble (some of) its expansionist intentions may have been. All too often, the view from elsewhere has been a view from Europe.

Yet there is no reason why a genuinely intercontinental model of world literature should not be possible. India, in fact, serves as a striking counterpart to Europe, composed as it is of a comparable number of languages and sub-cultures. If a comparative approach to Indian literature emerged, in the 1980s, as a sub-field unto itself, one might equally sketch out comparative literatures for almost all the continents. In the postcolonial age, perhaps every continent requires, to paraphrase Virginia Woolf, a comparative literature of its own. The most influential models of world literature in the postwar era, even those that emerged from Europe, have aspired to this multipolar perspective. In numerous studies of Chinese and comparative literature, for instance, the prolific French sinologist René Etiemble (1909–2002) theorized what he called *littérature universelle*, working tirelessly to demonstrate the ways in which Asian and European literature explored common thematic and stylistic concerns. Etiemble's slogans—the Sartrean manifesto 'comparative literature is humanism', the disciplinary self-consciousness captured by his untranslatable book title *Comparaison n'est pas raison* (1963)—not only helped establish the postwar discipline in France, but also skewered the limited vision of the 'world' that continued to characterize much European thought. Building on the legacy of illustrious forebears such as Montesquieu and Voltaire, Etiemble showed how much the Parisians could learn from the Persians.

More recently, this French conception of global literature has been repurposed in sociological terms. Pascale Casanova's influential vision of *The World Republic of Letters* (1999) proposes not world literature, but 'world literary space' as the key term. Literary history and political history, while obviously related, are not the same thing: the wounded pride of one nation—she gives the example of German classical literature 'fighting back' against Napoleonic hegemony—asserts itself culturally where it cannot politically. A constant push-and-pull thus develops, whereby a supposedly 'lesser' literature seeks to establish its own identity by both irritating and imitating the dominant power. In Casanova's sociological terms, national literatures, and national writers, compete with each other for international legitimacy.

It goes without saying, of course, that literary theorists do the same thing. The development of theories of world literature, and indeed of comparative literature more generally, can be understood through exactly the same models that are applied to literature. Universalism, planetarity, republicanism: such metaphors describe both comparison and comparatist, competing for attention with ever more inflated concepts of how world literature *really* works. Even the much-remarked manifesto 'For a world literature in French' (2007), signed by leading authors from Canada, Tunisia, Senegal, the Congo, and France, announced the death of Francophone literature and the birth of *littérature-monde* as a 'Copernican revolution'. Given such metaphysical claims, it is hard to see where the metaphors have left to go.

Perhaps this inflationary logic is why the most influential model to have emerged in recent years emphasizes world literature not as a stable canon of classic works, but as a 'mode of circulation and of reading'. From Gilgamesh to postmodernism, David Damrosch's *What is World Literature?* (2003) pursues the flow of creation, translation, and production into the literary works themselves, arguing that the texts that achieve 'world' status are those that build the process of circulation into their own reflective structure. For Damrosch, a text enters into world literature by a twofold process: 'first, by being read *as* literature; second, by circulating out into a broader world beyond its linguistic and cultural point of origin'. If global intellectual history teaches us that the universality of an idea can be assessed by the degree to which it is adopted in distant contexts, global literary history can apply a similar test to texts. Indeed, a work can move in and out of world literature, depending on how it is read in a given time; the most 'worldly' works, to use Said's term, are those that gain most in translation. Comparative literature, in this sense, is not so much a canon as a currency.

The language of commerce takes us back to the original Goethean conception of world literature, and forward to the major criticism of the term as it has emerged over the last ten years. As early as 1827, Goethe described world literature as 'the market-place where all nations offer their products', and he himself conceived the notion in part as a way of encouraging the international reception of his own work. From its inception, in other words, world literature has been as much a capitalist as a comparative concept, as much about selling books as scrutinizing them. The most widely discussed critical engagement with the term, Emily

Apter's *Against World Literature* (2013), takes this insight as its starting point, arguing that universalizing models of comparison ignore the problem of what the French philosopher Barbara Cassin calls 'untranslatables' (examples of which, as explored in Cassin's *Dictionary of Untranslatables* of 2004, include terms such as *Heimat*, *saudade*, and *pravda*). In resisting translation, such terms also resist the capitalist logic of international standardization; crossing borders, to cite the great comparative cliché, is precisely what they do not do. No one can read all the languages, which means that for better or for worse foreign texts are translated not only into a language, but also into an idiom familiar to the major markets—with all the attendant risks of misunderstanding and homogenization. Here as elsewhere, then, translation remains the dirty little secret of comparative literature.

Translation studies

The issue of translation is at the very heart of comparative literature. There is a limit, after all, to how many languages even the most gifted of linguists can read; the polyglot literary theorist Roman Jakobson, so the saying goes, spoke seventeen languages, but all of them in Russian. However much we urge ourselves to read in the original, translation is a necessary evil for the comparatist. Yet it is also, of course, a force for good, opening up as it does a whole range of practical and conceptual considerations regarding the relationships between national literatures. Translation, to adapt Oscar Wilde, is the sincerest form of flattery, but it is also the closest form of reading. As a model for comparative literature, it functions both as condition and criticism of how we read.

Translation studies took off in the 1970s. While the problem of translation is as old as Cicero and Horace, Saint Jerome and Luther, it had gained curiously little purchase in the world of literary studies. The theoretical, linguistic turn in comparative literature had left the issue of how texts were carried across languages curiously untouched; outside of the technical sphere of linguistics, discussion had barely moved on from the idea that a translation was simply an inferior imitation of an original. From the mid-1970s onwards, however, scholars such as George Steiner and Itamar Evan-Zohar started asking pertinently impertinent questions about the status and preconditions of translation. Why do some cultures translate more than others? Why are some texts more readily 'translatable' than others, and what does this tell us about how they are perceived by both target and source languages? How has the status of translation altered over the centuries? What gets lost in translation—and what, no less importantly, gets found? As provisional answers to these questions began to be proposed, translation emerged not as a transparent window, but as an opaque, culturally specific process.

An obvious starting point for the discipline was to reflect on the most common metaphors for translation, and on the ways in which they have changed over time. Perhaps the most enduring metaphors, in this context, have been those of fidelity/infidelity. Translations have traditionally been judged either by how 'loyal' they are to their source text—with perceived deviations from the original deemed intrusive and disloyal—or by how free they are. These two master metaphors inform, in turn, the two principal models of translation theory, namely 'domestication' and 'foreignization'. The former holds that the source text should be translated as fluently as possible into the target language, almost as though it had been written in this language (the approach to Greek texts taken by Roman poets such as Horace); the latter maintains that the translator's role is to render her own language 'foreign' by reproducing the syntax and meaning of the original source text as closely as possible, even at the expense of conventional linguistic usage (the approach to Greek texts taken by Romantic poets such as Hölderlin). Third ways come and go—the most influential being perhaps the German critic Walter Benjamin's claim, in an 1923 introduction to his versions of Baudelaire, that translation can access an Ur-text hidden between the lines of the original—but the history of translation, and of translation theory, essentially constitutes a continuing oscillation between these two extremes. Not least, of course, because they too are culturally specific, beholden to changing views of the status, symbolism, and—perhaps most importantly—sales figures of translation.

As a model for comparative literature more generally, translation is so resonant precisely because it represents both the precondition of international communication and the process itself. Translation not only *makes possible* comparison—it is also, itself, an *act* of comparison, 'the intertraffique of the minde', to cite Samuel Daniel's poem in praise of Florio's English version of Montaigne (1603). Conceived in its broadest sense, translation calls into question the politics, the aesthetics, and the ethics of literature; every act of translation, every last linguistic choice, represents an intervention in the field of international relations. Living, as we all do, 'after Babel' (see Box 9) we have no option but to communicate through translation; whether this is even possible is the subject of an enduring debate between 'universalists', who hold that everything can be translated, and 'nominalists', who hold that nothing, strictly speaking, can be translated. It is no surprise, then, that some scholars have gone so far as to posit translation studies as the true future of comparative literature, indeed as its successor.

In her 1993 introduction to comparative literature, Susan Bassnett argued that focusing on translation would help recalibrate the discipline in more genuinely global terms, away from the traditional distinction between major and minor literatures and towards a more egalitarian emphasis on international interaction. Her principal model for this was Itamar Evan-Zohar's theory of literature as a 'polysystem'. In an influential essay of 1978, Evan-Zohar argued that the shifting status of translation within this polysystem reflects the shifting status of the target language.

Box 9 *After Babel*

First published in 1975, George Steiner's *After Babel* places 'aspects of language and translation' at the very heart of literary studies. Ferociously learned, effortlessly polyglot, and fiercely uncompromising in his defence of high culture, Steiner is in many ways the natural successor to mid-20th-century European comparatists such as Auerbach and Spitzer. He goes beyond them, however, in his suggestion that *all* forms of expression can be conceived as processes of translation—even those occurring within one language—since linguistic usage is in constant flux. Ranging from Shakespearean monologues to modernist poems—and from sacred to secular texts—Steiner argues that literature is both an act of, and a reflection on, the communication of meaning; driven by the twin engines of similarity and difference, the mechanisms of translation are the mechanisms of comparison. Combining linguistics, literature, philosophy, and the history of ideas, *After Babel* remains the most influential of Steiner's many contributions to comparative literature.

Put briefly, this means that whenever a culture considers itself 'young', 'peripheral', or in 'crisis', it seeks to reinforce its sense of self by turning to translated works from elsewhere; as national self-confidence develops, so this external need for validation fades away. Increased translation, in short, implies increased insecurity.

Whatever criticisms one might make of this model—how does it square, for instance, with the fact that major cultures such as France and Germany translate so much?—what is striking is how quickly such theories date. It is not only translation that reflects changing cultural priorities, in other words, but also translation theory. In the theoretical fever of the 1970s, the language of structuralist 'systems' was in the air, with Claudio Guillén's

Literature as System (1971) one of several precursors to Evan-Zohar's notion of the literary polysystem. Since the turn of the millennium, by contrast, disciplinary discussion has moved on, with translation becoming part of a more politicized understanding of what Franco Moretti calls a 'world literary system', torn between models of close and distant reading, border crossing and border closing. Increasingly, the focus of comparative literature has been not so much on what gets lost in translation as on what gets least in translation, on the 'untranslatable' terms of Barbara Cassin's dictionary that resist reconceptualization in another language. What Lydia Liu has called 'translingual practice'—the contextually specific resonance of words such as the Western 'self' on the one hand and the Confucian *ji* on the other—has emerged as a way of shifting attention away from straightforward claims of equivalence and towards subtler forms of exchange. If the etymology of translation implies 'carrying over', it is precisely that which resists being carried over that is starting to claim the attention of comparatists. That such a development is merely the latest—and certainly not the last—skirmish in the age-old battle between universalists and nominalists underlines the extent to which translation remains both the prerequisite for, and the very practice of, comparative literature.

Reception studies

If translation suggests one mode of carrying over, 'reception' describes another. Translation ferries meaning *between* languages, as it were on a horizontal axis; reception traces meaning *through* languages, on a vertical axis. Translation is of course itself a form of reception—not least because the major works are constantly being retranslated—but its comparative thrust is largely geographical, across languages and cultures; reception, by definition, works historically, drawing attention to what readers and cultures do with translations. Clearly anything, in principle, can be 'received' by a later culture—certain theoretical schools, such as the 'reader response theory' of Wolfgang Iser and Hans

Robert Jauss, make reception the very basis for literary meaning—but the resonance is greatest where the lineage is longest. As such, the reception of Greek, Roman, and Arabic classics provides one of the most enduring models of comparative literature across the centuries, and can stand for the contemporary prominence of reception studies more generally.

Despite its newly fashionable status in the Anglophone world, classical reception studies are as old as Antiquity. Much of Latin literature amounts to an extended reception study of the Greeks; as Horace writes in his *Epistles*, 'conquered Greece conquered its fierce victor and introduced the arts to rustic Latium'. Perhaps more surprisingly, the Greeks themselves looked back to Persian culture, as Edward Said showed in his influential reading of Aeschylus' tragedy *The Persians* as one of the earliest documents of Orientalism. In some ways, then, the whole discipline of classical studies is about reception, looking back as it does across millennia of cultural accretion. The particular contribution of classical *reception* studies, however, is to focus on the ways in which the classical tradition is reactivated in later societies—thus drawing out the changing meanings created by changing contexts—and to reflect on the cultural and theoretical implications of this process. Out of this juxtaposition comes a new, original perspective not only on both the earlier and the later texts, but also on the relationship between these texts and their respective periods.

The richness of this approach for comparative literature is self-evident. Comparatively speaking, it is better to receive than to give, since the later context is enriched by the vestigial presence of the former. In the quarrel of the ancients and moderns, reception critics read the former through the latter, teasing out the ways in which a later text draws on its predecessor. Indeed, in Jonathan Swift's satirical version of the debate—the so-called 'Battle of the Books', published as part of *A Tale of a Tub* in 1704—it is the books themselves that come to life and fight for supremacy (see Figure 10).

10. The Battle of the Books, original woodcut from *A Tale of a Tub* (1704).

That Swift avoids reaching a conclusion in the debate is only prudent. For while the modern text may not be superior to the ancient one, it cannot help but be informed by it—as well, potentially, as by all the ways in which it has previously been received. Focusing on the reception of classical myth in the Victorian period might show us how the 19th-century ideal of masculinity was constructed through reference to Homeric heroes, but it may also retrospectively alter our view of how Homer was received in earlier times. The reception of 'Oriental' epics such as the *Arabian Nights* (first made available to a European audience in Antoine Galland's French translation of 1704), or of the Persian poem the *Shahnameh* (famous in particular for its history of illustrated manuscripts), tells us as much about the changing status of the Orient as it does about the texts themselves. Reception, in this sense, is like using Georg Brandes' telescope to look not only at the stars, but also at the telescope itself.

Another common approach to reception studies is to consider the evolution of genre distinctions such as tragedy or comedy, or of rhetorical modes such as *anagnorisis* (a moment of recognition) or *katabasis* (a trip to the underworld). Such distinctions allow critics to trace how later works have developed or deviated from their classical source while remaining within a shared frame of reference; Nietzsche's *The Birth of Tragedy*, juxtaposing Wagner with Sophocles, is a case in point. To be sure, this should not be taken to imply that reception is a passive state of affairs in which meaning is simply dictated by the past. On the contrary, new meaning is created by new juxtapositions: writing against the backdrop of the Franco-Prussian war of 1871, Nietzsche repurposes Greek tragedy as a constituent element of European Modernity. Creative reception of this sort can even work its way back to where it started: Edward Fitzgerald's *Rubaiyat of Omar Khayyám* (first published in 1859) essentially reinvented the medieval Persian poet Khayyám not just for modern European, but also for modern Persian readers. Understood in this fashion, reception becomes 'circulation', tracking recurring characters in changing contexts—Orpheus in modern poetry, Odysseus in modern cinema—or following processes of cultural transfer across continents. Tradition itself, to borrow Hobsbawm and Ranger's celebrated term, emerges not just as received but also as 'invented'.

Yet this idea of 'tradition' has, in turn, its own tradition. One of the key contributions of comparative literature understood as reception studies has been to reflect on the ways in which cultural tradition is created, curated, and corralled, on how it is appropriated in support of a prevailing ideology. The idea of the 'canon', it has become ever clearer, is never ideologically neutral; certain texts, characters, or even cultures—the 'tyranny of Greece' over 19th-century Germany, the Roman obsession of Mussolini's Italy—are foregrounded at certain times. More generally, intellectual history suggests that there are two main models for understanding tradition: either as an unbroken 'chain' of influence, in which every iteration of a motif or myth adds to its cumulative depth (as in our understanding of the 'tragic', for instance), or as a series of discrete, elective moments, in which one writer or period selectively evokes another, often very distant period (Keats's 'wild surmise' on first reading Chapman's translation of Homer). The very idea of reception, in short, has been received in different ways at different times.

Why, then, has it risen to prominence in the 21st century? Part of the answer is simple expediency. Facing an ever-greater struggle to justify its existence, Classics has turned to reception studies as a way of asserting its continuing relevance and self-awareness: Antiquity as a guide to Modernity. More broadly, however, the study of reception has emerged as part of a general turn to forms of history—book history, intellectual history—that prioritize cultural context over semantic content. This historical turn has brought with it a broadening of the comparative perspective, predicated not only on seeing reception as a form of comparison, but also on viewing comparison as a form of reception. Studying the ways culture is received amounts, in the final analysis, to comparing disciplines; that classical reception—or indeed reception studies of any kind—is inherently interdisciplinary suggests its potential for the *in*disciplinary compass of comparative literature, flickering uncertainly between ancient and modern, East and West, North and South. One thing is sure: future debates will add further coordinates. If comparative literature is a compass, it requires constant recalibration.

Chapter 5
The futures of comparative literature

Political education

In 1872, at the tender age of 27, a young professor published his first book. It may now be viewed as a seminal work, but at the time of its publication Nietzsche's *The Birth of Tragedy* was met with deafening silence. The only critic who responded to it was his old school friend Ulrich von Wilamowitz-Moellendorff; in a violent attack, he dismissed Nietzsche's anachronistic approach to criticism as 'philology of the future' (*Zukunftsphilologie*). However seductive the term, it was not intended as a compliment.

Can comparative literature reclaim the insult? For all its past struggles and present debates, comparative literature has an increasingly central role to play in the future of the Humanities. In a world defined by globalization and its discontents, in an academy defined by ever-greater interdisciplinarity, comparison is inescapable. The choice now is not whether to compare, but what and how to compare: books, films, languages, cultures, histories. The philology of the future has become the philology of the present, ranging ever more widely across contemporary culture.

Comparative literature is undoubtedly among the most ambitious of scholarly disciplines. It is also, however, among the most anxious. State-of-the-discipline reports—such as those commissioned at ten-year intervals by the American Comparative Literature Association (ACLA)—regularly betray a sense of unease about the emerging direction of travel. To be sure, comparative literature has long existed in a perpetual state of crisis, and much of its self-conception has accordingly revolved around the rhetoric of mortality and immortality. Metaphors of birth and death (of tragedy, for instance), or of oblivion and renaissance, have characterized comparative literature for centuries, torn as it is between resuscitating the past and revitalizing the present. In recent years, the notion of the 'afterlife' of a work (*Fortleben* in Walter Benjamin's variation of the term, *Nachleben* in that of the art historian Aby Warburg) has become increasingly popular as a way of capturing more creative forms of influence: Shakespeare's afterlives, for instance, form a whole school of comparative literature unto themselves. More broadly, such metaphysical metaphors point to the discipline's obsession with continuity and change, an obsession that reflects its own enduring insecurities regarding its changing status within the Humanities. By tying its fate in this manner to that of established figures and disciplines, comparative literature hopes to ensure its own survival.

This shadow status suggests a paradoxical conclusion: namely, that comparative literature is both central and marginal to literary studies, or perhaps, in what is only seemingly a paradox, central precisely *because* it is marginal. It is central because it draws on almost every discipline in the Humanities, cannily positioning itself in the middle of the Venn diagram of history, politics, languages, and literature; it is marginal because it is not tied to any single tradition, and thus risks being ignored by all of them. The vulnerability of comparative literature, in other words, is both its strength and its weakness. Sensitive as it is to shifting trends, it is also at the mercy of such trends. The risk of a hostile takeover by theoretical jargon, for instance, is a constant threat. A second round of the theory wars would surely be in no one's interest.

More pressing at this point is the *practice* of comparison, and the ways that it pushes at the edges of what we understand as 'literature'. One of the principal developments in recent years has been a move not just towards interdisciplinarity, but also towards transdisciplinarity. 'Inter-art' studies have become ever more prominent: comparison between fiction and films, sculptures and sonnets, figure increasingly on curricula and conferences. 'Transnational', meanwhile, has emerged as a key term within the field, creeping in from neighbouring disciplines such as history and law. Comparative literature, once again, finds itself in the crossfire of the Humanities.

What do such developments tell us about the future of the discipline? Above all, they suggest that both the method of comparison and the object of literature are becoming ever broader in their definitions. There are dangers, as well as opportunities, in such expansionism. Comparing differing media and forms of art can be an extremely fruitful way of opening up new perspectives—on Proust and painting, for instance, or Liszt and literature—but it is not always clear that the particularities of the respective art forms are maintained. 'What is the good of the Arts if they're interchangeable?', asks Margaret Schlegel of her sister Helen's attempts to translate music into painting in E.M. Forster's *Howard's End* (1910), and the question remains pertinent to the contemporary comparatist. Simply extracting content—Proust's references to art, Liszt's use of literary sources—is only of limited interpretive use; much more interesting is to enquire into the formal echoes and exchanges, the ways in which one medium borrows techniques from another. Pursued in this manner, both creator and critic emerge between the arts as comparatists.

'Transnational' interpretations of literature, similarly, are at their strongest when not simply used as a modish synonym for 'comparative'. Taken at its word, the term implies an approach that transcends the structures of nations, implying, to cite just one example, 'a web of social and textual interrelationships linking modernisms worldwide as well as an optic through which to see these links'. While this may seem similar to the traditional understanding of comparison, the difference lies in the attempt to give parity—and thus 'planetarity'—to a range of competing perspectives (the increasingly popular plural 'modernisms' is telling). If the comparative method has long been hostage, as we have seen throughout this book, to the prejudices of the day, imposing comparison on terms that are favourable to the dominant (Western) nation, then transnationalism effectively functions as a warning *against* comparison, against its colonial complicity and tendency to apply national prejudice internationally.

Closely related to this transnational turn is an increasing interest in forms of multilingualism. Historically speaking, comparative literature has tended to reduce regions and continents to one dominant language, dividing up the world according to Francophone, Anglophone, or Hispanophone spheres of influence. Yet areas such as the Maghreb, with its imbrication of dialects and forms of Arabic with French and Spanish, or the Indian sub-continent with its twenty-two official languages, are more accurately understood as multilingual, stubbornly irreducible to the European model of single-language nations. The potential of such a multilingual model of comparison is considerable, since it promises to push comparative literature beyond the increasingly unproductive dichotomy of 'national' and 'foreign', local and colonial languages, as well as to take into account both written and oral texts. It is also, of course, implicitly political as well as cultural, a bottom-up rebuke to top-down monolingualism.

For the sobering reality is that the multilingual are most often the marginal, the disenfranchised on the edges of Western wealth. Understood in literal rather than literary terms, the truly transnational in the 21st century are the refugees and immigrants clustering at border-points, traded back and forth between countries and continents. In a world in which humans are trafficked as ruthlessly as commodities, the metaphors of comparison ring humiliatingly hollow: it is facile to say that words cross borders, when people cannot. Comparative literature will surely have to catch up with this new reality and begin applying itself to the stories of those who are transnational not out of desire, but despair.

Aesthetic education

One way in which it might do this is by conceiving itself, in the terms of the German poet Friedrich Schiller (1759–1805), as a process of 'aesthetic education'. In letters written in the early 1790s in the wake of the French Revolution—around the same time, that is to say, that 'comparative philology' was coming into fashion—Schiller argued that the ideal aesthetic state is one characterized by the Kantian notion of disinterest (defined as the process of engaging with the world selflessly, without vested interest). In such a state, the enlightened, autonomous citizen, finely poised between reason and emotion, sense and sensibility, learns to balance competing intellectual demands through aspiring to an 'ideal of equality'. The aesthetic 'play' of the imagination, freely embraced, creates a safe space for human—and for humanist—self-realization.

That such a state can lead to a process of political and even moral education lies, for Schiller, in the nature of the (truly) aesthetic. It is also what makes it a possible model for the future of comparative literature. Conceived as an aesthetic project but born into political realities, comparative literature has struggled to achieve the impartial perspective that Schiller (and behind him, Kant) advocated. Yet this still could, and arguably should, be its aim: to outgrow its politicized history and create a fully egalitarian, disinterested model of comparison, one in which the free 'play' of literature embraces all peoples equally, regardless of national history or linguistic status. Comparative literature developed as the study of writing across borders, but it has yet to conceive a world *without* borders. If it is self-evident that such an aim can never be fully realized, such is the open-ended nature of education, conceived in its true etymological sense (*e-ducare*) as a process of 'leading people out'.

It is also the nature of capitalism. Comparative literature is nothing if not market-driven, and dewy-eyed notions of the free play of comparison quickly founder on hard-nosed commercial considerations. A whole host of sociological factors determine what internationally minded readers want—levels of education, travel experiences, the funding and marketing of literary translation—but critical theories are surely a long way down the list. The reality is that cultural differences are more perceived than understood; publishers pander, as they must, to clichés and preconceptions. For all the academic obsession with the 'Other', many readers are looking for more of the same, for confirmation of the supposedly universal feelings to be found in literature from one end of the globe to the other. Commercial realities, in this sense, are beyond compare.

It is precisely for this reason, however, that the concept of comparative literature is so necessary. Its task is to work with, but also against, commercial preconceptions; to take questions from one culture and pose them to another; and to ensure the good faith even of bad writing. This onus of evaluation sometimes gets lost in critical discussions of the discipline; but who else is to assess the best and worst of world literature if not comparatists? If international prizes are not to be decided on merely political grounds, then critically informed comparison is essential. In the ecology of books, comparative literature has a pragmatic, as well as a professorial role to play.

Such pragmatism extends, of course, to the increasingly important sphere of 'digital Humanities'. By nature interdisciplinary, digitized approaches to the Humanist tradition—whether in the form of online editions or bibliographical diagrams, computer databases or Internet encyclopaedia—tend to the maximal, pursuing ever-bigger data. In a world in which more and more information requires synthesizing, comparison remains the one indispensable tool. Indeed, the striking thing, in many ways, is just how much the 21st-century approach to information echoes that of the 19th: digital humanists are essentially philologists with computers, digging under cultures with their keyboards. The philology of the future is also the philology of the past; Ernest Renan's claim that 'comparison is the great instrument of criticism' remains as true now as it was in 1848.

The big difference between then and now, of course, is the sheer amount of information at our disposal. Already in 1935 Paul Valéry, when attempting an assessment of the modern mind, could state that 'all knowledge today is necessarily comparative knowledge'; it barely needs stating how much truer this is almost a century later. In the age of the Internet, the trick for the comparatist is not just knowing what to compare, but also what *not* to compare. If 'comp lit' is not to turn into 'comp list', with texts and authors simply piled up *ad nauseam* by a computer, then human judgement remains indispensable. With vast amounts of information instantly available, contemporary comparative literature is not so much about retrieving content as about knowing where to look in the first place; Brandes' image of the comparatist's telescope might now be better reconfigured as a kaleidoscope, refracting knowledge in every possible direction. Flooded with data, perspective is at an all-time premium.

Yet such an information overload is characteristic, ultimately, not just of our own, multimedia era, but also of modernity as a whole. It is no coincidence that the discipline of comparative literature began as modernity began, in the post-Revolutionary fervour of the early 1800s. The increasing prominence of comparison as an interpretive model accompanied the increasing proliferation of information in the 19th century; the more people knew about other cultures, the more they compared. That they still imposed their own prejudices on this knowledge tells us as much about human nature as about comparative literature, but it does not diminish the increasing importance of comparison to the modern age. How, indeed, can one even understand one's era as modern, unless it is by implicitly comparing it with the past? Modernity, like Antiquity, is a comparative concept.

It may be, in short, that comparative literature needs to understand itself more comparatively. Cognate approaches to other disciplines—comparative history, comparative law, comparative politics—are often considerably firmer in their grasp of their own methodology, triangulating themselves more rigorously within the sphere of global relations. Whether pursued as close or as distant reading, as creative practice or as critical theory, comparative literature can surely learn from the global history approach to the universalization of ideas, or from the social sciences approach to the ways in which information circulates—with the aim not of abjuring its Humanist mission, but of expanding it. If comparison is ubiquitous, literary studies must consider what it can learn from looking beyond literature.

For what remains most surprising is just how much comparative literature in the 21st century hides in plain sight. Its practice is everywhere, the very basis for how we gather knowledge; its practitioners, however, often struggle to attain the visibility of critics based within one language, torn as they necessarily are between competing traditions. Many of the most prominent comparatists are not even known under this name, but figure rather as literary theorists, cultural critics, or eccentric polymaths. It is in the interests of comparative literature that this situation change, and that its leading exponents gain prominence *as comparatists* in the public, as well as in the professorial, sphere. As the most demanding of literary disciplines, comparative literature should attract the brightest, most ambitious students; but aspiring comparatists need role models, and they are not always apparent in literary debate, dominated as it is by national traditions heavily invested in their own primacy. It is striking, if perhaps unsurprising, how many leading comparatists grew up in multilingual environments (comparative literature is in this sense among the most personal, as well as the most political, of intellectual activities). With the right role models, however, anyone can aspire to a multipolar perspective. Emerging from the profoundly monocultural world of the British education system, I for one was inspired by the likes of George Steiner or Edward Said to discover other literary traditions, and to explore the essential interconnectedness of all cultures; the initial difficulty, the challenge to raise my sights beyond my comfort zone, was part of the appeal. Such exemplars are sorely required in present times. Cosmopolitanism, especially in the Anglo-Saxon world, needs all the support it can get.

Comparing literatures is a complex process, fraught with theoretical, practical, and political dangers. Its ambition, however, is a simple one: to understand the ways in which literary cultures interact. As the discipline moves ever further away from its European origins, the future of comparative literature depends on retaining this coherence despite its worldwide reach, on articulating its place at the centre of the Humanities, and on making intellectual virtues out of institutional necessities. If comparative literature is to become the philology of the future, it must build on the achievements of the past, while working within the structures of the present. From politics to philosophy, from history to linguistics, comparatists have always drawn on the broadest possible range of approaches to culture; in this age of specialists, generalists continue to play a vital role in shaping and supporting the life of the mind. International, interdisciplinary forms of knowledge remain, in short, the very essence of modernity. Now more than ever, the aesthetic education of comparative literature is indispensable.

References and further reading

General sources and anthologies

Damrosch, David, Melas, Natalie, and Buthelezi, Mbongiseni (eds), *The Princeton Sourcebook in Comparative Literature* (Princeton, 2009)

D'haen, Theo, Damrosch, David, and Kadir, Djelal (eds), *Routledge Companion to World Literature* (Routledge, 2012)

Schulz, Hans-Joachim, and Rhein, Philip H. (eds), *Comparative Literature: The Early Years* (University of North Carolina, 1973)

Introductions to comparative literature

Bassnett, Susan, *Comparative Literature* (Blackwell, 1993)

Domínguez, César, Saussy, Haun, and Villanueva, Darío, *Introducing Comparative Literature: New Trends and Applications* (Routledge, 2015)

Morgan, Ben, Omri, Mohamed-Salah, and Reynolds, Matthew, 'Comparative Criticism: Histories and Methods', *Comparative Critical Studies* 12/2 (June 2015), 147–59

Principles and practices

Aristotle, *Poetics* (Penguin, 1996)

Bloom, Harold, *The Western Canon* (Harcourt Brace, 1994)

Borges, Jorge Luis, *Pierre Menard, Author of* Don Quixote (1939), tr. Andrew Hurley (Penguin, 1998), 88–95

Bouju, Emmanuel, 'Achille et la tortue. Quelques considérations intempestives sur la périodisation de la littérature', *Le temps des lettres. Quelles périodisations pour l'histoire de la littérature française du XXe siècle?*, ed. Fr. Dugast and M. Touret (Rennes, 2001), 45–54

Cervantes, Miguel de, *Don Quixote*, tr. John Rutherford (Penguin, 2003)

Damrosch, David, 'World Literature in a Postcanonical, Hypercanonical Age', *Comparative Literature in an Age of Globalization*, ed. Haun Saussy (Johns Hopkins University Press, 2006), 43–53

Dowden, Edward, *Shakspere: A Primer* (Macmillan, 1922)

Eliot, T.S., 'Tradition and the Individual Talent', *The Sacred Wood* (Methuen, 1945), 47–59

Ferris, David, 'Indiscipline', *Comparative Literature in an Age of Globalization* (Johns Hopkins University Press, 1994), 78–99

Lewis, Martin W., and Wigen, Kären, *The Myth of Continents: A Critique of Metageography* (University of California Press, 1997)

Lukács, Georg, *Studies in European Realism* (Merlin, 1972)

Moretti, Franco, *Signs taken for Wonders: On the Sociology of Literary Forms* (Verso, 2005)

Moretti, Franco, *Graphs, Maps, Trees: Abstract Models for Literary History* (Verso, 2005)

Moretti, Franco, *Distant Reading: The Formation of an Unorthodox Literary Critic* (Verso, 2013)

Pollock, Sheldon, 'Cosmopolitanism, Vernacularism, and Pre-modernity', *Global Intellectual History*, ed. Samuel Moyn and Andrew Sartori (Columbia, 2013), 59–80

Schaffner, Anna Katharina, and Weller, Shane (eds), *Modernist Eroticisms: European Literature after Sexology* (Palgrave Macmillan, 2012)

Steiner, George, *The Death of Tragedy* (Yale, 1996)

Stuurman, Siep, 'Common Humanity and Cultural Difference on the Sedentary-Nomadic Frontier: Herodotus, Sima Qian, and Ibn Khaldun', *Global Intellectual History*, ed. Samuel Moyn and Andrew Sartori (Columbia, 2013), 33–58

Szondi, Peter, *An Essay on the Tragic*, tr. Paul Fleming (Stanford, 2002)

Thiong'o, Ngũgĩ wa, *Decolonising the Mind: The Politics of Language in African Literature* (Heinemann Educational, 1986)

Underwood, Ted, *Why Literary Periods Mattered: Historical Contrast and the Prestige of English Studies* (Stanford, 2013)

Gilgamesh

Cregan-Reid, Vybarr, *Discovering Gilgamesh* (Manchester University Press, 2013)

Damrosch, David, *The Buried Book: The Loss and Rediscovery of the Great Epic of Gilgamesh* (Henry Holt, 2007)

Smith, George, 'The Chaldean Account of the Deluge', in *Transactions of the Society of Biblical Archaeology* 1–2 (1872), 213–34

Philology and German comparative literature

Benes, Tuska, *In Babel's Shadow: Language, Philology, and the Nation in Nineteenth-Century Germany* (Wayne State University Press, 2008)

Herder, Johann Gottfried, *Philosophical Writings*, tr. Michael N. Forster (CUP, 2002)

Lepper, Marcel, *Philologie. Eine Einführung* (Junius, 2014)

Turner, James, *Philology: The Forgotten Origins of the Modern Humanities* (Princeton, 2014), esp. ch. 5

Russian and Eastern European comparative literature

Dobrenko, Evgeny and Tihanov, Galin, *A History of Russian Literary Theory and Criticism: The Soviet Age and Beyond* (University of Pittsburgh Press, 2011)

Emerson, Caryl, 'Answering for Central and Eastern Europe', *Comparative Literature in an Age of Globalization*, ed. Haun Saussy (Johns Hopkins University Press, 2006), 203–11

Gould, Rebecca, *Writers and Rebels: The Literature of Insurgency in the Caucasus* (Yale, 2016)

Polonsky, Rachel, *English Literature and the Russian Aesthetic Renaissance* (CUP, 1998)

Szerb, Antal, *Reflections in the Library: Selected Literary Essays 1926–1944*, tr. Peter Sherwood (Legenda, 2017)

Danish comparative literature

Larsen, Svend Erik, 'Georg Brandes: The Telescope of Comparative Literature', *The Routledge Companion to World Literature* (Routledge, 2012)

Thomsen, Mads Rosendahl, and Ringgaard, Dan (eds), *Danish Literature as World Literature* (Bloomsbury, 2017)
Weinstein, Arnold, *Northern Arts: The Breakthrough of Scandinavian Literature and Art, from Ibsen to Bergman* (Princeton, 2008)

French comparative literature

Brunetière, Ferdinand, *L'Évolution des genres dans l'histoire de la littérature* (Hachette, 1914)
Chasles, Philarète, 'Foreign Literature Compared', in Hans-Joachim Schulz and Philip H. Rhein (eds), *Comparative Literature: The Early Years* (University of North Carolina, 1973), 16–37
Etiemble, René, *Comparaison n'est pas raison. La crise de la littérature comparée* (Gallimard, 1963)
Noël, François-Joseph-Michel, and de La Place, Guislain-François-Marie-Joseph (eds), *Leçons françaises de littérature et de morale* (Le Normant, 1816)
Renan, Ernest, *The Future of Science: Ideas of 1848*, tr. Albert Vandam and C.B. Pitman (Chapman & Hall, 1891)
Tageldin, Shaden M., 'One Comparative Literature? "Birth" of a Discipline in French-Egyptian Translation, 1810–1834', *Comparative Literature Studies* 47/4 (2000), 417–45

Hispanic comparative literature

Andrade, Oswald de, 'Cannibalist Manifesto', tr. Leslie Bary, *Latin American Literary Review* 19/38 (1991), 38–47
Castro, Américo, *The Spaniards: An Introduction to their History*, tr. Willard F. King (University of California Press, 1971)
Guillén, Claudio, *The Challenge of Comparative Literature*, tr. Cola Franzen (Harvard, 1993)
Novillo-Corvalán, Patricia, *Modernism and Latin America: Transnational Networks of Literary Exchange* (Routledge, 2018)

American comparative literature

Bernheimer, Charles (ed.), *Comparative Literature in the Age of Multiculturalism* (Johns Hopkins University Press, 1994)
de Man, Paul, *The Paul de Man Notebooks*, ed. Martin McQuillan (Edinburgh University Press, 2014), esp. 'Part III: Teaching'

Emerson, Ralph Waldo, *Representative Men* (Belknap Press, 1996)
Gayley, Charles Mills, 'What is Comparative Literature' (1903), *The Princeton Sourcebook in Comparative Literature* (Princeton, 2009), 67–78
Saussy, Haun (ed.), *Comparative Literature in an Age of Globalization* (Johns Hopkins University Press, 2006)
Wellek, René, 'The Crisis of Comparative Literature', *The Princeton Sourcebook in Comparative Literature* (Princeton, 2009), 161–72
Wellek, René, 'The Name and Nature of Comparative Literature', *Discriminations: Further Concepts of Criticism* (University of North Carolina Press, 1970), 1–36
Wellek, René, 'The New Nihilism in Literary Studies', in *Aesthetics and the Literature of Ideas: Essays in Honour of A. Owen Aldridge* (University of Delaware, 1990)

'European' literature

Auerbach, Ernst, *Mimesis: The Representation of Reality in Western Literature*, tr. Willard R. Trask (Princeton, 2003)
Auerbach, Ernst, 'The Philology of World Literature', *Time, History, and Literature: Selected Essays of Erich Auerbach* (Princeton, 2013), 253–65
Babits, Mihály, *Geschichte der europäischen Literatur* (Europa, 1949)
Cohen, Walter, *A History of European Literature* (OUP, 2017)
Coleridge, S.T., *Aids to Reflection*, vol. 1 (Pickering, 1848), 176–7
Coudenhove-Kalergi, Richard von, *Pan-Europe* (Knopf, 1926)
Curtius, Ernst Robert, *European Literature and the Latin Middle Ages*, tr. Willard R. Trask (Princeton, 1952)
de Man, Paul, *Allegories of Reading: Figural Language in Rousseau, Nietzsche, Rilke, and Proust* (Yale, 1979)
Hutchinson, Ben, *Lateness and Modern European Literature* (OUP, 2016)
Hutchinson, Ben, 'Late Reading: Erich Auerbach and the *Spätboot* of Comparative Literature', *Comparative Critical Studies* 14/1 (2017), 69–85
Macaulay Posnett, Hutcheson, *Comparative Literature* (Kegan Paul, Trench & Co, 1886)
Spengler, Oswald, *The Decline of the West*, tr. Charles Atkinson (OUP, 1991)

Spitzer, Leo, *Linguistics and Literary History* (Princeton, 1967)
Steiner, George, *Errata: An Examined Life* (Yale, 1999)
Valéry, Paul, 'The Crisis of the Mind', *Paul Valéry: An Anthology* (Princeton, 1977)

World literature

Apter, Emily, *Against World Literature: On the Politics of Untranslatability* (Verso, 2013)
Casanova, Pascale, *The World Republic of Letters* (Harvard, 2007)
Cheah, Pheng, *What is a World? On Postcolonial Literature as World Literature* (Duke, 2016)
Damrosch, David, *What is World Literature?* (Princeton, 2003)
Damrosch, David, *World Literature in Theory* (Wiley-Blackwell, 2014)
Goethe, Johann Wolfgang von, *Conversations of Goethe with Eckermann and Soret*, tr. John Oxenford (CUP, 2012)
Barbery, Muriel, Ben Jelloun, Tahar, Borer, Alain, et al., 'Pour une littérature-monde en Français', *Le Monde* 15 March 2007 (see: <http://www.lemonde.fr/livres/article/2007/03/15/des-ecrivains-plaident-pour-un-roman-en-francais-ouvert-sur-le-monde_883572_3260.html)>
Spivak, Gayatri Chakravorty, *Death of a Discipline* (Columbia, 2003)
Szerb, Antal, *Geschichte der Weltliteratur* (Schwabe, 2016)
Tagore, Rabindranath, 'World Literature', in *Rabindranath Tagore: Selected Writings on Literature and Language*, ed. Sukanta Chaudhuri (OUP, 2001), 147–9
Thomsen, Mads Rosendahl, *Mapping World Literature: International Canonization and Transnational Literatures* (Bloomsbury, 2008)
Thornber, Karen Laura, *Empire of Texts in Motion: Chinese, Korean, and Taiwanese Transculturations of Japanese Literature* (Harvard, 2009)

Literary theory

Barthes, Roland, *Writing Degree Zero*, tr. Annette Lavers and Colin Smith (Hill & Wang, 1977)
Cixous, Hélène, 'The Laugh of the Medusa', tr. Keith Cohen and Paula Cohen, *Signs* 1/4 (Summer 1976), 875–93
Derrida, Jacques, 'Différance', *Margins of Philosophy*, tr. Alan Bass (University of Chicago, 1982), 3–27

Derrida, Jacques, *Of Grammatology*, tr. G.C. Spivak (Johns Hopkins University Press, 1998)
Eagleton, Terry, *Literary Theory: An Introduction* (Blackwell, 1983)
Gilbert, Sandra, and Gubar, Susan, *The Madwoman in the Attic: The Woman Writer and the Nineteenth-Century Literary Imagination* (Yale, 1979)

Cultural studies

Barthes, Roland, *Mythologies*, tr. Annette Lavers (Farrar, Strauss & Giroux, 1972)
During, Simon (ed.), *The Cultural Studies Reader* (Routledge, 1993)
Eliot, T.S., *Notes Towards the Definition of Culture* (Faber & Faber, 1973)
Hall, Stuart, *Cultural Studies 1983: A Theoretical History* (Duke University Press, 2016)
Hall, Stuart, *Familiar Stranger: A Life between Two Islands* (Allen Lane, 2017)
Hoggart, Richard, *The Uses of Literacy: Aspects of Working-Class Life* (Penguin, 2009)

Postcolonialism

Aravamudan, Srinivas, *Enlightenment Orientalism* (Chicago, 2011)
Bhabha, Homi, *The Location of Culture* (Routledge, 2004)
Césaire, Aimé, *Discourse on Colonialism*, tr. Joan Pinkham (Monthly Review Press, 2000)
Césaire, Aimé, *Return to my Native Land*, tr. Mireille Rosello and Annie Pritchard (Bloodaxe, 1995)
Chakrabarty, Dipesh, *Provincializing Europe: Postcolonial Thought and Historical Difference* (Princeton, 2000)
Fanon, Frantz, *The Wretched of the Earth*, tr. Richard Philcox (Grove, 2005)
Glissant, Édouard, 'Cross-Cultural Poetics: National Literatures', *The Princeton Sourcebook in Comparative Literature* (Princeton, 2009), 248–58
Li, Xiofan Amy (ed.), 'The Exotic and the Autoexotic', *Publications of the Modern Language Association of America* 132/2 (March 2017), 392–461
Said, Edward, *Orientalism* (Pantheon, 1978)

Translation theory

Apter, Emily, *The Translation Zone: A New Comparative Literature* (Princeton, 2005)

Benjamin, Walter, 'The Task of the Translator', *Illuminations*, tr. Harry Zohn (Fontana, 1992), 70–82

Cassin, Barbara (ed.), *Dictionary of Untranslatables: A Philosophical Lexicon* (Princeton, 2014)

Evan-Zohar, Itamar, 'The Position of Translated Literature within the Literary Polysystem', *Papers in Historical Poetics* (Porter Institute, 1978)

Liu, Lydia H., *Translingual Practice: Literature, National Culture, and Translated Modernity—China, 1900–1937* (Stanford, 1995)

Reynolds, Matthew, *Translation: A Very Short Introduction* (OUP, 2016)

Steiner, George, *After Babel* (OUP, 1975)

Taylor, Charles, *The Language Animal: The Full Shape of the Human Linguistic Capacity* (Harvard, 2016)

Reception studies

Bloom, Harold, *The Anxiety of Influence: A Theory of Poetry* (OUP, 1973)

Fumaroli, Marc (ed.), *La Querelle des anciens et des modernes* (Gallimard Folio, 2001)

Hardwick, Lorna, and Stray, Christopher (eds), *A Companion to Classical Receptions* (Wiley-Blackwell, 2007)

Horace, *Satires and Epistles*, tr. John Davie (Oxford World's Classics, 2011)

Skinner, Quentin, 'Meaning and Understanding in the History of Ideas', *History and Theory* 8/1 (1969), 3–53

Warner, Marina, *Stranger Magic: Charmed States and the Arabian Nights* (Chatto & Windus, 2011)

Zajko, Vanda (ed.), *A Handbook to the Reception of Classical Mythology* (Wiley-Blackwell, 2017)

Futures of comparative literature

Berman, Jessica, *Modernist Commitments: Ethics, Politics, and Transnational Modernism* (Columbia, 2011)

Forster, E.M., *Howard's End* (Penguin, 1961)

Pollock, Sheldon, 'Future Philology? The Fate of a Soft Science in a Hard World', *Critical Inquiry* 35/4 (Summer 2009), 931–61

Saussy, Haun, 'Exquisite Cadavers Stitched from Fresh Nightmares', *Comparative Literature in an Age of Globalization* (Johns Hopkins, 2006), 3–42

Saussy, Haun, 'Comparative Literature: The Next Ten Years': <https://stateofthediscipline.acla.org/entry/comparative-literature-next-ten-years>

Schiller, Friedrich, *On the Aesthetic Education of Man*, ed. E.M. Wilkinson and L.A. Willoughby (OUP, 1983)

Seigel, Micol, 'Beyond Compare: Comparative Method after the Transnational Turn', *Radical History Review* 91 (Winter 2005), 62–90

Stanford Friedman, Susan, *Planetary Modernisms: Provocations on Modernity Across Time* (Columbia, 2015)

Szegedy-Maszák, Mihály, 'Unseen Paintings and Unheard Melodies: The Uses and Limits of Interart Studies', *Comparative Critical Studies* 12/2 (2015), 251–66

Valéry, Paul, 'Le bilan de l'intelligence', *Œuvres*, vol. 1 (Gallimard, 1957)

Websites

American Comparative Literature Association: <www.acla.org>

British Comparative Literature Association: <www.bcla.org>

Index

A

B

C

D

E

F

G

H

T

U

V

W

CONFUCIANISM Daniel K. Gardner
THE CONQUISTADORS
Matthew Restall and
Felipe Fernández-Armesto
CONSCIENCE Paul Strohm
CONSCIOUSNESS Susan Blackmore
CONTEMPORARY ART
Julian Stallabrass
CONTEMPORARY FICTION
Robert Eaglestone
CONTINENTAL PHILOSOPHY
Simon Critchley
COPERNICUS Owen Gingerich
CORAL REEFS Charles Sheppard
CORPORATE SOCIAL
RESPONSIBILITY Jeremy Moon
CORRUPTION Leslie Holmes
COSMOLOGY Peter Coles
CRIME FICTION Richard Bradford
CRIMINAL JUSTICE Julian V. Roberts
CRITICAL THEORY
Stephen Eric Bronner
THE CRUSADES Christopher Tyerman
CRYPTOGRAPHY Fred Piper and
Sean Murphy
CRYSTALLOGRAPHY A. M. Glazer
THE CULTURAL REVOLUTION
Richard Curt Kraus
DADA AND SURREALISM
David Hopkins
DANTE Peter Hainsworth and
David Robey
DARWIN Jonathan Howard
THE DEAD SEA SCROLLS
Timothy H. Lim
DECOLONIZATION Dane Kennedy
DEMOCRACY Bernard Crick
DEPRESSION Jan Scott and
Mary Jane Tacchi
DERRIDA Simon Glendinning
DESCARTES Tom Sorell
DESERTS Nick Middleton
DESIGN John Heskett
DEVELOPMENTAL BIOLOGY
Lewis Wolpert
THE DEVIL Darren Oldridge
DIASPORA Kevin Kenny
DICTIONARIES Lynda Mugglestone
DINOSAURS David Norman
DIPLOMACY Joseph M. Siracusa
DOCUMENTARY FILM
Patricia Aufderheide
DREAMING J. Allan Hobson
DRUGS Les Iversen
DRUIDS Barry Cunliffe
EARLY MUSIC Thomas Forrest Kelly
THE EARTH Martin Redfern
EARTH SYSTEM SCIENCE Tim Lenton
ECONOMICS Partha Dasgupta
EDUCATION Gary Thomas
EGYPTIAN MYTH Geraldine Pinch
EIGHTEENTH-CENTURY
BRITAIN Paul Langford
THE ELEMENTS Philip Ball
EMOTION Dylan Evans
EMPIRE Stephen Howe
ENGELS Terrell Carver
ENGINEERING David Blockley
THE ENGLISH LANGUAGE
Simon Horobin
ENGLISH LITERATURE Jonathan Bate
THE ENLIGHTENMENT
John Robertson
ENTREPRENEURSHIP Paul Westhead
and Mike Wright
ENVIRONMENTAL
ECONOMICS Stephen Smith
ENVIRONMENTAL LAW
Elizabeth Fisher
ENVIRONMENTAL
POLITICS Andrew Dobson
EPICUREANISM Catherine Wilson
EPIDEMIOLOGY Rodolfo Saracci
ETHICS Simon Blackburn
ETHNOMUSICOLOGY Timothy Rice
THE ETRUSCANS Christopher Smith
EUGENICS Philippa Levine
THE EUROPEAN UNION John Pinder
and Simon Usherwood
EUROPEAN UNION LAW
Anthony Arnull
EVOLUTION Brian and
Deborah Charlesworth
EXISTENTIALISM Thomas Flynn
EXPLORATION Stewart A. Weaver
THE EYE Michael Land
FAIRY TALE Marina Warner
FAMILY LAW Jonathan Herring
FASCISM Kevin Passmore
FASHION Rebecca Arnold

ARISTOCRACY William Doyle
ARISTOTLE Jonathan Barnes
ART HISTORY Dana Arnold
ART THEORY Cynthia Freeland
ASIAN AMERICAN HISTORY Madeline Y. Hsu
ASTROBIOLOGY David C. Catling
ASTROPHYSICS James Binney
ATHEISM Julian Baggini
THE ATMOSPHERE Paul I. Palmer
AUGUSTINE Henry Chadwick
AUSTRALIA Kenneth Morgan
AUTISM Uta Frith
THE AVANT GARDE David Cottington
THE AZTECS Davíd Carrasco
BABYLONIA Trevor Bryce
BACTERIA Sebastian G. B. Amyes
BANKING John Goddard and John O. S. Wilson
BARTHES Jonathan Culler
THE BEATS David Sterritt
BEAUTY Roger Scruton
BEHAVIOURAL ECONOMICS Michelle Baddeley
BESTSELLERS John Sutherland
THE BIBLE John Riches
BIBLICAL ARCHAEOLOGY Eric H. Cline
BIG DATA Dawn E. Holmes
BIOGRAPHY Hermione Lee
BLACK HOLES Katherine Blundell
BLOOD Chris Cooper
THE BLUES Elijah Wald
THE BODY Chris Shilling
THE BOOK OF MORMON Terryl Givens
BORDERS Alexander C. Diener and Joshua Hagen
THE BRAIN Michael O'Shea
BRANDING Robert Jones
THE BRICS Andrew F. Cooper
THE BRITISH CONSTITUTION Martin Loughlin
THE BRITISH EMPIRE Ashley Jackson
BRITISH POLITICS Anthony Wright
BUDDHA Michael Carrithers
BUDDHISM Damien Keown
BUDDHIST ETHICS Damien Keown
BYZANTIUM Peter Sarris
CALVINISM Jon Balserak
CANCER Nicholas James
CAPITALISM James Fulcher
CATHOLICISM Gerald O'Collins
CAUSATION Stephen Mumford and Rani Lill Anjum
THE CELL Terence Allen and Graham Cowling
THE CELTS Barry Cunliffe
CHAOS Leonard Smith
CHEMISTRY Peter Atkins
CHILD PSYCHOLOGY Usha Goswami
CHILDREN'S LITERATURE Kimberley Reynolds
CHINESE LITERATURE Sabina Knight
CHOICE THEORY Michael Allingham
CHRISTIAN ART Beth Williamson
CHRISTIAN ETHICS D. Stephen Long
CHRISTIANITY Linda Woodhead
CIRCADIAN RHYTHMS Russell Foster and Leon Kreitzman
CITIZENSHIP Richard Bellamy
CIVIL ENGINEERING David Muir Wood
CLASSICAL LITERATURE William Allan
CLASSICAL MYTHOLOGY Helen Morales
CLASSICS Mary Beard and John Henderson
CLAUSEWITZ Michael Howard
CLIMATE Mark Maslin
CLIMATE CHANGE Mark Maslin
CLINICAL PSYCHOLOGY Susan Llewelyn and Katie Aafjes-van Doorn
COGNITIVE NEUROSCIENCE Richard Passingham
THE COLD WAR Robert McMahon
COLONIAL AMERICA Alan Taylor
COLONIAL LATIN AMERICAN LITERATURE Rolena Adorno
COMBINATORICS Robin Wilson
COMEDY Matthew Bevis
COMMUNISM Leslie Holmes
COMPARATIVE LITERATURE Ben Hutchinson
COMPLEXITY John H. Holland
THE COMPUTER Darrel Ince
COMPUTER SCIENCE Subrata Dasgupta

Y

Z

Index

BESTSELLERS

A Very Short Introduction

John Sutherland

'I rejoice', said Doctor Johnson, 'to concur with the Common Reader.' For the last century, the tastes and preferences of the common reader have been reflected in the American and British bestseller lists, and this *Very Short Introduction* takes an engaging look through the lists to reveal what we have been reading - and why. John Sutherland shows that bestseller lists monitor one of the strongest pulses in modern literature and are therefore worthy of serious study. Along the way, he lifts the lid on the bestseller industry, examines what makes a book into a bestseller, and asks what separates bestsellers from canonical fiction.

> 'His amiable trawl through the history of popular books is frequently entertaining'
>
> Scott Pack, The Times

www.oup.com/vsi

ENGLISH LITERATURE

A Very Short Introduction

Jonathan Bate

Sweeping across two millennia and every literary genre, acclaimed scholar and biographer Jonathan Bate provides a dazzling introduction to English Literature. The focus is wide, shifting from the birth of the novel and the brilliance of English comedy to the deep Englishness of landscape poetry and the ethnic diversity of Britain's Nobel literature laureates. It goes on to provide a more in-depth analysis, with close readings from an extraordinary scene in King Lear to a war poem by Carol Ann Duffy, and a series of striking examples of how literary texts change as they are transmitted from writer to reader.

{No reviews}

French Literature

A Very Short Introduction

John D. Lyons

The heritage of literature in the French language is rich, varied, and extensive in time and space; appealing both to its immediate public, readers of French, and also to aglobal audience reached through translations and film adaptations. *French Literature: A Very Short Introduction* introduces this lively literary world by focusing on texts - epics, novels, plays, poems, and screenplays - that concern protagonists whose adventures and conflicts reveal shifts in literary and social practices. From the hero of the medieval *Song of Roland* to the Caribbean heroines of *Tituba, Black Witch of Salem* or the European expatriate in Japan in *Fear and Trembling*, these problematic protagonists allow us to understand what interests writers and readers across the wide world of French.

www.oup.com/vsi

ANALYTIC PHILOSOPHY Michael Beaney
ANARCHISM Alex Prichard
ANCIENT ASSYRIA Karen Radner
ANCIENT EGYPT Ian Shaw
ANCIENT EGYPTIAN ART AND ARCHITECTURE Christina Riggs
ANCIENT GREECE Paul Cartledge
ANCIENT GREEK AND ROMAN SCIENCE Liba Taub
THE ANCIENT NEAR EAST Amanda H. Podany
ANCIENT PHILOSOPHY Julia Annas
ANCIENT WARFARE Harry Sidebottom
ANGELS David Albert Jones
ANGLICANISM Mark Chapman
THE ANGLO-SAXON AGE John Blair
ANIMAL BEHAVIOUR Tristram D. Wyatt
THE ANIMAL KINGDOM Peter Holland
ANIMAL RIGHTS David DeGrazia
ANSELM Thomas Williams
THE ANTARCTIC Klaus Dodds
ANTHROPOCENE Erle C. Ellis
ANTISEMITISM Steven Beller
ANXIETY Daniel Freeman and Jason Freeman
THE APOCRYPHAL GOSPELS Paul Foster
APPLIED MATHEMATICS Alain Goriely
THOMAS AQUINAS Fergus Kerr
ARBITRATION Thomas Schultz and Thomas Grant
ARCHAEOLOGY Paul Bahn
ARCHITECTURE Andrew Ballantyne
THE ARCTIC Klaus Dodds and Jamie Woodward
HANNAH ARENDT Dana Villa
ARISTOCRACY William Doyle
ARISTOTLE Jonathan Barnes
ART HISTORY Dana Arnold
ART THEORY Cynthia Freeland
ARTIFICIAL INTELLIGENCE Margaret A. Boden
ASIAN AMERICAN HISTORY Madeline Y. Hsu
ASTROBIOLOGY David C. Catling
ASTROPHYSICS James Binney
ATHEISM Julian Baggini
THE ATMOSPHERE Paul I. Palmer
AUGUSTINE Henry Chadwick
JANE AUSTEN Tom Keymer
AUSTRALIA Kenneth Morgan
AUTISM Uta Frith
AUTOBIOGRAPHY Laura Marcus
THE AVANT GARDE David Cottington
THE AZTECS Davíd Carrasco
BABYLONIA Trevor Bryce
BACTERIA Sebastian G. B. Amyes
BANKING John Goddard and John O. S. Wilson
BARTHES Jonathan Culler
THE BEATS David Sterritt
BEAUTY Roger Scruton
LUDWIG VAN BEETHOVEN Mark Evan Bonds
BEHAVIOURAL ECONOMICS Michelle Baddeley
BESTSELLERS John Sutherland
THE BIBLE John Riches
BIBLICAL ARCHAEOLOGY Eric H. Cline
BIG DATA Dawn E. Holmes
BIOCHEMISTRY Mark Lorch
BIODIVERSITY CONSERVATION David Macdonald
BIOGEOGRAPHY Mark V. Lomolino
BIOGRAPHY Hermione Lee
BIOMETRICS Michael Fairhurst
ELIZABETH BISHOP Jonathan F. S. Post
BLACK HOLES Katherine Blundell
BLASPHEMY Yvonne Sherwood
BLOOD Chris Cooper
THE BLUES Elijah Wald
THE BODY Chris Shilling
THE BOHEMIANS David Weir
NIELS BOHR J. L. Heilbron
THE BOOK OF COMMON PRAYER Brian Cummings
THE BOOK OF MORMON Terryl Givens
BORDERS Alexander C. Diener and Joshua Hagen
THE BRAIN Michael O'Shea
BRANDING Robert Jones
THE BRICS Andrew F. Cooper

BRITISH CINEMA Charles Barr
THE BRITISH CONSTITUTION
Martin Loughlin
THE BRITISH EMPIRE Ashley Jackson
BRITISH POLITICS Tony Wright
BUDDHA Michael Carrithers
BUDDHISM Damien Keown
BUDDHIST ETHICS Damien Keown
BYZANTIUM Peter Sarris
CALVINISM Jon Balserak
ALBERT CAMUS Oliver Gloag
CANADA Donald Wright
CANCER Nicholas James
CAPITALISM James Fulcher
CATHOLICISM Gerald O'Collins
CAUSATION Stephen Mumford and
Rani Lill Anjum
THE CELL Terence Allen and
Graham Cowling
THE CELTS Barry Cunliffe
CHAOS Leonard Smith
GEOFFREY CHAUCER David Wallace
CHEMISTRY Peter Atkins
CHILD PSYCHOLOGY Usha Goswami
CHILDREN'S LITERATURE
Kimberley Reynolds
CHINESE LITERATURE Sabina Knight
CHOICE THEORY Michael Allingham
CHRISTIAN ART Beth Williamson
CHRISTIAN ETHICS D. Stephen Long
CHRISTIANITY Linda Woodhead
CIRCADIAN RHYTHMS
Russell Foster and Leon Kreitzman
CITIZENSHIP Richard Bellamy
CITY PLANNING Carl Abbott
CIVIL ENGINEERING
David Muir Wood
THE CIVIL RIGHTS MOVEMENT
Thomas C. Holt
CLASSICAL LITERATURE William Allan
CLASSICAL MYTHOLOGY
Helen Morales
CLASSICS Mary Beard and
John Henderson
CLAUSEWITZ Michael Howard
CLIMATE Mark Maslin
CLIMATE CHANGE Mark Maslin
CLINICAL PSYCHOLOGY
Susan Llewelyn and
Katie Aafjes-van Doorn
COGNITIVE BEHAVIOURAL
THERAPY Freda McManus
COGNITIVE NEUROSCIENCE
Richard Passingham
THE COLD WAR Robert J. McMahon
COLONIAL AMERICA Alan Taylor
COLONIAL LATIN AMERICAN
LITERATURE Rolena Adorno
COMBINATORICS Robin Wilson
COMEDY Matthew Bevis
COMMUNISM Leslie Holmes
COMPARATIVE LITERATURE
Ben Hutchinson
COMPETITION AND ANTITRUST
LAW Ariel Ezrachi
COMPLEXITY John H. Holland
THE COMPUTER Darrel Ince
COMPUTER SCIENCE
Subrata Dasgupta
CONCENTRATION CAMPS
Dan Stone
CONDENSED MATTER PHYSICS
Ross H. McKenzie
CONFUCIANISM Daniel K. Gardner
THE CONQUISTADORS
Matthew Restall and
Felipe Fernández-Armesto
CONSCIENCE Paul Strohm
CONSCIOUSNESS Susan Blackmore
CONTEMPORARY ART
Julian Stallabrass
CONTEMPORARY FICTION
Robert Eaglestone
CONTINENTAL PHILOSOPHY
Simon Critchley
COPERNICUS Owen Gingerich
CORAL REEFS Charles Sheppard
CORPORATE SOCIAL
RESPONSIBILITY
Jeremy Moon
CORRUPTION Leslie Holmes
COSMOLOGY Peter Coles
COUNTRY MUSIC Richard Carlin
CREATIVITY Vlad Glăveanu
CRIME FICTION Richard Bradford
CRIMINAL JUSTICE Julian V. Roberts
CRIMINOLOGY Tim Newburn
CRITICAL THEORY
Stephen Eric Bronner
THE CRUSADES Christopher Tyerman

CRYPTOGRAPHY
Fred Piper and Sean Murphy
CRYSTALLOGRAPHY A. M. Glazer
THE CULTURAL REVOLUTION
Richard Curt Kraus
DADA AND SURREALISM
David Hopkins
DANTE Peter Hainsworth and
David Robey
DARWIN Jonathan Howard
THE DEAD SEA SCROLLS
Timothy H. Lim
DECADENCE David Weir
DECOLONIZATION Dane Kennedy
DEMENTIA Kathleen Taylor
DEMOCRACY Naomi Zack
DEMOGRAPHY Sarah Harper
DEPRESSION Jan Scott and
Mary Jane Tacchi
DERRIDA Simon Glendinning
DESCARTES Tom Sorell
DESERTS Nick Middleton
DESIGN John Heskett
DEVELOPMENT Ian Goldin
DEVELOPMENTAL BIOLOGY
Lewis Wolpert
THE DEVIL Darren Oldridge
DIASPORA Kevin Kenny
CHARLES DICKENS Jenny Hartley
DICTIONARIES Lynda Mugglestone
DINOSAURS David Norman
DIPLOMATIC HISTORY
Joseph M. Siracusa
DOCUMENTARY FILM
Patricia Aufderheide
DREAMING J. Allan Hobson
DRUGS Les Iversen
DRUIDS Barry Cunliffe
DYNASTY Jeroen Duindam
DYSLEXIA Margaret J. Snowling
EARLY MUSIC Thomas Forrest Kelly
THE EARTH Martin Redfern
EARTH SYSTEM SCIENCE Tim Lenton
ECOLOGY Jaboury Ghazoul
ECONOMICS Partha Dasgupta
EDUCATION Gary Thomas
EGYPTIAN MYTH Geraldine Pinch
EIGHTEENTH-CENTURY BRITAIN
Paul Langford
THE ELEMENTS Philip Ball
EMOTION Dylan Evans
EMPIRE Stephen Howe
EMPLOYMENT LAW David Cabrelli
ENERGY SYSTEMS Nick Jenkins
ENGELS Terrell Carver
ENGINEERING David Blockley
THE ENGLISH LANGUAGE
Simon Horobin
ENGLISH LITERATURE Jonathan Bate
THE ENLIGHTENMENT
John Robertson
ENTREPRENEURSHIP Paul Westhead
and Mike Wright
ENVIRONMENTAL ECONOMICS
Stephen Smith
ENVIRONMENTAL ETHICS
Robin Attfield
ENVIRONMENTAL LAW
Elizabeth Fisher
ENVIRONMENTAL POLITICS
Andrew Dobson
ENZYMES Paul Engel
EPICUREANISM Catherine Wilson
EPIDEMIOLOGY Rodolfo Saracci
ETHICS Simon Blackburn
ETHNOMUSICOLOGY Timothy Rice
THE ETRUSCANS Christopher Smith
EUGENICS Philippa Levine
THE EUROPEAN UNION
Simon Usherwood and John Pinder
EUROPEAN UNION LAW
Anthony Arnull
EVANGELICALISM
John G. Stackhouse Jr.
EVIL Luke Russell
EVOLUTION Brian and
Deborah Charlesworth
EXISTENTIALISM Thomas Flynn
EXPLORATION Stewart A. Weaver
EXTINCTION Paul B. Wignall
THE EYE Michael Land
FAIRY TALE Marina Warner
FAMILY LAW Jonathan Herring
MICHAEL FARADAY
Frank A. J. L. James
FASCISM Kevin Passmore
FASHION Rebecca Arnold
FEDERALISM Mark J. Rozell and
Clyde Wilcox
FEMINISM Margaret Walters

FILM Michael Wood
FILM MUSIC Kathryn Kalinak
FILM NOIR James Naremore
FIRE Andrew C. Scott
THE FIRST WORLD WAR Michael Howard
FLUID MECHANICS Eric Lauga
FOLK MUSIC Mark Slobin
FOOD John Krebs
FORENSIC PSYCHOLOGY David Canter
FORENSIC SCIENCE Jim Fraser
FORESTS Jaboury Ghazoul
FOSSILS Keith Thomson
FOUCAULT Gary Gutting
THE FOUNDING FATHERS R. B. Bernstein
FRACTALS Kenneth Falconer
FREE SPEECH Nigel Warburton
FREE WILL Thomas Pink
FREEMASONRY Andreas Önnerfors
FRENCH LITERATURE John D. Lyons
FRENCH PHILOSOPHY Stephen Gaukroger and Knox Peden
THE FRENCH REVOLUTION William Doyle
FREUD Anthony Storr
FUNDAMENTALISM Malise Ruthven
FUNGI Nicholas P. Money
THE FUTURE Jennifer M. Gidley
GALAXIES John Gribbin
GALILEO Stillman Drake
GAME THEORY Ken Binmore
GANDHI Bhikhu Parekh
GARDEN HISTORY Gordon Campbell
GENES Jonathan Slack
GENIUS Andrew Robinson
GENOMICS John Archibald
GEOGRAPHY John Matthews and David Herbert
GEOLOGY Jan Zalasiewicz
GEOMETRY Maciej Dunajski
GEOPHYSICS William Lowrie
GEOPOLITICS Klaus Dodds
GERMAN LITERATURE Nicholas Boyle
GERMAN PHILOSOPHY Andrew Bowie
THE GHETTO Bryan Cheyette
GLACIATION David J. A. Evans
GLOBAL CATASTROPHES Bill McGuire
GLOBAL ECONOMIC HISTORY Robert C. Allen
GLOBAL ISLAM Nile Green
GLOBALIZATION Manfred B. Steger
GOD John Bowker
GÖDEL'S THEOREM A. W. Moore
GOETHE Ritchie Robertson
THE GOTHIC Nick Groom
GOVERNANCE Mark Bevir
GRAVITY Timothy Clifton
THE GREAT DEPRESSION AND THE NEW DEAL Eric Rauchway
HABEAS CORPUS Amanda L. Tyler
HABERMAS James Gordon Finlayson
THE HABSBURG EMPIRE Martyn Rady
HAPPINESS Daniel M. Haybron
THE HARLEM RENAISSANCE Cheryl A. Wall
THE HEBREW BIBLE AS LITERATURE Tod Linafelt
HEGEL Peter Singer
HEIDEGGER Michael Inwood
THE HELLENISTIC AGE Peter Thonemann
HEREDITY John Waller
HERMENEUTICS Jens Zimmermann
HERODOTUS Jennifer T. Roberts
HIEROGLYPHS Penelope Wilson
HINDUISM Kim Knott
HISTORY John H. Arnold
THE HISTORY OF ASTRONOMY Michael Hoskin
THE HISTORY OF CHEMISTRY William H. Brock
THE HISTORY OF CHILDHOOD James Marten
THE HISTORY OF CINEMA Geoffrey Nowell-Smith
THE HISTORY OF COMPUTING Doron Swade
THE HISTORY OF EMOTIONS Thomas Dixon
THE HISTORY OF LIFE Michael Benton
THE HISTORY OF MATHEMATICS Jacqueline Stedall
THE HISTORY OF MEDICINE William Bynum

THE HISTORY OF PHYSICS J. L. Heilbron
THE HISTORY OF POLITICAL THOUGHT Richard Whatmore
THE HISTORY OF TIME Leofranc Holford-Strevens
HIV AND AIDS Alan Whiteside
HOBBES Richard Tuck
HOLLYWOOD Peter Decherney
THE HOLY ROMAN EMPIRE Joachim Whaley
HOME Michael Allen Fox
HOMER Barbara Graziosi
HORMONES Martin Luck
HORROR Darryl Jones
HUMAN ANATOMY Leslie Klenerman
HUMAN EVOLUTION Bernard Wood
HUMAN PHYSIOLOGY Jamie A. Davies
HUMAN RESOURCE MANAGEMENT Adrian Wilkinson
HUMAN RIGHTS Andrew Clapham
HUMANISM Stephen Law
HUME James A. Harris
HUMOUR Noël Carroll
IBN SĪNĀ (AVICENNA) Peter Adamson
THE ICE AGE Jamie Woodward
IDENTITY Florian Coulmas
IDEOLOGY Michael Freeden
IMAGINATION Jennifer Gosetti-Ferencei
THE IMMUNE SYSTEM Paul Klenerman
INDIAN CINEMA Ashish Rajadhyaksha
INDIAN PHILOSOPHY Sue Hamilton
THE INDUSTRIAL REVOLUTION Robert C. Allen
INFECTIOUS DISEASE Marta L. Wayne and Benjamin M. Bolker
INFINITY Ian Stewart
INFORMATION Luciano Floridi
INNOVATION Mark Dodgson and David Gann
INTELLECTUAL PROPERTY Siva Vaidhyanathan
INTELLIGENCE Ian J. Deary
INTERNATIONAL LAW Vaughan Lowe
INTERNATIONAL MIGRATION Khalid Koser
INTERNATIONAL RELATIONS Christian Reus-Smit
INTERNATIONAL SECURITY Christopher S. Browning
INSECTS Simon Leather
INVASIVE SPECIES Julie Lockwood and Dustin Welbourne
IRAN Ali M. Ansari
ISLAM Malise Ruthven
ISLAMIC HISTORY Adam Silverstein
ISLAMIC LAW Mashood A. Baderin
ISOTOPES Rob Ellam
ITALIAN LITERATURE Peter Hainsworth and David Robey
HENRY JAMES Susan L. Mizruchi
JAPANESE LITERATURE Alan Tansman
JESUS Richard Bauckham
JEWISH HISTORY David N. Myers
JEWISH LITERATURE Ilan Stavans
JOURNALISM Ian Hargreaves
JAMES JOYCE Colin MacCabe
JUDAISM Norman Solomon
JUNG Anthony Stevens
THE JURY Renée Lettow Lerner
KABBALAH Joseph Dan
KAFKA Ritchie Robertson
KANT Roger Scruton
KEYNES Robert Skidelsky
KIERKEGAARD Patrick Gardiner
KNOWLEDGE Jennifer Nagel
THE KORAN Michael Cook
KOREA Michael J. Seth
LAKES Warwick F. Vincent
LANDSCAPE ARCHITECTURE Ian H. Thompson
LANDSCAPES AND GEOMORPHOLOGY Andrew Goudie and Heather Viles
LANGUAGES Stephen R. Anderson
LATE ANTIQUITY Gillian Clark
LAW Raymond Wacks
THE LAWS OF THERMODYNAMICS Peter Atkins
LEADERSHIP Keith Grint
LEARNING Mark Haselgrove
LEIBNIZ Maria Rosa Antognazza
C. S. LEWIS James Como
LIBERALISM Michael Freeden

LIGHT Ian Walmsley
LINCOLN Allen C. Guelzo
LINGUISTICS Peter Matthews
LITERARY THEORY Jonathan Culler
LOCKE John Dunn
LOGIC Graham Priest
LOVE Ronald de Sousa
MARTIN LUTHER Scott H. Hendrix
MACHIAVELLI Quentin Skinner
MADNESS Andrew Scull
MAGIC Owen Davies
MAGNA CARTA Nicholas Vincent
MAGNETISM Stephen Blundell
MALTHUS Donald Winch
MAMMALS T. S. Kemp
MANAGEMENT John Hendry
NELSON MANDELA Elleke Boehmer
MAO Delia Davin
MARINE BIOLOGY Philip V. Mladenov
MARKETING
Kenneth Le Meunier-FitzHugh
THE MARQUIS DE SADE John Phillips
MARTYRDOM Jolyon Mitchell
MARX Peter Singer
MATERIALS Christopher Hall
MATHEMATICAL ANALYSIS
Richard Earl
MATHEMATICAL FINANCE
Mark H. A. Davis
MATHEMATICS Timothy Gowers
MATTER Geoff Cottrell
THE MAYA Matthew Restall and
Amara Solari
THE MEANING OF LIFE
Terry Eagleton
MEASUREMENT David Hand
MEDICAL ETHICS Michael Dunn and
Tony Hope
MEDICAL LAW Charles Foster
MEDIEVAL BRITAIN John Gillingham
and Ralph A. Griffiths
MEDIEVAL LITERATURE
Elaine Treharne
MEDIEVAL PHILOSOPHY
John Marenbon
MEMORY Jonathan K. Foster
METAPHYSICS Stephen Mumford
METHODISM William J. Abraham
THE MEXICAN REVOLUTION
Alan Knight
MICROBIOLOGY Nicholas P. Money
MICROBIOMES Angela E. Douglas
MICROECONOMICS Avinash Dixit
MICROSCOPY Terence Allen
THE MIDDLE AGES Miri Rubin
MILITARY JUSTICE Eugene R. Fidell
MILITARY STRATEGY
Antulio J. Echevarria II
JOHN STUART MILL Gregory Claeys
MINERALS David Vaughan
MIRACLES Yujin Nagasawa
MODERN ARCHITECTURE
Adam Sharr
MODERN ART David Cottington
MODERN BRAZIL Anthony W. Pereira
MODERN CHINA Rana Mitter
MODERN DRAMA
Kirsten E. Shepherd-Barr
MODERN FRANCE
Vanessa R. Schwartz
MODERN INDIA Craig Jeffrey
MODERN IRELAND Senia Pašeta
MODERN ITALY Anna Cento Bull
MODERN JAPAN
Christopher Goto-Jones
MODERN LATIN AMERICAN
LITERATURE
Roberto González Echevarría
MODERN WAR Richard English
MODERNISM Christopher Butler
MOLECULAR BIOLOGY
Aysha Divan and Janice A. Royds
MOLECULES Philip Ball
MONASTICISM Stephen J. Davis
THE MONGOLS Morris Rossabi
MONTAIGNE William M. Hamlin
MOONS David A. Rothery
MORMONISM
Richard Lyman Bushman
MOUNTAINS Martin F. Price
MUHAMMAD Jonathan A. C. Brown
MULTICULTURALISM Ali Rattansi
MULTILINGUALISM John C. Maher
MUSIC Nicholas Cook
MUSIC AND TECHNOLOGY
Mark Katz
MYTH Robert A. Segal
NANOTECHNOLOGY
Philip Moriarty
NAPOLEON David A. Bell

THE NAPOLEONIC WARS Mike Rapport
NATIONALISM Steven Grosby
NATIVE AMERICAN LITERATURE Sean Teuton
NAVIGATION Jim Bennett
NAZI GERMANY Jane Caplan
NEGOTIATION Carrie Menkel-Meadow
NEOLIBERALISM Manfred B. Steger and Ravi K. Roy
NETWORKS Guido Caldarelli and Michele Catanzaro
THE NEW TESTAMENT Luke Timothy Johnson
THE NEW TESTAMENT AS LITERATURE Kyle Keefer
NEWTON Robert Iliffe
NIETZSCHE Michael Tanner
NINETEENTH-CENTURY BRITAIN Christopher Harvie and H. C. G. Matthew
THE NORMAN CONQUEST George Garnett
NORTH AMERICAN INDIANS Theda Perdue and Michael D. Green
NORTHERN IRELAND Marc Mulholland
NOTHING Frank Close
NUCLEAR PHYSICS Frank Close
NUCLEAR POWER Maxwell Irvine
NUCLEAR WEAPONS Joseph M. Siracusa
NUMBER THEORY Robin Wilson
NUMBERS Peter M. Higgins
NUTRITION David A. Bender
OBJECTIVITY Stephen Gaukroger
OBSERVATIONAL ASTRONOMY Geoff Cottrell
OCEANS Dorrik Stow
THE OLD TESTAMENT Michael D. Coogan
THE ORCHESTRA D. Kern Holoman
ORGANIC CHEMISTRY Graham Patrick
ORGANIZATIONS Mary Jo Hatch
ORGANIZED CRIME Georgios A. Antonopoulos and Georgios Papanicolaou
ORTHODOX CHRISTIANITY A. Edward Siecienski
OVID Llewelyn Morgan
PAGANISM Owen Davies
PAKISTAN Pippa Virdee
THE PALESTINIAN-ISRAELI CONFLICT Martin Bunton
PANDEMICS Christian W. McMillen
PARTICLE PHYSICS Frank Close
PAUL E. P. Sanders
IVAN PAVLOV Daniel P. Todes
PEACE Oliver P. Richmond
PENTECOSTALISM William K. Kay
PERCEPTION Brian Rogers
THE PERIODIC TABLE Eric R. Scerri
PHILOSOPHICAL METHOD Timothy Williamson
PHILOSOPHY Edward Craig
PHILOSOPHY IN THE ISLAMIC WORLD Peter Adamson
PHILOSOPHY OF BIOLOGY Samir Okasha
PHILOSOPHY OF LAW Raymond Wacks
PHILOSOPHY OF MIND Barbara Gail Montero
PHILOSOPHY OF PHYSICS David Wallace
PHILOSOPHY OF SCIENCE Samir Okasha
PHILOSOPHY OF RELIGION Tim Bayne
PHOTOGRAPHY Steve Edwards
PHYSICAL CHEMISTRY Peter Atkins
PHYSICS Sidney Perkowitz
PILGRIMAGE Ian Reader
PLAGUE Paul Slack
PLANETARY SYSTEMS Raymond T. Pierrehumbert
PLANETS David A. Rothery
PLANTS Timothy Walker
PLATE TECTONICS Peter Molnar
PLATO Julia Annas
POETRY Bernard O'Donoghue
POLITICAL PHILOSOPHY David Miller
POLITICS Kenneth Minogue
POLYGAMY Sarah M. S. Pearsall
POPULISM Cas Mudde and Cristóbal Rovira Kaltwasser

POSTCOLONIALISM Robert J. C. Young
POSTMODERNISM Christopher Butler
POSTSTRUCTURALISM Catherine Belsey
POVERTY Philip N. Jefferson
PREHISTORY Chris Gosden
PRESOCRATIC PHILOSOPHY Catherine Osborne
PRIVACY Raymond Wacks
PROBABILITY John Haigh
PROGRESSIVISM Walter Nugent
PROHIBITION W. J. Rorabaugh
PROJECTS Andrew Davies
PROTESTANTISM Mark A. Noll
PSEUDOSCIENCE Michael D. Gordin
PSYCHIATRY Tom Burns
PSYCHOANALYSIS Daniel Pick
PSYCHOLOGY Gillian Butler and Freda McManus
PSYCHOLOGY OF MUSIC Elizabeth Hellmuth Margulis
PSYCHOPATHY Essi Viding
PSYCHOTHERAPY Tom Burns and Eva Burns-Lundgren
PUBLIC ADMINISTRATION Stella Z. Theodoulou and Ravi K. Roy
PUBLIC HEALTH Virginia Berridge
PURITANISM Francis J. Bremer
THE QUAKERS Pink Dandelion
QUANTUM THEORY John Polkinghorne
RACISM Ali Rattansi
RADIOACTIVITY Claudio Tuniz
RASTAFARI Ennis B. Edmonds
READING Belinda Jack
THE REAGAN REVOLUTION Gil Troy
REALITY Jan Westerhoff
RECONSTRUCTION Allen C. Guelzo
THE REFORMATION Peter Marshall
REFUGEES Gil Loescher
RELATIVITY Russell Stannard
RELIGION Thomas A. Tweed
RELIGION IN AMERICA Timothy Beal
THE RENAISSANCE Jerry Brotton
RENAISSANCE ART Geraldine A. Johnson
RENEWABLE ENERGY Nick Jelley
REPTILES T. S. Kemp
REVOLUTIONS Jack A. Goldstone
RHETORIC Richard Toye
RISK Baruch Fischhoff and John Kadvany
RITUAL Barry Stephenson
RIVERS Nick Middleton
ROBOTICS Alan Winfield
ROCKS Jan Zalasiewicz
ROMAN BRITAIN Peter Salway
THE ROMAN EMPIRE Christopher Kelly
THE ROMAN REPUBLIC David M. Gwynn
ROMANTICISM Michael Ferber
ROUSSEAU Robert Wokler
RUSSELL A. C. Grayling
THE RUSSIAN ECONOMY Richard Connolly
RUSSIAN HISTORY Geoffrey Hosking
RUSSIAN LITERATURE Catriona Kelly
THE RUSSIAN REVOLUTION S. A. Smith
SAINTS Simon Yarrow
SAMURAI Michael Wert
SAVANNAS Peter A. Furley
SCEPTICISM Duncan Pritchard
SCHIZOPHRENIA Chris Frith and Eve Johnstone
SCHOPENHAUER Christopher Janaway
SCIENCE AND RELIGION Thomas Dixon and Adam R. Shapiro
SCIENCE FICTION David Seed
THE SCIENTIFIC REVOLUTION Lawrence M. Principe
SCOTLAND Rab Houston
SECULARISM Andrew Copson
SEXUAL SELECTION Marlene Zuk and Leigh W. Simmons
SEXUALITY Véronique Mottier
WILLIAM SHAKESPEARE Stanley Wells
SHAKESPEARE'S COMEDIES Bart van Es
SHAKESPEARE'S SONNETS AND POEMS Jonathan F. S. Post
SHAKESPEARE'S TRAGEDIES Stanley Wells
GEORGE BERNARD SHAW Christopher Wixson
MARY SHELLEY Charlotte Gordon
THE SHORT STORY Andrew Kahn

SIKHISM Eleanor Nesbitt
SILENT FILM Donna Kornhaber
THE SILK ROAD James A. Millward
SLANG Jonathon Green
SLEEP Steven W. Lockley and Russell G. Foster
SMELL Matthew Cobb
ADAM SMITH Christopher J. Berry
SOCIAL AND CULTURAL ANTHROPOLOGY John Monaghan and Peter Just
SOCIAL PSYCHOLOGY Richard J. Crisp
SOCIAL WORK Sally Holland and Jonathan Scourfield
SOCIALISM Michael Newman
SOCIOLINGUISTICS John Edwards
SOCIOLOGY Steve Bruce
SOCRATES C. C. W. Taylor
SOFT MATTER Tom McLeish
SOUND Mike Goldsmith
SOUTHEAST ASIA James R. Rush
THE SOVIET UNION Stephen Lovell
THE SPANISH CIVIL WAR Helen Graham
SPANISH LITERATURE Jo Labanyi
THE SPARTANS Andrew J. Bayliss
SPINOZA Roger Scruton
SPIRITUALITY Philip Sheldrake
SPORT Mike Cronin
STARS Andrew King
STATISTICS David J. Hand
STEM CELLS Jonathan Slack
STOICISM Brad Inwood
STRUCTURAL ENGINEERING David Blockley
STUART BRITAIN John Morrill
SUBURBS Carl Abbott
THE SUN Philip Judge
SUPERCONDUCTIVITY Stephen Blundell
SUPERSTITION Stuart Vyse
SYMMETRY Ian Stewart
SYNAESTHESIA Julia Simner
SYNTHETIC BIOLOGY Jamie A. Davies
SYSTEMS BIOLOGY Eberhard O. Voit
TAXATION Stephen Smith
TEETH Peter S. Ungar
TERRORISM Charles Townshend
THEATRE Marvin Carlson
THEOLOGY David F. Ford
THINKING AND REASONING Jonathan St B. T. Evans
THOUGHT Tim Bayne
TIBETAN BUDDHISM Matthew T. Kapstein
TIDES David George Bowers and Emyr Martyn Roberts
TIME Jenann Ismael
TOCQUEVILLE Harvey C. Mansfield
LEO TOLSTOY Liza Knapp
TOPOLOGY Richard Earl
TRAGEDY Adrian Poole
TRANSLATION Matthew Reynolds
THE TREATY OF VERSAILLES Michael S. Neiberg
TRIGONOMETRY Glen Van Brummelen
THE TROJAN WAR Eric H. Cline
TRUST Katherine Hawley
THE TUDORS John Guy
TWENTIETH-CENTURY BRITAIN Kenneth O. Morgan
TYPOGRAPHY Paul Luna
THE UNITED NATIONS Jussi M. Hanhimäki
UNIVERSITIES AND COLLEGES David Palfreyman and Paul Temple
THE U.S. CIVIL WAR Louis P. Masur
THE U.S. CONGRESS Donald A. Ritchie
THE U.S. CONSTITUTION David J. Bodenhamer
THE U.S. SUPREME COURT Linda Greenhouse
UTILITARIANISM Katarzyna de Lazari-Radek and Peter Singer
UTOPIANISM Lyman Tower Sargent
VATICAN II Shaun Blanchard and Stephen Bullivant
VETERINARY SCIENCE James Yeates
THE VICTORIANS Martin Hewitt
THE VIKINGS Julian D. Richards
VIOLENCE Philip Dwyer
THE VIRGIN MARY Mary Joan Winn Leith
THE VIRTUES Craig A. Boyd and Kevin Timpe
VIRUSES Dorothy H. Crawford
VOLCANOES Michael J. Branney and Jan Zalasiewicz

Jennifer Gosetti-Ferencei

IMAGINATION

A Very Short Introduction

OXFORD
UNIVERSITY PRESS

OXFORD
UNIVERSITY PRESS

Great Clarendon Street, Oxford, OX2 6DP,
United Kingdom

Oxford University Press is a department of the University of Oxford.
It furthers the University's objective of excellence in research, scholarship,
and education by publishing worldwide. Oxford is a registered trade mark of
Oxford University Press in the UK and in certain other countries

Published in the United States of America by Oxford University Press
198 Madison Avenue, New York, NY 10016, United States of America

British Library Cataloguing in Publication Data
Data available

Library of Congress Control Number: 2023936565

ISBN 978-0-19-883002-3

Printed and bound by
CPI Group (UK) Ltd, Croydon, CR0 4YY

FSC
www.fsc.org
MIX
Paper | Supporting
responsible forestry
FSC® C013604

For Steve Magill

Contents

List of illustrations

Chapter 1
What is imagination?

The ability for human beings to imagine is virtually unlimited, for through imagining we can mentally engage ideas unconstrained by reality. Imagination's exercise allows for an escape from, without ever leaving, our ordinary life. Yet imagination also endows our lives with possibility. While we cannot intervene in reality simply by imagining it otherwise, we can regard it in a new light. Endowed by imagination, we can press beyond existing constraints and realize the transformation of a given state of things. This book is dedicated to exploring imagination and its importance in human thought and experience. It draws from philosophy, the human sciences, and literary theory. It attends to examples of imagination across ancient and modern human cultures—from art, science, literature, music, and everyday life—in order to demonstrate the reach and depth of its contributions.

This first chapter will be devoted to defining imagination, accounting for the variety of imaginative experience and the ways imagination tends to elude understanding. In the second chapter we will consider the evolution of imagination and its contribution to the emergence of human culture. In Chapters 3, 4, and 5, we will examine philosophies of imagination from the ancients to the 20th century in order to grasp imagination's roles in human thinking. These include imagination's deviation from as well as participation in knowledge, its association with madness, its role in poetry and art and in thinking possibilities, its ties to emotions, its role in perception, its relation to beauty, the sublime, and tragedy, to our sense of the transcendent and human freedom, and its ways of augmenting our sense of reality. As the expressive manifestation of imaginative thinking and being, creativity is an important theme throughout this book, but the final chapter takes a closer look at creativity and its support for human flourishing.

The value and variety of imaginative experience

Imagination is wide-ranging, and distinguishes human life in countless ways. In order to understand imagination, we must first recognize just how varied are its contributions to our experience. Imagination is the medium of children's pretend play and an audience's absorption in a drama. Imagination consoles mourners with visions beyond earthly life. Artists depict life from novel perspectives, crafting imagined worlds for readers to virtually inhabit. Imagination is responsible for innovation. The invention of the kite in ancient China, the design of the Egyptian pyramids, the moon landing, and advancement in medical technology are all indebted to human imagining among other cognitive skills.

Imagination is, of course, also the medium of fantasies and daydreams. Children may dream of being able to fly, or of having superhero strength, and they interweave their fantasies into play. Adults too entertain unlikely scenarios—becoming a champion boxer or figure skater, winning the lottery—or impossible ones—evading mortality. To imagination, it matters not how vanishing or nil these prospects may be in real life. Imagination can stake claims well beyond the probable or even possible.

Apart from fantasy, our grasp of reality itself owes much to imagination. We can start with our grasp of the past. An understanding of history might be dry and far less vivid, even incomplete, if we had no means to place knowledge into some experiential context. In accordance with known facts, yet going beyond the strictly known, we can imagine what it might have been like to live as a soldier in ancient Sparta, or as a scribe in medieval Italy, or to have been present at the signing of the Declaration of Independence. Culture is in many senses an inheritance of imagination.

Even literary narratives may bring historical events and places to life by imagining fictional characters in the midst of them. While we would not look to Leo Tolstoy's novel *War and Peace* (1869) for historical evidence about 19th-century Russia, the novel can help us to imagine its culture under the impact of the Napoleonic wars. In her novel *Jazz* (1992) the American Nobel laureate Toni Morrison, combining historical research with the force of her imagination, brought the Harlem Renaissance and the American South of the turn of the 20th century to life for those born long after.

With the help of imaginative works, we can also think across different perspectives within our own time. Putting ourselves 'in another person's shoes', we take up an imagined point of view. Through imagination, we can try to come to a better understanding of those different from ourselves. When we fail in such imagining, differences may seem more insurmountable than they are. Imagination thus plays an important role in ethical and political life.

Imagination also plays with time. We do not simply remember the past but may see it in a new light. Mistakes made can be imagined undone, in the mind. While this may feed regret, such reflection can also help us to learn from past error. Through imagining alternatives to it, we can reflect on the present. We can envision other possible ways to live in the here and now, and project future goals for which to aim.

Given such tremendous flexibility, imagination has been revered for its expansion of human life and its contributions to human achievement. Yet imagination has also been blamed for disturbances in our sense of reality. Distracted by inflated imagining, we can submit to false hopes. Imagination may inflame emotions, sustain outsized anxieties and fears. Imagination is the currency of conspiracy theories and when combined with cultural anxieties it can feed prejudice. While imagination is widely celebrated in popular culture today, it was castigated throughout history for confounding fantasy and perception, illusion and reality.

The attack on imagination goes all the way back to Plato. Despite being an exceptionally imaginative philosopher himself, in his *Republic* (*c.*375 BCE), Plato maligned imagination as the medium of error and confusion. In the 17th century the French mathematician and philosopher Blaise Pascal declared imagination the very 'enemy of reason'. In his *Pensées* (1660), Pascal described imagination as 'that deceitful part in man [*sic*], that mistress of error and falsity, the more deceptive that she [*sic*] is not always so'. Being 'generally false', Pascal thought, imagination 'cannot set a true value on things'. In his novel *Rasselas* (1759), the British writer Samuel Johnson deemed imagination depraved, seducing the mind to feast on 'luscious falsehood' whenever 'offended with the bitterness of truth'. Imaginative indulgence is there illustrated by the character of a mad astronomer who believes himself in 'imaginary dominion' over the weather, dispensing sunshine and rain around the globe at will. In recent decades, psychologists have investigated imagination's potential to distort memories, or, controversially, to mix the feeling of remembrance with ideas imagined rather than recalled.

As imagination's product, literature and art have been criticized for tarrying with illusion or cultivating irrational passions. Plato worried that the arts, in particular dramatic and epic poetry, would miseducate citizens, disrupting social order. Johnson warned that the luxuries of fiction would turn the mind to reject the 'insipidity of truth'. The Spanish writer Miguel de Cervantes rendered the protagonist of *Don Quixote* (1605) a ridiculous figure by way of the overinfluence of imaginative literature. The self-proclaimed knight, having read too many chivalrous tales, casts his fantastical eye everywhere and sees the world as he imagines it. Quixote fights windmills he imagines are really giants disguised as windmills. The irony of Cervantes' treatment is of course that his own reader too is indulging in an imagined world.

Against the tide of criticism, other philosophers recognized imagination as an enhancement of the human mind. Departing from his teacher Plato, Aristotle argued that all thinking requires imagination. The mind never thinks without an image, he claimed; images—one of the main currencies of imagination—are the very stuff of thought. In his treatment of dramatic poetry, Aristotle praised the capacity to think possibilities, enabling understanding not only of what has happened, but of what *could* happen. This appreciation will be echoed in the 18th century with the German philosopher Immanuel Kant and the rise of aesthetics. The idea of the productive imagination to which the thinking of possibility is attributed will be rapturously elaborated by Romantic writers.

Since the 19th century, as scientific thinking came to be regarded a culture apart from or even opposed to the humanities and arts, literary writers have been imagination's staunch defenders. The American poet Wallace Stevens hailed imagination as the power of the mind to grasp the possibilities of things. Imagination, he wrote in *The Necessary Angel: Essays on Reality and Imagination*, relieves the 'pressure of reality' by creating other perspectives for our minds to consider. The Irish Nobel laureate Seamus Heaney described in 'The Redress of Poetry' how imagination enables us to respond variably to misfortune, allowing us to recognize the nature of our predicament and consider possible redress—'tilting the scales of reality towards some transcendent equilibrium'.

Because of this, Heaney claims, imagination 'has a liberating and verifying effect upon the individual spirit'.

It may be perplexing to think that the very same capacity that allows us to evade the pressure of reality, or can confuse us about it, may be required to understand it. Scientific discovery, however, owes much to imagination. Famously praising imagination as 'more important' than knowledge, Albert Einstein detailed his own use of imagination in achieving discoveries in physics that revolutionized our understanding of space and time. Einstein described processes of inner visualization through which he conjured hypothetical scenarios against which to test existing knowledge. Einstein described inspiration while playing the violin, such that ideas arose as images in his mind before being expressed in language and scientific concepts.

Einstein's own imagination may be considered a special case of genius. Yet he himself thought that imagination was required for all scientific progress. He wrote in *The Evolution of Physics* (1938) that: 'To raise new questions, new possibilities, to regard old problems from a new angle, requires creative imagination and marks real advance in science.' Other scientists have echoed Einstein's appraisal of imagination. Nobel laureates for physiology or medicine François Jacob (1965) and Eric R. Kandel (2000) have written eloquently about the close analogy between scientific enquiry and artistic creation, while Elizabeth Blackburn (2009) described as beautiful 'the very process of scientific inquiry by which human creativity and ingenuity unveil a pattern within what had looked like chaos and incomprehensibility'. Whether or not imagination is more important than knowledge, scientists have argued that existing knowledge cannot evolve without it.

We have so far described how imagination allows us to escape reality, distorts our sense of it, allows us to take a new perspective on it, and even to understand it. From play and dreams to art and science, imagining is central to many human experiences and accomplishments. Does imagination work differently across these different kinds of experiences? Are we really speaking of one and the same facility, or are these experiences manifesting a variety of mental capacities? In the rest of this chapter we will address some challenges in defining imagination and identify its multiple modes.

The elusiveness of imagination

Imagination, which has so deeply influenced human history, has not been well understood for much of it. Even philosophers who assigned imagination a significant role in their theories of the mind admitted that understanding imagination is a daunting challenge. The British philosopher David Hume described imagination eluding philosophy's grasp, as a 'kind of magical faculty' which is 'inexplicable by the utmost efforts of human understanding'. Kant called imagination 'a hidden art in the depths of the human soul, whose true operations we can divine from nature and lay unveiled before our eyes only with difficulty'. Yet we can get closer to defining imagination by identifying those very characteristics which render it so elusive.

The first such characteristic is the *heterogeneity* of the concept. By 'imagining' we may mean conjuring something like a visual image in our minds, as we may do in fantasizing or daydreaming. Inner images comprise much of what we often refer to as the content of imagining. Or we may mean considering other possibilities than the current situation, without any inner imaging at all. We have mentioned forms of creativity and invention, pretending and play, all of which engage imagination. Some of these are experiential in nature, involving something akin to inner perception, while others are conceptual in nature. Some of these take place wholly in the individual mind, while others arise through social or material interaction.

Imagination is most typically identified in the history of philosophy as inner representation of what is not present to perception. Imagining in this sense draws up a mental image or other schematic representation on the basis of previous experience. The French philosopher René Descartes, for example, treated the imagination as a kind of mental envisioning. He illustrated this faculty by pointing out that while he could imagine or inwardly 'picture' a triangle with its three sides, he could only conceptualize, but not imagine, a thousand-sided figure. This mode of imagining has been said to take place in 'the mind's eye' and involves a quasi-visual experience. Apart from sight, inner presentations of imagination could invoke other senses, such as the sound of a whistle, or the taste of a lemon, or the feel of silk.

Other philosophers have regarded imagination not principally as inner envisioning but as a form of pretence. Pretence can be taken to encompass the ability to entertain counterfactual scenarios, such as my imagining that I am a farmer in ancient Mesopotamia, rather than at my desk typing these words as I am doing here and now. Or one may take something present as a stand-in for something not present, as children at play could pretend that the log is a pirate ship and a meadow the surrounding sea. Pretence could involve the experiential component of inward visualization or other imaging of the same, but it could also be conceived as strictly conceptual.

A strictly conceptual or 'propositional' view of imagination as pretence was defended by the British philosopher Gilbert Ryle in his influential work *The Concept of Mind* (1949). In Ryle's oft-cited example, I can imagine a nursery from my childhood. For Ryle such imagining means that I only need pretend, or imagine *that*, I am seeing the room. No inner visual experience, nothing like an inner image of this room, need be present in my mind. Since inner images are unnecessary for imagining to occur, Ryle argued, they are not an essential part of imagination.

This view, however, has been countered by examples of imagining for which visualization is essential. Without any fruits at hand, comparing the yellow of a banana to that of a lemon, for example, will require something like an inner envisioning of it. Moreover, in imagining a childhood room, both pretence and an attending quasi-visualization may be involved: while I 'pretend' that I see a room of my childhood home, I may also experience something like a visual image of such a room, which for many imaginers would be felt to fulfil the experience of truly imagining it. The debate between proponents of propositional imagination and those of experiential imagination reflects different models of the mind, and may reflect, as William James pointed out in *Principles of Psychology* over a century ago, variation in imaginers' capacities for inner visualization. We can get around this impasse if we understand imagination not as a single faculty but as heterogeneous, admitting multiple modes. Before addressing these, we can consider further difficulties imagination poses to any reductive explication.

A characteristic of imagination is its *variability in relation to our will*. We can sometimes deliberately imagine as we wish to. We can gaze at the clouds and identify the shapes they might make. We can, writing a short story, compose what will happen next. We can come up with a joke to introduce a speech. Alternatively, our will to imagine can fail. We can try to conjure an image of something without succeeding, or try to come up with a new idea, but fall short.

Yet we can also imagine more passively. Dreaming involves imagination wholly passive to the will. In daydreaming, imagined ideas may simply appear in the flow of our awareness, as if of their own accord, untethered to our current reality. Without effort or direction, the clouds may suddenly appear to us in the shape of a face, or an animal. The boundary between deliberate imagining and its unwilled flow in fantasizing may be blurred in creativity, where a receptive flow of ideas can be channelled towards elaboration. In such experience it may be difficult to discern any clear boundary between our willed exertion of imagination and passive imagining.

A third feature of imagination that renders it elusive to observation is its *introspective nature*. While imagination may be outwardly expressed, the process of imagining itself cannot be directly observed by others. What I am imagining may be wholly invisible and inaccessible to you, and vice versa. While we can scan the brain of an imagining subject to observe an imaginer's areas of neuronal activity, imagining occurs from the first-person perspective, and cannot be fully understood in isolation from this.

For this reason, phenomenology is often enlisted in efforts to understand imagination. Phenomenology is the study, from a first-person perspective, of what appears to consciousness and the structure this takes. While a formal philosophical method invented at the turn of the 20th century by the philosopher Edmund Husserl, phenomenology can be engaged informally whenever we reflect on and describe our first-person lived experience. French phenomenological philosophers such as Jean-Paul Sartre, Maurice Merleau-Ponty, and Paul Ricoeur dedicated phenomenological studies to imagination and its processes, as we will see in Chapter 5.

A fourth and final difficulty that needs to be mentioned is *the term 'imagination' itself*. Its multiplicity also helps to explain some of the complexity of the conceptual history of imagination—the way over time imagination as a concept has been defined and examined. While the reader of this book can make do without keeping in mind the following distinctions, familiarity with the etymological multiplicity of the term may help to avoid potential confusions as we go along. The word *imagination*, along with *image*, *imaginary*, *imaginative*, and so on, is derived from Latin. In Latin *imago* means 'image' and *imaginari* means 'to picture to oneself'. Yet we also use the term *fantasy*, along with *fantastical*, *fancy*, and so on, derived from Greek. *Phantasia* in ancient Greek means the perception of appearances or bringing an object to mind in its absence to perception. While in English *imagination* and *fantasy* are often used interchangeably, they are occasionally distinguished. *Fantasy* or *fancy* is sometimes used, as for instance by Shakespeare, when the illusory quality of ideas is emphasized. Yet other writers, such as Samuel Johnson, do not distinguish always between imagination and fancy, regarding imagination itself in light of the vulnerabilities of illusory thinking.

German-language philosophers use several terms which we translate as 'imagination'. In addition to the borrowed *die Imagination* or *die Phantasie*, we find *Einbildungskraft*, which for Kant involves making an image (*Bild*) from diverse sense-impressions. Also translated into 'imagination' is *Vorstellungskraft*, the power to represent, used both by Kant and by the Austrian philosopher Ludwig Wittgenstein. Prominent in Husserl's discussions is also the term *Vergegenwärtigung*, presentifying or making-present to consciousness, a task ascribed to imagination.

Reproductive and productive imagination

We have so far identified imagination as an activity of consciousness, whether wilfully directed or passively experienced, that presents images or ideas of what is not immediately given in perception, and may potentially transform them. Such presentation and transformation may happen in the mind alone, or also through material or linguistic creativity. Imagination thus defined admits of multiple modes. Before identifying these, we must make a further distinction.

Crucial to understanding the scope of imagination's involvement in human cognition is the distinction between reproductive and productive imagination. With reproductive imagination, we call up or conjure in the mind images or ideas we already know from past perceptions or experiences. Aristotle thus classed imagination of this kind as a form of memory. Yet what we so imagine is not strictly speaking only a reproduction of memory. If we remember a particular car we once drove or an elephant with which we spent time at a sanctuary, for example, the memory will be specific to what was once perceived. Yet we can also imagine a car or an elephant without it representing any specific vehicle or animal. In this case we may draw from various memories while generating a schema that abstracts from any particular experience.

Reproductive imaginings can be altered or combined to make a new image. We can imagine a car and an elephant. We can imagine an elephant inside a car. We can further imagine an elephant driving a car. Here the new idea clearly exceeds any original ingredients previous experience could have provided. This new idea may provoke still further elaborations, for example, in writing a children's book or drawing a political cartoon. Many accounts of imagination that describe such combination or synthesis regard imagination as an entirely reproductive function. Yet sometimes we are able to imagine in ways that produce new ideas, the meaning of which cannot be wholly accounted for by adding up old ones.

We can find an example in literature. Shakespeare relied on previous experience and knowledge when he wrote his play *Hamlet*, in which the protagonist considers how to react to his uncle's (purported) murder of his father, the king. The author would have had knowledge of princes, of political intrigue, of patricides and regicides, and even of a similar name, Hamnet, that of his own son. Shakespeare would have had some knowledge from life, history, or existing drama of human psychology. To claim, however, that the character Hamlet is only an amalgamation of previous ideas held by Shakespeare would not capture the novelty of his creation. The particular character of the inner life—or as Shakespeare puts it, 'that within'—constructed by

Hamlet's indecisive brooding is among the qualities newly introduced by Shakespeare's dramatic fiction.

Beyond such novelty, productive imagination may have a further, more fundamental role in thinking. Rather than only producing novel ideas, productive imagination may generate the very shape of experience. As we will see in more detail in Chapter 3, Kant thought that imagination was involved in generating the structure of human perception itself. Kant argued that, among other roles imagination performs, imagination in its productive use synthesizes sensation into a coherent image, so that we are able to perceive complex sensory objects that remain constant across successive moments of perception. Since imagination mediates between other faculties (for Kant these are sensibility and understanding), Kant called this activity of productive imagination 'transcendental'. More recently, cognitive theorists ascribe to imagination a similarly productive role in that it is said to constantly blend concepts to form new ones. In this role imagination is held to work in the background of our awareness such that it is inaccessible to observation.

A more accessible example of productive imagination offered by Kant can be found in the aesthetic experience of beauty. When we perceive a sunset or an orchid as beautiful, we do not merely register its empirical details, or regard it in conceptual terms. We do not see in the sunset only a scattering of light rays, or in the orchid just a part of a plant with a reproductive function. We also feel enlivened by the harmony or vitality of what is perceived, by its beauty or other striking aesthetic quality, which, according to Kant, provokes a free play of imagination with another faculty of the mind, the understanding. When something strikes us as beautiful, Kant suggests, we are perceiving it through the play of imagination.

This aesthetic effect is due not to the features of the object alone, but rather to the activities of the perceiving subject that these features stimulate. To put it another way, for Kant beauty is not so much in the eye as in the imagination of the beholder—or rather in imagination's play with the faculty of understanding. Sartre too recognized the beauty of a landscape as indebted to the consciousness which beholds it. For the mind configures relations among this and that element, holds the multiplicity in a harmonious or striking configuration. It is consciousness that lends qualities to regard the landscape as majestic or serene. In these ways we might say that imagination is productive, generating an interpretive perspective through which the world is revealed in a certain way.

So far, we have suggested that imagination is active in a wide range of human experiences. Imagination is an activity of consciousness that can be directed or passive, or some combination of these. It can engage ideas reproductively or also productively contribute to shaping experience. We can now consider some major modes of imagining.

Modes of imagining

The activity of imagining can be undertaken in several modes. These include inner imaging, including visual or other sense presentation in the mind; pretence, and closely related to that, hypothetical or counterfactual thinking; concrete imagining or 'seeing-as'; and creativity. Many philosophers have focused on one of these capacities alone as paradigmatic of imagining. While such approaches enable a more streamlined analysis, a multimodal view of imagination can register both its range and the depths of its involvement in human thinking.

Inner visualization and other inner imaging comprise the most frequently discussed mode of imaginative activity. It is the subject of Sartre's phenomenological analysis in *The Imaginary* (1940) and more recently of empirical study in psychology. Yet inner visualization is accessible to most people through reflection, as long as they have had the experience of closing their eyes and drawing to their 'mind's eye' something like a visual image.

For example, I can image a snowman, even if it is a hot summer day. Something that was not there already in my mind, and is not there to my immediate perception, is presented and appears in my thought. Such imagining enables us to think freely untethered to perception. Beyond presentation, imagination can also transform such an image. I can imagine the snowman on a beach, wiping its melting forehead with a handkerchief. Drawn schematically on the basis of memories, such inner phenomena have a visual quality even if they are not exactly pictures in the mind.

Inner imaging is not only visual in nature, however, but may involve any of the senses. I can similarly evoke sounds, smells, tastes, or tactile sensations. Beyond the five senses, I can evoke kinaesthetic feelings, or sensations of movement, such as falling, floating, or running fast. I can also imagine proprioceptive sensation: hunger, or pain, or being out of breath. While inner imaging is often described in visual terms, it can evoke multiple sensations of embodied experience.

Pretence is not limited to pretending, but can encompass entertainment of a counterfactual idea, hypothetical thinking, and taking one thing as a stand-in for another. As in Ryle's example of imagining that I see my childhood room, I can imagine that something is the case (when it is not). I can imagine that I am Napoleon Bonaparte, and wonder how I might feel in captivity on the island of Saint Helena. Counterfactual imagining can also be intertwined with hypothetical thinking (as in, if *this* is supposed, then *that* could follow). I can imagine that I have won the lottery, and consider various prospects as if I were in the position to distribute the winnings. Pretence also allows us to 'take *this* for *that*'—as in our earlier example, taking a log for a pirate ship. This same capacity allows us to become immersed in the fictional situations of theatre and drama, to take that particular actor for

Hamlet, and the theatre stage for the room of a medieval castle in Denmark. Taking one thing for another is the basis of metaphoric and symbolic thinking. Thus pretence has been described as the origin of the arts.

Concrete imagining, aspect perception, or 'seeing-as', all describe that mode of imagining which is dependent upon perception, yet generates meaning, resemblance, or value beyond what is directly given perceptually. Seeing faces in the clouds is an example of 'seeing-as', also called 'seeing an aspect' or aspect perception, explored by Wittgenstein, who recognized in such phenomena the involvement of imagination in perception. The related phenomenon of 'concrete' imaging was described by Sartre as seeing in perceived objects some symbolic value or quality. We have mentioned the beautiful landscape that may be seen as majestic or serene. Through imagination, Sartre says, we lend our emotion to perceptual phenomena and perceive more than what is empirically present. This augmentation in our perception of reality will be discussed in more detail in Chapters 2 and 5.

Inner imaging, pretence, and 'seeing-as' are all presentational activities of consciousness in which what is presented—an image or idea or a proposition or an evoked experience—is undetermined by present perception. These presentations are all malleable in ways our perception of reality is not, and thus they are all latently or actively transformative. Creativity involves any of these modes of imagination becoming expressive, playing and working with the media of language, images, sounds, bodily movement, or physical matter. We will devote the final chapter of this book to considering creativity in more detail, while many endeavours of human creativity will serve as examples throughout.

Imagination is wide-ranging in scope and significance for human life, playing a crucial role in consciousness and admitting multiple modes. Imagining allows us to step back from our immediate perceptions or thoughts and entertain and elaborate possibilities.

Visualizing or other inner imaging, pretending or entertaining other states of affairs, conceiving counterfactual or hypothetical possibilities, and seeing things in symbolical ways or as latent with meaning all allow us to take a stance towards the world, to develop a perspective on it, and potentially to transform it.

Imagining otherwise than what is merely given, we can respond to it more freely. Engaging imagination, we can creatively express new ideas and sometimes integrate them in reality. In the next chapter we will explore the emergence of imagination in human evolution and its role in the emergence of human culture.

Chapter 2
Imagination in human evolution

Imagination has nurtured human thinking for around 50,000 years and has distinguished our species as the most innovative on the planet. As our early human ancestors adapted to changing environments, established social groups, and developed more complex ways of ensuring their survival, they began to create decorative works and to represent their world in novel ways. Evidence of tool and body decorations, sculptures, cave paintings, burial rituals, and toys made by prehistoric humans suggests a gradually evolving capacity for imaginative thought and creativity. In order to grasp how imagination emerged, it is necessary to consider human consciousness itself not as separated from the surrounding world but as evolving in interaction with it.

Approaching imagination as an evolved dimension of human consciousness requires complementing philosophical understanding with insights from other disciplines. While the dominant model of the mind in modern philosophy essentially divided it from the body, phenomenology and contemporary philosophies of mind have acknowledged its embodied and enactive nature. This means that the capacity for us to think about the world emerges through our physical and psychological involvement with it, and that the world's meaning for us emerges through our interactive concerns. Along with philosophy, knowledge of prehistoric artefacts, of early human groups and their migrations, of the psychological development of modern human children, and of primate cognition have all been enlisted to help explain how imagination may have evolved in early human interaction with the world.

Evolving imagination

Imagination is a relatively recent development in evolution. From about 5 million years ago up to the emergence of the first member of our genus, our pre-human ancestors came to walk on two legs, make rudimentary hand tools from stone, and develop in brain size due to the increased consumption of protein. From the appearance of *Homo ergaster* 1.9 million years ago, early humans would have developed new cognitive capacities through further tool-making, migration, and planned hunting. From half a million years to 100,000 ago, *Homo neanderthalensis* in Europe and pre-human ancestors in Africa developed again dramatically in brain size and in technical and communication skills. Around 200,000 years ago modern *Homo sapiens* emerged in Africa and by 60,000 years ago had wandered into Eurasia. Around this time—around 50,000 years ago—new ways of thinking emerged among our early human ancestors.

While less developed than early *Homo sapiens*, their Neanderthal relatives left evidence of bodily decoration, ornament-making, burials of their dead, and, around 41,000 years ago, simple cave paintings with red dots, lines, and hand stencils on cave walls. Yet Neanderthals were to be surpassed, and by about 40,000 years ago, *Homo sapiens* remained the only human species left. They engaged in more complex social organization, travelled further in search of food, and made more advanced decorative works. Their representations of animals and other living beings gradually expanded to include expressive and symbolic depictions, giving rise to the capacity for myth and fictionalization.

It is widely argued that the capacity for imagination was enhanced with the migrations of early humans in search of food. As early humans took in the view of surrounding lands from a distance, perhaps climbing hills to get a view from above, they would have been able to consider the landscape from new and variable perspectives. This would have conferred tactical advantages, supporting the planning of hunts or mapping out new territory. The comparison of different perspectives may have also enabled the gradual emergence of representational skills and exercised cognition of possibilities.

Imaginative capacities would have also developed in correlation with specific practical skills. One example is the development of projectile tools, such as javelins, that require aiming a throw. Chimpanzees and other monkeys do throw objects in displays of aggression and some can anticipate the trajectory of objects that are thrown towards them. Yet aimed throwing at a moving target is a skill other species do not appear to be able to do with accuracy. The earliest known projectile tools early humans used for this purpose were made 280,000 years ago in Ethiopia. It has been argued that the mind's capacity for internal representation was gradually enabled by the repeated actions of aiming a spear or other projectile at moving prey.

On this theory, the process of aiming one object at another moving object may promote a special cognitive function. During the process of an aimed throw, neural feedback generates anticipatory calculations. This cognitive process is thought to have given rise to inner visual schemata, as the thrower simulates inwardly where the moving target may be next. Along with memory and other material interactions with their environment, this may have provided early humans with a cognitive basis for a mode of imagination, that of inner mental imaging or representation.

Moreover, the availability of such tools would have allowed early humans to be able to plan their activities. It would have been advantageous to be able to consider and even represent prospective strategies for hunting before taking risks to implement them, thus stimulating hypothetical thinking. Tools were also among the first objects of decoration. Both the comparative contemplation of possibilities and the decorative embellishment occasioned by tools would have supported the development of imaginative thought.

Early cave painters and carvers not only represented animals and other living beings they observed in the world around them. They also reconfigured their representations to transform their subject matter. The earliest known symbolic artefact and sculpture was made around 40,000 years ago, when a prehistoric carver made a half-human, half-lion figurine around 30 centimetres tall from a mammoth tusk. Found in the Hohlenstein-Stadel in Germany, the zoomorphic lion-man figure manifests the emergence of creative imagination, and perhaps the first evidence of fictional thought (Figure 1).

Perhaps the most widely recognized prehistoric artworks are the Palaeolithic cave paintings of Lascaux, France. Until their rediscovery in 1940 they had been sealed from view for around 17,000 years since they had been created. On the walls of the chambers were preserved thousands of paintings, drawings, and carvings. We can now view a splendorous array of bison, horses, deer, birds, mammoths, bears, wolves, felines, aurochs, and other animals, with the polychromatic paintings in red, yellow, ochre, violet, brown, and black mineral pigments.

What is now known as the Lascaux Shaft scene is particularly significant, despite the fact that its monochrome black oxide, painted over a natural protrusion in a wall, is at first glance less visually striking than the polychromatic works. Yet the scene presents the only rendering of a human figure in the cave complex, albeit one fantastically imagined. A man appears with the head of a bird—or in a bird mask—and only four fingers on each hand,

1. The Löwenmensch, or 'Lion-Man', an ivory sculpture between 35,000 and 41,000 years old, discovered in Hohlenstein-Stadel in 1939.

perhaps suggesting an animalistic being of mythic significance. The bird-man is lying prostrate and appears to be dying at the feet of a wounded bison (its entrails are hanging down) which has turned to gouge the hunter. Nearby is a goose or other bird at the end of a staff. A few feet away is the outline of what appears to be a woolly rhinoceros.

It has been suggested that this fantastical rendering of the bird-man figure could represent ancestors of the group to which the painter belonged; magic rituals around hunting; a burial marking for a slain hunter; or a spiritual vision. The work has also been interpreted as shamanic cosmology, in that the three points of the man, bison, and bird appear to repeat the asterism, or pattern of stars, in the northern celestial hemisphere called the Summer Triangle. Another theory is that the Lascaux Shaft scene may have recorded a cosmic event, the death of the bird-man and bison representing a catastrophic comet strike at Lascaux around 15200 BCE. Whatever meaning it had to its creator, the scene combines realistic, symbolic, and mythical elements, and yields fascinating early evidence of the productive imagination.

Seeing-as and the early human view of the world

Along with inner representation and hypothetical thinking, human cognitive evolution saw the emergence of our capacity for 'seeing-as'. This facility describes the way in which through visual perception we may perceive in one thing or group of things the shape of another: while I perceive the clouds above as white moving puffs against the sky, I may sometimes 'see' in them familiar objects, such as a face or a turtle. This embellishment may be ascribed in part to the fact that recognizing patterns or figures is a strength of the human visual system. The human eye and brain register and visually categorize faces and animals through faster neural pathways than those which process visual detail. The visual recognition of faces would have enabled social bonding, while that of animal bodies, the evasion of threats or the pursuit of food.

Such facility may influence the perception of patterns or figures in other objects and is thought to have spilled over into the making of early human art.

Cave paintings, for example, suggest the recognition of figures in the shapes of natural surfaces, evidencing imagination's involvement with sensory perception. On the Chauvet cave in France, where hundreds of representational paintings of deer, lions, rhinoceros, and other animals were made around 36,000 years ago, a bear's head can be seen painted on a natural protrusion. The relief of the rock wall is suggestive of the bear head painted in outline, and the circular indication of an eye was placed in its anatomically appropriate location by the painter. Along with the bears then present in the area, the shape of the protrusion may have prompted the idea for the painting.

This capacity for seeing-as, likely to have enhanced early human thinking, persists as a function of the modern human artistic mind. Seeing-as would be practised deliberately by artists of the Renaissance. Leonardo da Vinci looked for patterns everywhere in nature. The master advised his students to find images of humans, animals, and scenes in natural figurations, even in the settling of dust on a surface. His younger rival Michelangelo similarly engaged in interpretive perception, seeing his subject matter in the stone that was to become his sculpture. He reportedly claimed that he saw a statue in every block of marble, and he needed only to chisel away what did not belong in order to liberate it from the stone.

In seeing-as, one thing is perceptually interpreted as another through partial resemblance. In a similar process one object can also serve as or stand in for another. Wittgenstein offered among his examples of seeing-as that of seeing a triangle on its side as a mountain. With only rudimentary perceptual resemblance (its basic shape), the perception becomes symbolic, and can enable analogical thinking. To recognize geographical features on a map, for example, the viewer grasps resemblance to what a given mark stands for, in respect to other features in the respective visual frameworks. On the map the curved line is to the triangle as in the landscape the river is to the mountain.

For our early human ancestors, a stable prospect for seeing-as would have been offered by the stars in the night sky. With the human eye and visual processing system relatively unchanged for hundreds of thousands of years, the stars would have been perceived as they are by modern humans, although with much clearer visibility for our early human ancestors who would not have had to contend with light pollution. For them a certain grouping of stars may have also been seen as outlining the shape of a bull or a hunter, and by convention come to be so identified. This ancient process has given rise to variable conventions in different human cultures on the identification of the constellations.

This process of symbolic seeing-as may orient pragmatic action and thus serve human survival. A journey can be guided by location of the stars, their recognition facilitated by figures seen in the sky. Knowledge of the respective locations of the stars across the seasons can be handed down from generation to generation. Beyond immediate practical purpose, such seeing-as may enable imaginative contemplation. From figures recognized in the night sky may have arisen myths among early humans about the cycles of life and death or the larger forces of the cosmos.

Recent comparative studies of prehistoric art—including the Lion-Man of the Hohlenstein-Stadel mentioned above and cave paintings from France, Spain, and Turkey—have suggested that as early as 40,000 years ago our early human ancestors had knowledge of the movements of the stars, and could track time accordingly. Comparisons of patterns found in prehistoric artworks of different places with computer-generated maps of the skies in ancient times suggest that their creators were mapping star clusters and other celestial observations. Some of the animals in these works may have also functioned as zodiac symbols.

Near the Lascaux cave entrance, for example, a painting of bulls or aurochs includes patterns of dots thought to map two different star clusters within the constellation that is known to us as Taurus. Above the shoulder of one bull appears a curved line of dots that corresponds to a map of the star cluster Pleiades. Inside the same bull figure are dots that may correspond to the Hyades cluster. In front of its snout the dots appear to represent the stars aligned in the 'belt' of the constellation Orion, which would have been visible in the sky near the Taurus constellation (Figure 2). Such symbolic connection between representations of animals on earth and the patterns of stars may have yielded a sense of connection between earth-bound humans and the larger cosmos.

We can surmise that seeing-as allowed early humans to find meaning in the world around them and in the skies above. That animals or other figures can be seen in the protrusion on a cave

2. Cave painting in Lascaux, France, 10,000–18,000 years old, with star clusters Taurus, the Pleiades, and Orion's Belt.

wall or in a particular grouping of stars manifests an ancient imaginative capacity amplifying human perception and gradually transforming our grasp of the surrounding world. Artistic or other representation of such subjects enables further contemplation of them. A bull or a bear seen up close may be frightening, yet the same object can become an object of reflection, and perhaps narrative, through artistic representation. Knowledge about these objects can be handed down. Beyond aiding early human survival, imagination supported the gradual emergence of human culture.

The role of play in human cognitive development

While recent research suggests that early humans were far more sophisticated in their thinking than previously understood, early human cognition has often been compared to the childhood of the modern human mind. The role of imagination in the cognitive development of modern children has been regarded as a source of potential insight into the role imagination may have played in the cognitive evolution of the human species. We can first consider how play might have been used by prehistoric children in fostering the development of imagination.

If you take a walk today in any park, you may see young children playing with sticks, leaves, stones, or other simple objects found in the surrounding environment. While contemporary commercial societies generate countless products designed for their size and developmental age, young children enjoy playing with these basic things, often transforming them into tools, weapons, animals, or treasures. Early human children would have done the same and, like their modern counterparts, would have also adapted adult tools and utensils for their own play. Yet archaeologists have also unearthed prehistoric toys, objects constructed with no evident practical function and scaled to fit a child's hand. These give some insight into the potential role of imagination in cognitive development.

The oldest putative toys (from between 11,000 and 18,000 years ago and found in Europe) are rondelles, or small circular discs carved from stone, bone, or ivory. They are often perforated and engraved on one or both sides with animal or geometric figures. These objects were mysterious for a long period, but more recently archaeologists have begun to understand them as optical amusements. A single rondelle perforated in the centre can be used as a thaumatrope—making a kind of moving image—by being pulled on a string on its lateral axis, so that the image from one side is superimposed onto that of the other due to the persistence of images on the retina. For example, a 15,000-year-old rondelle found in 1868 in the Dordogne in France, engraved with a chamois, shows the animal on each side respectively standing and in a lying position. The disc twirled quickly would have blended and virtually animated the images for the viewer. Similar to the modern thaumatrope toy invented in the 19th century by the astronomer John Hershel and later commercialized by John Ayrton Paris, the rondelle has been likened to a prehistoric form of animation.

While adults and children may have equally delighted in such optical effects, some ancient objects appear to be solely designed for the play of young children. We can point to a 7,500-year-old stone carriage just a few inches long found in Turkey, a tiny chalk figurine of a piglet or hedgehog with a snout and long ears buried with a child from the Bronze Age at Stonehenge, and miniature figurines and rattles found in the graves of infant children in the remote Khakassia region of Siberia, including a 4,500-year-old doll carved of soapstone. On the Italian island of Pantelleria, archaeologists found part of a 4,000-year-old doll buried along with miniature cooking tools. A 3,500-year-old bronze and silver toy found in the Rhodope Mountains of Bulgaria was shaped as a stork mounted on a tripod, and could move its head, allowing children to pretend that the bird was drinking.

These miniaturizations are evidence of both advanced technical skills and social support for children's imaginative play. Just as modern dolls, stuffed animals, miniature vehicles, and building blocks do for children today, these miniaturized toys invite children to engage with and even master things in the world around them. While psychologists once argued that pretend play and imagining discouraged rational thinking in children, in recent decades the importance of play for cognitive development has begun to be recognized. In *Playing and Reality* (1971), the psychologist D. W. Winnicott argued that play nurtures a child's sense of being—'it belongs to being alive', he writes—and thus their development of a fully inhabited self. Through play children are both intensely focused and spontaneous, keenly aware of the world and their interaction with it and, through that interaction, of themselves.

More recently play has been seen as essential to the intellectual development of the child's mind. As the psychologist Paul Harris argued in *The Work of Imagination* (2000), imagining does not detract from, but is rather essential to, the development of rational thinking. Playful imagining helps children to apply knowledge they have learned from reality to new scenarios. Through imagined play children examine possible future actions, considering multiple options. By pretending they also imagine the perspectives of others, which enables social bonding and empathy. Play exercises imagination by encouraging pretence, consideration of counterfactual scenarios, and shifting perspectives. Play not only supports other skills necessary for survival, but may be an evolutionary end in itself.

While the impulse for play diminishes as children grow into adults, grown-ups also delight in pastimes with no obvious practical function, and, as Winnicott argued, play remains essential for cognitive well-being. Games that require multiple players, such as board games, were enjoyed in many ancient societies. Chequers is among the oldest board games still played and originated in Mesopotamia around 5,000 years ago. Backgammon was played in Ancient Persia (Iran), while Ancient

Egyptians played Mehen, named for the snake-god on whose shape the board is fashioned. The game of Go or Weiqi, still popular today, originated in ancient China between 3,000 and 4,000 years ago. The oldest playable board game still physically extant is an iteration of The Royal Game of Ur, originating in Mesopotamia 4,600 years ago. Its rules were written on cuneiform tablet in 177 BCE by a Babylonian astronomer. While all of these games entail complex reasoning, they also sustain the instinct for play, enabling the working out of possibilities and multiple perspectives, along with pleasurable activity.

Animal imagination

Further evidence of the evolutionary development of imagination can be found in studies of our animal relatives. In courting rituals, male bower birds construct and elaborately decorate woven or glued towers of sticks with such objects as flowers, moss, insects, snail shells, and butterfly wings. Parrots engage in complex mimicry. Such activities may be attributed to instinct, but others are socially shared or learned. Elephants have exceptionally strong social bonds and recognize the bones of other elephants, performing burial actions suggesting awareness of death and attachment to other elephant life. Apes and monkeys use forms of language, make and use rudimentary tools, and are self-aware. While an especially concentrated ability for imagining appears to distinguish the human species, other animals can also imagine, as manifest in their problem-solving and social communication.

While throughout most of the Western tradition, animal intelligence was dismissed or denied by philosophers, Aristotle had suggested that animals must have some imagination in seeking or avoiding objects not immediately perceived. Animals have, he thought, inner visual or other percept-like representation of objects. Recent research shows that animals may be able to engage in other modes of imagining such as pretence and some creativity. Chimpanzees in the wild have been observed to transfer activities from a real scenario to a pretended object. They have been observed, for example, grooming leaves in imitation of social grooming, using sticks to fish in an 'imaginary' nest of ants, and carrying a log as if it were a baby. Even when alone they may pretend aggressive displays. Macaques may imitate one another's actions, and feign feeding or ignoring. They also play-fight and tease.

Human-raised primates exhibit a wide range of behaviours that suggest some modes of imagination. A chimp in captivity named Viki was observed to play with pretend objects, acting as if pulling at a non-existent pull toy that then got 'stuck'. A bonobo named Kanzi was observed playing with imaginary invisible objects and encouraging others to play with them. Washoe, a chimpanzee raised by humans, was the first non-human to communicate in American Sign Language. She pretended while at play, bathing her dolls with soap and drying them with towels. She and others in her group would sign 'tickle' when playing with a doll. A chimpanzee has been observed pretending to eat an eraser, signing 'eat', and subsequently hiding it in his room. This suggests imagining another perspective from which the location of a real object could be masked. In captivity gorillas have painted pictures, albeit rather rudimentary ones, to which they give titles in sign language.

Perhaps the most advanced display of animal imagination we know was evidenced by Koko, a gorilla who lived from 1971 to 2018 in California and was taught sign language from infancy. Koko came to be able to sign around 1,000 words and could understand twice as many. At play Koko routinely pretended. She played with toy gorillas, signing to them to chase or tickle each other. At around 4 years of age her favourite game was to act as if she were blind, stumbling around and bumping into things. In discussion with her caretaker about a picture of a bird, she signed

'Koko, Bird', and then admitted upon further questioning that she was in fact 'Gorilla Koko'. Upon seeing an image of the Queen of England in scarlet robes as painted by Richard Stone, Koko dressed herself up in a red blanket and signed 'Koko, Queen'. Imagination may also be at work in understanding significant events she could not perceive directly. When informed that her beloved pet kitten she had named All Ball had been struck by a car and died, Koko grieved, signing 'Bad, sad…cry-frown', and later in private audibly mourned, evidencing conscious preoccupation with something absent.

So far as we can tell, what appears to be unique to humans is the use of imagination unprompted by surrounding objects or circumstances. Only humans appear to engage in elaborated imagining apart from environmental cues, which allows us to fantasize, create fictions, and to construct other worlds. Yet evidence for higher mental functioning of apes and other animals continues to grow, and they are clearly far more advanced than we have previously believed. We now recognize that other animals besides humans—including not only primates but elephants and dolphins among others—are self-aware and may have something like an inner life. Koko's remarkable message in sign language delivered in a video to the UN Climate Change Conference in Paris in 2015 includes her criticism of 'stupid' humans who have broken nature. While staged and edited by her human companions, and so received with some scepticism about the degree of understanding involved, Koko's plea to 'Fix earth…protect earth…nature' at the very least evidenced a non-human animal evoking a situation not immediately perceived, and pointing to an alternative.

Like human cognition, non-human animal cognition arises in interaction with the environment and in efforts to shape the world to needs. Although he had dedicated his work to a phenomenology of embodied human consciousness, the French philosopher

Merleau-Ponty recognized the interiority of animal life. He noted that 'all living things, ourselves included, endeavour to give shape to a world that has not been preordained to accommodate our attempts to think and act upon it'. Yet we can hope to understand this common endeavour only 'if we are prepared to live alongside the world of animals instead of rashly denying it any kind of interiority'. To understand human imagination in light of our cognitive evolution may entail recognizing some affinities with non-human animals, however special human imagining has evolved to be.

The evolution of imagination, as we have explored in this chapter, has made human culture possible. From a modern point of view, prehistoric cave paintings, sculptures, and toys appear to express the raw vitality of early human imagination. Where our early human ancestors climbed hills and first saw the world from above, or viewed the stars with awe, modern humanity's capacities for imagining have been radically transformed by technology. We now have images of the earth from space, and can examine the whole surface of the earth by means of satellite imagery. Yet modern artists turned to so-called primitive works of early humans for inspiration. Having just seen the cave paintings at Lascaux, Picasso reportedly said, 'They invented everything.' However polemical such a statement may have been, modern artists recognized in early human art original expressions of imaginative vision.

Beyond mere survival, imagination has allowed us to amplify, transform, and expressively reflect on our experiences of living. Imagination has enabled a symbolic humanization of our world, scaled to a mental frame with which the human mind can cope and with which it can play. Due to imagination we are able to perceive the world as one to which a human community belongs. The ecological imbalance to which our practical humanization of the world has led, however, may again demand imagination as a crucial ingredient in problem-solving. In order to optimize our thinking, it may be advantageous to better understand this remarkable facility.

In the next three chapters, we will trace the philosophical understanding of imagination from the ancient Greeks to early modern philosophy and science, the rise of aesthetics and Romantic enthusiasm for imagination, and 20th-century affirmations of productive imagining.

Chapter 3
From divine madness to cognitive power

Throughout the history of Western thought, the concept of imagination has had a tumultuous record. Both ancient and early modern philosophers disagreed strongly about imagination, or viewed the topic with striking ambivalence. For some thinkers, imagination was at best a divinely inspired madness, at worst a source of deceptive illusion; curtailing its influence was urgent if objective truth was to be established. For others, imagination was an irrepressible activity of the mind that cannot be expelled from cognition, and may be essential to it.

Throughout their assessments, philosophers and writers considered the imagination's involvement in human thinking to be a matter of high consequence. Despite much suspicion surrounding imagination, it was intermittently understood as serving important, even essential functions for the human mind. Tracing the assessment of imagination allows us to consider a number of things: its relationship with rationality and knowledge; its role in making the images of poetry and art; and its tie to emotions, bodily sensations, empathy, and perception. These debates reveal the power of imagination and its profound implications for the imagining subject.

The critique of imagery and appearances

In ancient Greece, where Western philosophy began, poetic literature served as a primary resource for ideas about matters both divine and human, and it is on the subject of its influence that the debate about imagination begins. The theogony of Hesiod and the epic tales of Homer had provided ancient Greek citizens with insights about the origins of the cosmos and the relevance of gods to human affairs. Dramatists such as Euripides and Sophocles provided not only entertainment but important explorations of ideas. Orators influenced public life much as political and social commentators do today.

Philosophy arose in direct contest with such literary activities. Plato's treatment of imagination must be understood in light of his effort to ensure philosophy's ascension over the influence of poetic literature and the persuasions of rhetoric. Plato aimed for victory in what he called philosophy's 'ancient quarrel' with poetry. For, in Plato's view, poets and orators had no real knowledge, and their influence was therefore dangerous.

Despite the extraordinary literary talent evidenced in his philosophical dialogues, Plato's critique of poets and artists (and implicitly of imagination) is extensive. In his dialogue *Republic,* Plato has his character Socrates advocate the censorship and even banishment of the poets on grounds that poets foster illusions and even lies. Through his protagonist, Plato lambasts poetic and artistic imagery as obscuring our apprehension of reality. He rejects poetic depictions of events, for example of a god changing form, as false and illusory. He castigates pretence—such as in drama when one actor would voice multiple characters—as detrimental to social order, for each citizen should be assigned a clear role. The polis, Plato suggests, should be governed by one whose soul is directed by reason alone, rather than a poetic—and dangerously misleading—vision of mere appearances.

In his works Plato conceptualizes imagination in several related ways: in respect to the artistic creation of images; as related to perception; and as involved with emotions. Imagination is implicated in Plato's critique of mimesis, or the production of images by poets and artists. Since he thinks of it as dealing with appearances, Plato addresses imagination in his account of their perception. He also acknowledges directly the image-making faculty of the soul, and imagination's reach into human emotions. To show how imagination was understood by Plato, we can take up each of these in turn.

Mimesis is the artistic skill of creating likenesses or, more critically, imitations, through visual or verbal images. Depictions of the bison, horses, and deer on the Chauvet cave walls described in the previous chapter are mimetic, as are Homer's depiction of the wandering of Odysseus, or the dramatic presentation of Oedipus in Sophocles' tragedy. Music can be imitative by conveying mood or feeling. The origin of all art is attributed by the ancient Greek philosophers to mimesis. Yet Plato insists that the likenesses or imitations poets and artists make are inherently misleading. Distortion by mimesis is inevitable, Plato argues, since the representation of things in poetic or visual images is several degrees removed from the true reality.

In Plato's philosophy, true being is found not in the material world that appears to perception, but rather in the stable ideas or forms accessible only to the rational part of the soul. The artist is therefore several degrees removed from such truth. In *Republic*, Socrates explains that while the craftsman makes a copy of the form of a thing—making a couch or bed, for example, according to the essential idea of a bed—the painter or poet makes only an image of that physical copy. The poet or painter's image of a bed, unlike that of the craftsman, involves no reference to an original, but only to its manifestation as appearance. Therefore, art affords not 'an imitation of things as they are', or of true reality, but only 'as they appear—of appearance [*phantasmatos*]'. This has epistemic implications, for Socrates argues that 'the creator of the phantom, the imitator, we say, knows nothing of the reality but only the appearance'.

Plato's critique of mimesis cast a long shadow in the history of art, and still figures in artists' understanding of their task. The famous example of mimesis offered in *Republic*—the bed as painted by the artist rather than made by the craftsman—has been the subject of playful critique in contemporary art. For what he called his 'combine' painting, *Bed* (1955), Robert Rauschenberg attached his own bed quilt and pillow to a frame, making a painting that was in part the real thing it represented (Figure 3). Rauschenberg was not the first modern artist to toy with mimesis, of course. Marcel Duchamp had offered his infamous submission to the Society of Independent Artists show in 1917, a 'ready-made' composed of a porcelain urinal, only signed with a fictional name by the artist. Following Duchamp, with *Bed* and other combine works, Rauschenberg advanced Pop Art, integrating into art the objects and images of everyday life that were the very things they represent.

More recently, Tracey Emin's installation *My Bed* (1998) dispensed with mimetic representation of this object altogether. Instead the artist arranged, in a dishevelled state, a box frame, mattress, used linens, pillows, and various detritus of the physical life of the artist in bed. The fact that Emin's work was nominated for the Turner Prize and, in 2014, sold at auction for several million dollars reflects not only the anti-Platonic disposition of contemporary art collectors, but ongoing play with mimesis as the supposed principle of art and challenge to its status as the paradigmatic act of imagination.

The critique of mimesis or the creation of images of things is intertwined with Plato's view of perceived images and appearances. Plato discusses *phantasia*, meaning appearances as well as their reception by the soul, and *phantasm*, designating variously appearance, apparition, dream, vision, phantom,

3. Robert Rauschenberg, *Bed* (1955), Museum of Modern Art, New York.

shadow, and the like. *Phantasmata* are sometimes associated with natural phenomena such as physical reflections, and sometimes with poetic or artistic imagery that in words or colours and lines creates as it were reflections of things. Among the parts of the soul identified by Plato is an image-making faculty, *eikasia*, related to the word *eikonos* (image).

Plato's use of these sets of terms bears the marks of his metaphysics, or theory of the principles underlying reality, and his epistemology, or theory of knowledge. For Plato, we recall, true being cannot be grasped in sense-experience, but only in the mind with the use of reason. What we can grasp with the senses, the empirical manifestation of reality, is mere appearance. Plato repeatedly points out that appearances can be deceptive, because a thing's appearance does not necessarily evidence its true nature. In *Republic* Socrates cites the examples of a reed that looks bent in water when in reality it is straight, and of the sun seeming small in the sky.

Plato contrasts faculties of the soul that perceive appearances and those that, in contrast, attain knowledge of a deeper reality. Plato invokes the metaphor of a divided line in order to explain the soul's cognitive distribution. The line is divided between an upper half, with its faculties of reason and understanding that pertain to knowledge, and a lower half, its faculties dealing with mere opinion. On this lower half are belief and imagination (*eikasia*). While belief deals with objects of perception (i.e. taking things as they appear), imagination deals with only images, shadows, or 'phantasms' of those objects—such as they might be depicted in literary or artistic works, or called up in the mind's eye. In the discussion of poetry, Socrates refers to the part of our thought with which images consort—represented on the lower half of the line—as inferior to 'the part that puts its trust in measurement and reckoning'—the upper part of the line. Imagination, in other words, is inferior to reason.

Imagination may also be dangerous: Plato also locates the emotions in the lower part of the soul, which is most affected by such images and without the restraint of reason. In *Republic* Plato has in mind, among other things, painful experiences such as those represented in tragic poetry. Plato is scornful of depictions of expressive lamentation and grief—since it might suggest a negative view of death or the afterlife and discourage the bravery needed to sacrifice one's life for the polis. Plato's critique of imagination encompasses its entanglement with lower emotions that, in his view, corrupt the soul and distract from contemplation of the highest objects of thought.

This rather devastating critique is, however, not the whole story about imagination for Plato. The later dialogue *Phaedrus* allows for a very different discussion of *phantasia*, of images, and of poetry. The dialogue concerns among other things the nature of eros or romantic love. The appearance of the beautiful beloved is said to awaken a higher vision of divine beauty, as it is held to be a reflection or image of its divine form or essence. In this same dialogue, Plato has Socrates admit that poets may have a gift for discerning the nature of the beautiful and, indeed, that poetry may be inspired by the gods. To be so inspired is not a form of knowledge, however. Instead Socrates calls it a form of madness, albeit one divinely endowed.

While in *Republic* Plato discusses the passive perception of appearances or the mimetic creation of images by artists and poets, in his dialogue *Philebus* he describes the active construction of images within the soul itself. There Socrates likens the soul to a book, in which memories are recorded by an inner scribe. Socrates introduces a second 'workman', namely 'a painter, who paints in our souls pictures to illustrate the words which the writer has written'. This is not merely a mnemonic function, however, for Socrates and his interlocutor agree that such writing and images in the soul relate not only experiences of the past, but also of expectations. This inner picturing is relevant to 'all hopes relating to the future'. Thus Plato recognizes imagination's role in anticipatory thought.

Despite Plato's concessions to divine inspiration and anticipation, his overall account of the imagination is admonitory. The imagination deals with epistemically suspect images and can mislead the soul from its search for knowledge and truth.

The irony of Plato's critique, of course, is that his own writings are extraordinarily imaginative. Plato uses vivid metaphors, creative analogies, imagistic illustrations, and mythical narratives. His cave parable in *Republic*, where bound individuals are watching a shadow-play on the wall as an analogy for the deceptions of sense-experience, is just one of many examples of Plato's own use of imaginative devices typically associated with poetry. Clearly Plato would have to accept imagination as a useful tool for the philosopher, so long as it is constrained by rational thought.

Thinking images and the art of possibilities

Imagination may be more crucial to thinking than Plato recognized. Aristotle counters Plato's critique by describing imagination as an active faculty of the mind that produces images necessary for cognition. In *De Anima* (*On the Soul*), Aristotle describes that process 'by which we say that an image is presented to us', and treats *phantasia* as this image-making faculty. While Plato's account does not always distinguish between the perception of appearances and their production in the mind, Aristotle clearly distinguishes between imagination in the mind and passive sensation. He points out that through imagination visions appear to those 'even with their eyes shut'.

Aristotle notes further distinctions between imagining and sense-perception. He argues that imagination lies within our power, whereas sensation does not. Aristotle gives the example that 'we can call up a picture, as in the practice of mnemonics by the use of mental images'. He explains the visual association of the term: 'As sight is the most highly developed sense, the name *phantasia* (imagination) has been formed from *phaos* (light), because without light it is impossible to see.'

In Aristotle's view imagination need not be considered erroneous despite the fact that an image can lack grounding in reality or sharply diverge from it. In contrast to Plato, Aristotle argues that we can imagine something false without necessarily falling into error by so doing. For just as imagination is distinct from sensation, it is also distinct from belief. We can imagine the sun as a small orb in the sky, while knowing it to be many times larger than the earth. We can imagine something that in reality is not there at all, like a griffin, without believing in the image so presented. This independence of imagination from belief allows it to serve as a distinct cognitive power that can, in line with correct belief, avoid error.

The thinking soul can also be served by images as if they were contents of perception. These images can be the objects of the soul's valuation and intentions, such that the soul asserts and pursues what it deems good or denies and avoids what it deems bad. Indeed, Aristotle regards imagination as essential for any thinking at all, claiming that 'the soul never thinks without a mental image'. Aristotle specifies how thinking proceeds through such use of images. In *De Anima*, he writes:

> So the faculty of thinking then thinks the forms in images... sometimes by means of the images or thoughts in the soul, just as if it were seeing, it calculates and plans for the future in view of the present....

Here Aristotle suggests that imagination not only presents to the mind images based on past experiences, but allows us to project future possibilities. Like Socrates in Plato's *Philebus*, Aristotle acknowledges the role of anticipatory images. Closely related to this, the ability to deal in possibilities—what might or could happen, as in hypothetical thinking—is essential to innovation.

Aristotle not only recognized the ubiquity of imagination in thinking, but also valued its expression in creative works. In his *Poetics* Aristotle outlines the proper structure and elements of a successful tragedy, including the 'thought' that shapes the work as a whole. Aristotle argues that such poetry is more philosophical than history, because it tells us not only what has happened but what *could* happen. Against Plato's critique of poetic imagination, Aristotle further defends poetry and the catharsis it can provoke as beneficial for the individual soul as well as a community. While Plato warned about the dangers of provoking emotions, Aristotle thought that exercising the emotions through imaginatively stirred empathy with tragic characters has a salutary function in balancing the soul.

These connections between imagination and possibility, both in deliberative thinking and in poetic representation, suggest that imagination need not be conceived only in reproductive terms (where the imagination is only derivative of sense-experience). For if imagination is that element of our minds that allows us to think about possibilities that depart from what is already actual, imagining—or thinking that imagines—would also be the source of new ideas. Against a wholly reproductive view of imagination, philosophies of the 18th century onward promote the productive imagination. They owe much to Aristotle's recognition that imagination enables us to think possibilities.

Embodied feeling, empathy, and trickery

Imagination evokes bodily experiences, and it was this aspect of imagination that most preoccupied some early modern thinkers. In his essay 'On the Force of Imagination' (1574), the French philosopher and essayist Michel de Montaigne offered a theory of embodied imagination that helps to explain a number of imaginative phenomena, including empathy, paranoia, and psychosomatic experiences. Montaigne argued that imagination is responsible for our ability to feel empathy for others. In his view, imagination facilitates direct communication of emotions, responses, or anxieties between one imagining subject and another. The imagination, moreover, has a direct effect on the bodily experience of the imaginer. He writes that: 'we start, tremble, turn pale, and blush, as we are variously moved by imagination'.

Most of us have had the experience of yawning after another person does so in our presence, in a kind of empathetic contagion. Montaigne explains such phenomena by reporting on his own highly sensitive empathetic responses, often through a bodily sense. He writes: 'The very sight of another's pain materially pains me. I often usurp the sensations of another person.' Through this imaginative transference, in Montaigne's example, a subject's own throat can itch when another person coughs. Before Descartes came to cast doubt on the existence of other minds, Montaigne argues that imagination gives one a quasi-direct connection with the physical or psychological experiences of another by receptively echoing or mimicking them. If another person coughs, I may cough too. If another has anxiety, this may induce anxiety in me. A cough or an anxiety is no less real even if it was provoked by imagination.

While Montaigne attested to his own experience, regarding himself afflicted or gifted with a strong imagination, contemporary psychology has studied the phenomenon of social empathy. Some cognitive theories describe this ability as the mind's simulation of the experience of another. Neuroscientists have identified a mirror neuron mechanism in the brain in which neurons are triggered when observing another perform a given action. Such explanations point, respectively, to the cognitive processes and brain mechanics underlying empathetic experiences as described by Montaigne. While these accounts help to explain the cognitive and physical correlates of social empathy, imagination remains their experiential medium.

Empathy is not limited to an immediate, unconscious response, but can be cultivated by deliberate effort to imagine the perspective of another. Literature has been credited with fostering empathetic imagining. Aristotle counted pity or empathy for the suffering of characters among the core emotions stirred up by tragic drama. In *Poetic Justice* (1995), philosopher Martha Nussbaum promoted the view that literature helps us to imagine, and thus empathize with, perspectives of others unlike ourselves, and that the literary imagination thus serves a democratic function. More recently theorists have argued that literature functions to exercise our 'theory of mind'—the idea that we recognize others as having experiences like our own, that we can 'mind-read'. This may be multiply layered in literary experience—as when we can imagine the points of view of multiple characters and their perspectives on one another—but also forms a part of our basic human communication. Enabled by imagination, we recognize others as having experiences as we ourselves do, though these experiences are not directly accessible to us.

Apart from embodied empathy, Montaigne offers a number of engaging examples that demonstrate the imagination not only as a feature of mental life but as a bodily force. He cites the variable effects of imagination on erotic activity, and what we now call the placebo effect, in which substances we believe to have healing or other beneficial powers induce such effects based on our beliefs. He wonders if religious devotion might have similar effects on our well-being, thus anticipating some contemporary studies in empirical psychology. (While there is no scientific evidence (at time of writing) that prayer directly affects health, visualization techniques have been demonstrated to positively affect subjects' well-being.)

Montaigne's speculations, however, go beyond the scope of plausibility. In the absence of scientific scrutiny, he wonders whether one could bring about physical effects in the world through the imagination alone. He notes, for example, an anecdote about a falconer said to bring down a kite with his gaze. Such speculations would have inflamed anxiety about imagination in Montaigne's time.

Philosophers were not the only thinkers invested in understanding imagination. In a number of his dramatic works, Shakespeare explored the power of imagination, but expressed more scepticism than Montaigne did about its efficacy. In *A Midsummer Night's Dream* (1605), a comedy featuring fairies and spells and magical metamorphoses, imagination is humorously attacked as a source of error, and as stimulating hysteria and obsession. Shakespeare's treatment of imagination in the play is also analytical. Observing the misadventures of others, Theseus comments on the distortions wrought by imagination, and implicates the audience as among those duped by its charms.

For just as the characters succumb to trances and hallucinations, the audience is drawn into the world of the play and subjected to its extraordinary fantasies. Commenting on the visions 'more strange than true' of imagination, Theseus says:

> The poet's eye, in fine frenzy rolling,
> Doth glance from heaven to Earth, from Earth to heaven.
> And as imagination bodies forth
> The forms of things unknown, the poet's pen
> Turns them to shapes and gives to airy nothing
> A local habitation and a name.

The poet, Theseus suggests, is as irrational as the lover and the lunatic. While the mad person would see demons everywhere, he tells us, the lover is duped by fantasies of his beloved's superior beauty. Shakespeare comes close to suggesting that the capacity to be misled by imagination is a universal human vulnerability. The author of *A Midsummer Night's Dream* seems to take extended delight in elaborating the dubious exercises of the poet's fancy in particular.

Here Shakespeare ironically echoes Plato's critique of poets in *Republic*. The poet is not merely misled by imagination, but, in and through imagining, deliberately misleads others—his audience and readers. While the lover and the lunatic are helpless under imagination's sway, the poet's imagination is intentional and directed. Shakespeare charges that imagination tends to fabricate causation in place of mere coincidence and, in provoking fear, transforms neutral objects into dangers. Shakespeare here anticipates the notion of productive imagination, insofar as he further charges that imagination prompts false inferences—apprehending some joy, the imagination furnishes an idea of an agent who brought it forth. Seeing a bush on a dark evening, we might fear it as a bear. Imagination conjures from nothing and transforms what is present in ways that provoke our emotions, entrap our thoughts, and potentially misdirect our deeds. Imagination breeds superstition and paranoia—along with comedic amusements.

We cannot find physical sustenance or shelter in fantasies, and Shakespeare accordingly points to imagination's poverty. In *Richard II*, Shakespeare has Bolingbroke remind us that imagination is not equal to reality, by invoking contrasting sensations:

> Oh! who can hold a fire in his hand
> By thinking on the frosty Caucasus?
> Or cloy the hungry edge of appetite
> By bare imagination of a feast?

We could hold a fire in our hands but we cannot prevent our hands from being burned by thinking of frosty mountains. We cannot sate our appetite with mere thoughts. The irony would not have been lost on Shakespeare that he uses vivid imagery to expose imagination's limits.

Methodical imagination and the synthesis of experience

If imagination provoked anxiety among those of the early modern period, some set out to curtail imagination's power. Descartes sought to differentiate the rational part of the mind from that of imagination. While imagination was recognized as mediating between the senses and the intellect—bringing ideas of corporeal things to mind—it must not, in Descartes's view, have undue influence. At stake was not only a contest between philosophy and the imaginative arts, but trust in the mind's grasp of rational ideas that were to serve as the foundations of modern science.

For Descartes, rational thinking and imagination both deal with ideas in the mind, yet they are distinct faculties and the former alone will be considered essential to cognition. To confuse the source of our ideas not only risks error. It also renders unstable any effort to grasp the nature of reality through rational ideas.

Thus, in the *Meditations on First Philosophy* (1641), Descartes aligns the imagination with perceptual distortions, illusions, and madness. According to Descartes, innate ideas are clear and distinct, but ideas borne of imagination are merely derivative, copied from sense-impressions and recombined, and may be experienced as delusions or hallucinations. Descartes describes persons who have succumbed to the imagination so that:

> they steadfastly insist that they are kings when they are utter paupers, or that they are arrayed in purple robes when they are naked, or that they have heads made of clay, or that they are gourds, or that they are made of glass.

Descartes further argues that thinking can proceed without imagination, and so imagination is not an essential part of the thinking self.

While Descartes's own philosophical procedures will employ imagination in distinctive and fascinating ways, here and in his work *Discourse on Method* (1637) the imagination is treated dismissively as associated with the uncertain and epistemically problematic life of the senses. In the *Discourse* Descartes anticipates his arguments in the *Meditations* and argues for the priority of reason, as the faculty capable of clear and distinct ideas, over imagination and the sense-experience from which it draws. Descartes argues that epistemic vigilance—the use of reasoned judgement to curtail the influence of images—is needed to counter imagination, for 'it is not a dictate of Reason that what we thus see or imagine is in reality existent'.

Despite declaring imagination to be inessential to the rational mind, Descartes allows some role for imagining in both his philosophical and his scientific writings. In fact, Descartes engages imagination methodically in *Meditations*. Just as Plato engages imagery, metaphor, and myth, Descartes engages pretence, hypothetical constructions, and visualization as tools for his methodical process of doubt. The thought experiments in the *Meditations* would not be achievable without imagination as both the medium of such counterfactual images and their very theme.

The *Meditations* begins with Descartes purporting to excise from his mind all accumulated opinions, including those drawn from sense-experience, in order to establish a truthful basis for scientific thinking. The thinker's own existence as a thinking being is the one indubitable truth that can serve as a point of reference, a basis for rational thinking as such. But arriving at this basic truth requires a methodical use of the imagination. Descartes must contrast his certain grasp of himself as a thinking mind with counterfactual possibilities—most famously with the prospect that an evil deceiver makes him think that he exists—in order to exclude them as logically incoherent. Descartes argues that he may be deceived about his body, but he cannot be deceived that he is, at very least, a 'thinking thing'. For one who doubts his own existence must exist in order to doubt it in the first place.

Imagination is also necessary to contemplate what knowledge we may have of the world. In the *Discourse* Descartes defines imagination as the ability to contemplate 'the shape of a corporeal thing'. Imagination allows the mind both to conjure ideas of things that could belong to the world of the senses and to contemplate or manipulate such ideas. Imagination is required for the mind to construct a representation of the world to which its scientific understanding could apply.

We can find an example of this in Descartes's own scientific studies. In explaining how a rainbow appears in the sky, Descartes imagines a point of view from which light, hitting the raindrops at a particular angle, would produce colour. Without this hypothetical visualization Descartes could not have explained the phenomenon. While he insists that imagination is not an essential part of the thinking subject, Descartes concedes in the *Discourse* that even ideas originating in imagination must 'contain in them some truth'.

A development in consideration of imagination occurs a century later, when the Scottish philosopher David Hume will assign further roles to imagination—that of not only providing ideas of corporeality but also synthesizing them. In *An Enquiry Concerning Human Understanding* (1748), Hume describes the various capacities we ought to attribute to imagination. With imagination we can engage in fictional constructions, feigning (what we have called pretence) and rendering (through envisioning) such appearances convincingly. He writes:

> Nothing is more free than the imagination of man; and though it cannot exceed that original stock of ideas furnished by the internal and external senses, it has unlimited power of mixing, compounding, separating, and dividing these ideas, in all the varieties of fiction and vision.

While the imagination is at first described in Hume's account in positive terms, as free and capable, his description of what imagination does is limited to a reproductive function. Imagination does not truly create anything new, but mixes, adds together, takes apart, or divides other ideas.

The difficulty arises with the potential inextricability of imagination and belief. While Aristotle segregated these capacities, Hume does not. Of imagination, Hume continues:

> It can feign a train of events, with all the appearance of reality, ascribe to them a particular time and place, conceive them as existent, and paint them out to itself with every circumstance, that belongs to any historical fact, which it believes with the greatest certainty.

As Shakespeare pointed out, the imagination can evoke fictional worlds not only conceived as existing, but believed as such. While Aristotle had taken pains to distinguish between imagination of and belief in a false image, Hume follows Shakespeare in attributing to imagination's feigning a potential concession to the existence of its objects.

As an empiricist philosopher Hume also recognized—despite his critique of imagination—that only imagination can facilitate the connections among our ideas drawn from sense-experience, providing a crucial synthetic function for the mind. Sense-data does not of itself give us a stable presentation of the world. Imagination, for Hume, binds sense-data together to enable us to perceive the objects of perception from moment to moment as constant, enabling a coherent experience of them. Hume argued that imagination also creates the sense of personal identity, as well as of the continuity of objects in space and time, by synthesizing as it were all the diverse data of which these entities are composed. As he wrote in *A Treatise of Human Nature* (1739):

> The identity, which we ascribe to the mind of man, is only a fictitious one, and of a like kind with that which we ascribe to vegetables and animal bodies. It...must proceed from a like operation of the imagination upon like objects.

In Hume's account there would be no coherent sense of a stable objective world or of our own selves without imagination. This view, adapted and developed by Kant, will inspire extravagant expectations of imagination among philosophers over the next two centuries.

The critical scrutiny and even condemnation of imagination in ancient and early modern philosophy are countered by a recognition of its power and importance for the human mind. Imagination's role in literature and the arts has been historically opposed to the philosophical search for truth. Imagination's relation to truth and falsity, sensation and emotion has been scrutinized not only by philosophers but by literary writers considering its power. The delusions and distortions attributed to imagination provoked anxiety over its influence in human thinking.

At the same time, imagination has also been recognized as the medium of empathy and for providing the mind with an intuition of the objective world. With much ambivalence, philosophers come to recognize that imagination may be involved in shaping cognition of the world and of ourselves. Recognition of the synthetic power of imagination will play an important role in the formulation of the productive imagination. This notion will in turn electrify the aesthetics of the late 18th and 19th centuries and influence treatment of the imagination long into the 20th, as we will see in the following chapters.

Chapter 4

The productive and aesthetic imagination

The assessment and understanding of imagination was transformed by the recognition of its central role in the perception and expression of aesthetic qualities. From the Greek word *aisthesthai* ('perceive'), aesthetics originally meant the study of sense-perception. But by the 18th century, philosophers of aesthetics focused on the perception of beauty or sublimity—the sense of the vast or transcendent—in nature or art. Practitioners of aesthetics tried to identify the nature of aesthetic pleasure and to unlock the secrets of artistic genius. Imagination came to be appreciated as the source of our experience of freedom and even of the very feeling of life. As rationality, with the scientific revolution, had come to be associated with knowledge of a physically determined and mathematically predictable world, some philosophers looked to imagination to enliven the mind and offer glimpses of a higher meaning.

The rise of aesthetics (and particularly its treatment by Kant) would inspire an ecstatic devotion to imagination on the part of the Romantic writers and thinkers. Celebrating the productive imagination, early 19th-century Romantics found in it an echo of divine creation or an ability to intuit what they called the 'absolute' or immediate, unconditioned knowledge of reality in its wholeness. Later that century, the German philosopher Friedrich Nietzsche claimed that imagination was a vital cognitive force, and thought that through art, imagination could counter the cold, abstract thinking that constricted modern life and impeded reception of nature's primal forces. In this chapter we trace the discovery of productive imagination—imagination which does not merely reproduce sense-experience but originally generates connections or ideas—and its profound legacy.

Shaping the phenomenal world

Productive imagination plays a number of roles in Kant's philosophy. According to Kant, the coherence of the phenomenal world—of the world as it appears to us—requires the activity of what he called the productive imagination. Taking Hume's idea that imagination synthesizes sense-perception, Kant argued further that imagination contributes to shaping how we experience the world before us. Imagination in this role works in the service of perception, bringing the manifold of sensation—the diverse data of sense-experience—into an image for the mind.

Kant advances beyond Hume's idea of the synthetic role for imagination in clearly distinguishing the productive use of imagination from any merely reproductive function. Kant defines imagination as the 'faculty of intuition without the presence of the object'. Yet Kant explains in his work *Anthropology from a Pragmatic Point of View* (1798) that imagination can work reproductively or productively. The reproductive imagination allows us to reproduce the idea or image of any objects we have already experienced. It is, as Kant writes, a 'derivative presentation'. In contrast, the productive imagination produces an 'original presentation', making possible any experience of an object in the first place.

To understand how the imagination can function productively, we need to address one of Kant's several terms for imagination. When he refers to imagination by the term *Einbildungskraft*, the German term suggests the power (*Kraft*) for making a unified or single (*ein*) image (*Bild*). *Einbildungskraft* is described by Kant as the synthetic power to make present a coherent image from the diversity of impressions we receive from our senses. Kant's term *Phantasie* (which can be translated as 'imagination' or 'fantasy' in English) can indicate the playful inner combination or transformation of such images when they are called to mind. *Vorstellungskraft*—or the power (*Kraft*) of ideation or presentation (*Vorstellung*)—is also important as the power to represent, as in conjuring an idea or intuition of something. In Kant's writings, these terms sometimes designate technical assignments of imagination, while at other times they are used interchangeably. It is as *Einbildungskraft* that imagination is conceived as productive in a way fundamental to our experience.

In his ground-breaking work *Critique of Pure Reason* (1781) Kant outlined our cognition of objects, or our perception and understanding of things in the world. He argued that several of our cognitive faculties—sensibility, understanding, and reason—work together to give coherent form to phenomenal experience, or to the world as it appears to us. How the world is in itself apart from such appearance, we cannot know. Kant likened this to a 'Copernican revolution'. Kant argued that reality appears as it does to us because it is so structured by the mind. Our sense of reality is structured for us according to our own cognitive set-up.

Imagination for Kant is part of the faculty of sensibility, which also includes the capacity for sensations—both outer senses of the spatial world and the inner sense of temporally ordered states of mind. Kant argued that imagination is responsible for synthesizing sensations which are subsumed under—or given order by—the categories of the understanding. This means that we experience the world not merely as a barrage of sensory input but rather in a spatial, temporal, and causal continuity and according to an objective order which the mind can interpret. For this to happen, Kant writes, 'imagination is to bring the manifold of intuition into the form of an image'—or the diverse impressions in the mind are put together to form a discrete whole. This unified intuition will come together with, and (as Kant puts it) be legislated by, the faculty of understanding. In this role imagination is productive because its synthetic process, underwritten automatically by the mind, yields an original presentation. Imagination does not merely re-present what we have already experienced in perception, but plays an original role in shaping the perception itself.

Productive imagination for Kant is thus 'transcendental', as it exceeds the bounds of a single faculty to provide an underlying foundation for experience. Imagination in this mode is performed spontaneously, Kant says, for it is not derivative of or directed by another faculty of mind. This notion of spontaneity will become important for Kant's understanding of aesthetic experience. For the Romantics, this spontaneity will link the imagination to human freedom. Aesthetic experience, moreover, will be celebrated for promoting the 'free play' of imagination with the understanding—a role in which imagination is not subordinate to, but plays together with, conceptual thinking.

Aesthetic free play and the perception of beauty

Recognition of the transcendental role of productive imagination leaves us with a difficulty, one that also pertains to contemporary theories of creativity, as we will see in Chapter 6. If imagination is always operating to shape our phenomenal experience, how is a particularly 'imaginative' experience different from the ordinary processing of input from our surroundings? The philosophical discipline of aesthetics sought to distinguish particularly heightened experiences, such as the feelings evoked by beautiful nature or art, from ordinary perception. It is to Kant's aesthetic philosophy that we can look for an account of what he called the beautiful and the sublime, as well as artistic genius. In its special aesthetic roles, imagination will turn out to be of central importance for reconciling the mind and the world.

Aesthetics arose in the mid-18th century, when the German philosopher Alexander Baumgarten applied the philosophy of perception more generally to experiences of beauty in nature and art. The Irish-born philosopher Edmund Burke had also tried to grasp the ways we are affected by the experiences of the beautiful and the sublime. Both thinkers sought to explain the significance of those special experiences that seem to be universal: a feeling of pleasure taken in beautiful nature or in works of artistic genius, and of awe in encountering sublime vistas or ideas. Kant understood from these sources, among others, that his own philosophy would have been incomplete without grasping such experiences, for they stand apart strikingly from a deterministic understanding of the world. He also recognized in them the prospect of joining two otherwise separate parts of his philosophy. Kant devoted the third of his so-called critical works, the *Critique of Judgment* (1790), to how the perception of beauty and sublimity engages imagination in distinctive ways.

Kant found that aesthetic experience interrupts our usual cognitive habits. In ordinary experience, Kant had argued, the understanding 'legislates' the intuitions shaped through imagination, imposing upon them conceptual coherence and ensuring our grasp of a knowable reality. Yet when confronted with a beautiful object, the subject's ordinary thinking processes are for a moment suspended in the experience of pleasure. The judgement that something, say a sunset, 'is beautiful' pertains not to the object itself, Kant claims, but to the feeling it provokes in the experiencing subject. This feeling is initiated when, encountering something beautiful, the imagination and the understanding engage in a playful mode of interaction. Instead of the imagination being 'legislated' by the understanding, the experience of beauty stimulates a cognitive 'free play' between them, which enlivens the mind.

This mental vitality is described by Kant as a 'feeling of life': a feeling of freedom that importantly differs from our understanding of a world wholly determined by material causes. In *Critique of Pure Reason* Kant had explained knowledge of reality through the lens of Newtonian physics: the world we know is a mechanistic universe causally determined with mathematical precision. But he also regarded the human soul as free, and therefore capable of autonomous legislation of its desires, which he described in his second critical work, *Critique of Practical Reason* (practical here meaning pertaining to morality). While the phenomenal world, or the world we can know, is causally determined, the noumenal world, or the world as it is in itself, includes the free human self or soul.

These realms known by pure and practical reason respectively are absolutely separate. Kant says in the preface to *Critique of Judgment* that an abyss (the German term is *Abgrund*) yawns between them. Yet encountering beauty, we are affected by an object in the phenomenal world the effect of which cannot be wholly explained in mechanical or deterministic terms. Such experience offers a glimpse of what Kant considers our higher moral calling and, implicitly, of our freedom.

Let us consider the example of aesthetic experience mentioned above. According to Kant, perceiving a beautiful sunset stimulates imagination in a free play with understanding. Of course, in ordinary cognition, we understand the sunset in practical or scientific terms. A sailor might consider a particularly red sunset as indicating clear weather from the west in the morning. A physicist might describe the sunset as a scattering of light rays when they strike molecules in the atmosphere, at a time of day when, due to the earth's rotation, the sunlight takes a longer pathway to reach the human eye. Yet insofar as it strikes us as beautiful, the sunset is not wholly explained away by this practical or physical knowledge. Such determinations are suspended as the mind absorbs the phenomenon in a state of play. For the beautiful sunset evokes a special form of pleasure and with that an awareness of another aspect of ourselves. When I judge the sunset as beautiful, it is for me more than a practical indication or a set of physical effects. In such experience, Kant says, the 'understanding serves the imagination rather than vice versa'.

Although the judgement of the beautiful is subjective, Kant claims that it is also universal, and so connects us with our common humanity. When we experience a beautiful sunset, Kant suggests, we feel a connection to other human subjects, for we feel that they too would be similarly affected if they too were to view the sunset. Indeed, when we witness something beautiful we may feel an impulse to share it with another, pointing out to them how beautiful it is, despite the fact that there is more to it than we can put into words. And although we cannot explain it, the beauty of the sunset will evoke the purposefulness of nature as a whole—a sense that it all fits together in some way that is not merely random but expresses a higher purpose. This happens, Kant argues, without the mind's supplying any concept of what this purpose may be. This cognitive free play thus sustains within the subject an orientation towards the world as a purposive, harmonious whole.

Beauty is often explained by reference to the concept of symmetry and our attraction to it. Yet Kant argues that freedom is central to any lasting effect beauty may have upon us. For Kant a judgement of the beautiful is not a determination of the object, but an effect of imagination in the process of perceiving it. In aesthetic terms, perfect regularity eventually bores us, Kant claims, while phenomena that stimulate imagination's free play captivate us. To illustrate this, Kant praises the wildness of English gardens, as opposed to the strictly geometric French designs popular at the time. These and similar phenomena—Kant mentions a pepper garden in the forest of Sumatra, the play of birdsong, a flickering fire, or the rippling of a brook—carry 'the imagination's freedom very far'. The pleasure we take in such phenomena reveals the freedom of imagination which thrives with no requirement to conform to an idea of perfection.

Free play in experiencing the beautiful may also stimulate creative activity or the making of beautiful art. Artistic creativity, Kant says, is that power to 'create another nature out of the material that actual nature gives it'. Here Kant also introduces the notion of the aesthetic ideas—ideas borne by poetry or art that provoke intuitions to which no concept is adequate.

> By an aesthetical idea I understand that representation of the imagination which prompts much thought, but to which no determinate thought whatsoever, i.e. no [determinate] concept, can be adequate; so that no language can express it completely and allow us to grasp it.

Aesthetic ideas, Kant argues, expand our thinking, for they allow us to 'strive toward something that lies beyond the bounds of experience'. Despite its ineffability, an aesthetic idea prompts the mind to 'think more', beyond conceptual reason, thus enlivening the mind.

Imagination and the sublime

While in perceiving or creating the beautiful, the imagination is freely playful, the sublime provokes a different response—one of violent agitation of the imagination. A major theme in Romanticism, the sublime was thought to be an important aesthetic experience. The sublime may be experienced through witnessing natural phenomena that seem overwhelming in their power or scale, or invoked by ideas of such magnitude they surpass imaginative intuition.

In his work *A Philosophical Enquiry into the Origin of our Ideas of the Sublime and Beautiful* (1757), Burke emphasized terrifying, dangerous phenomena that, when experienced from a position of safety, could provoke a negative form of pleasure or awe. Echoing Aristotle's analysis of tragic pleasure taken in depictions of catastrophic suffering, Burke wanted to explain the feeling of delight we take in objects that would elicit our strongest emotions. The sublime is an experience that evokes emotions pertaining to self-preservation, and produces astonishment:

> The passion caused by the great and sublime in nature, when those causes operate most powerfully, is Astonishment; and astonishment is that state of the soul, in which all its motions are suspended, with some degree of horror. In this case the mind is so entirely filled with its object, that it cannot entertain any other, nor by consequence reason on that object which employs it.

The sublime evokes a sense of boundlessness that surpasses anything we could create ourselves or even fully comprehend, and as the mind is overwhelmed by the sublime other 'motions of the soul' are suspended.

Sublime phenomena may include a tumultuous ocean, powerful thunderstorms, earthquakes, erupting volcanoes. These would be the kinds of objects that Kant, in *Critique of Judgment*, argued stimulate a sense of the 'dynamically sublime'. In the face of these, the mind strains to intuit the boundlessness and magnitude of the forces involved—and insofar as it does not resolve on such an intuition, lingers in astonishment. For 'nature is sublime in those of its appearances whose intuition carries with it the idea of their infinity'. To witness the sublime, at least from a safe distance, is to experience 'an expansion of the mind'. Yet the power of nature is also demystified by the sublime, insofar as the mind is able to resist the presentation of such overwhelming force.

In addition to manifestations of natural power, for Kant the sublime is triggered by phenomena the magnitude of which dwarfs human perception. The immensity of some phenomena overwhelms our power to assemble an image of their unity—Kant names the Egyptian pyramids, the Swiss Alps, and St Peter's Basilica in Rome. Having never ventured further than 10 miles from his native Prussian city of Königsberg, Kant never saw these sights in person. Yet Kant could have imagined that in order to take them in as a whole, one would have to stand so far back from them that one could no longer perceive minutiae. The imagination must strain, and fail, to encompass simultaneously the unity of such objects and the diversity of their details. While such effort does expand the imagination, Kant argues, a kind of violence is inflicted on the subject's inner sense. Yet, as Kant argues, 'this same violence that the imagination inflicts on the subject is still judged purposive for the *whole vocation* of the mind'. The awe we experience in the sublime calls forth our own higher vocation as human beings.

Natural phenomena associated with the sublime are persistent subjects of Romantic painting, despite Kant's view that art could not properly represent the sublime. Works by the German painter Caspar David Friedrich—such as *The Monk by the Sea* (1808–10)—contemplate the magnificence of natural scenes in which the human figure may be diminutive. The English painter J. M. W. Turner depicted forces of nature in episodes of great destruction, including great raging fires, devastating naval battles, or ships swallowed up at sea by enveloping storms—as in *Snow Storm—Steam-Boat off a Harbour's Mouth* (first exhibited in 1842). It was Turner's particular genius to evoke for the viewer a sense of the boundlessness of the sublime from within the spatial confines of the painted image. The tumultuous, misty, swirling, and enveloping colours of Turner's sea storm scenes not only express the Romantic sublime but will come to influence Abstract Expressionist renderings of nature.

Yet ideas might represent the sublime more than art could, according to Kant. The idea of the end of all things or of infinity could overwhelm the human imagination with its magnitude. The mind cannot invent an image or conjure a sensuous intuition that adequately corresponds to such a concept as infinity, which Kant included among examples of what he called the 'mathematically sublime'. These sorts of ideas, in their provocation of astonishment, seem at first to expose the inadequacy of the human mind, or more specifically that of imagination. Yet the resolution of astonishment turns out to involve what the French philosopher Jean-François Lyotard, in his contemporary revival of Kant in *Lessons on the Analytic of the Sublime* (1991), likened to a sacrifice of imagination to the power of reason. For Kant, the experience of the sublime ultimately, and paradoxically, reveals the human superiority over nature. For rational thought prevails over the imagination and the inadequate images it forms from the empirical world.

While frightening, the sublime also 'calls forth our strength' to regard our physical vulnerability to nature's forces as subordinate to our higher calling. According to Kant the experience of the sublime provokes us to test in our imaginations the highest value we hold of ourselves as human beings, were we in a position to have to choose, for example, between saving ourselves and upholding a higher moral law. Experiencing the sublime reminds us of our ability to consider ideas that exceed any presentation in the phenomenal world, and potentially choose even in the face of mortal danger what action we judge to be right. This for Kant demonstrates our capacity for moral autonomy, and thus our human dignity.

From cosmic speculation to the 'absolute'

The rise of aesthetics ignited rapture about the imagination across the Romantic movement. Coleridge had read Kant for many years before publishing his famous definition of imagination in *Biographia Literaria* in 1817. For Coleridge, the imagination is central to the human self and our knowledge of the world. It offers our only access to the intuition of nature's unity and to the divine.

The definition of imagination offered by Coleridge, however, is notoriously confusing. Coleridge employed three terms for imagination, distinguishing among the primary imagination, the secondary imagination, and fancy. Fancy appears to describe the reproductive, derivative imagination, as in the ability to conjure and recombine images of things not present to immediate perception. But imagination proper is identified by Coleridge as a genuinely creative power. Kant's emphasis on productivity and spontaneity is reflected in Coleridge's description of the primary imagination and its secondary echo.

The primary imagination is ravishingly praised as a vital power allowing for finite human beings to repeat the creativity of God by perceiving creation. Coleridge writes:

> The primary imagination I hold to be the living power and prime agent of all human perception, and as a repetition in the finite of the eternal act of creation of the infinite I AM. The secondary I consider as an echo of the former, coexisting with the conscious will, yet still identical with the primary in the kind of its agency, and differing only in degree, and in the mode of its operation.

Primary imagination is a vital, original agency, and yet it is also receptive insofar as it is involved in and affects all perception. We can perceive aspects of nature as beautiful or sublime, for example, due to this 'living power' of imagination. As the 'prime agent' in perception itself, imagination allows the poet or artist to receive inspiration from divinely endowed nature. This echoes Plato's argument, in *Phaedrus*, that poets can uniquely perceive the beautiful, and are divinely inspired.

Yet for Coleridge imagination must also function in conjunction with human will. The primary imagination in human perception itself repeats in finite terms the divine generative act which gives shape to the world as it is experienced. The secondary imagination is 'an echo of' this primary creative power, but fainter, 'differing in degree', and it operates at the level of human consciousness.

With secondary imagination, an artist may intentionally create, impose, and discover ideas in the act of creating. Thus, while the secondary imagination is most relevant to the creation of beauty in art, it follows and is subordinate to the primary imagination endowing a more original perception of beauty in nature.

The ancient notion of divine inspiration is thus here joined with an account of imagination as a faculty of human cognition. While implying receptivity to a higher power (the primary imagination), the imagination (as secondary) is also rooted in the active human mind. Through imagination thought can go beyond direct perception, or the retrieval and combination of its sense impressions in fancy, and enable higher cognition. Taken together, the power of imagination enables the human mind both to perceive and understand the created universe and to create works that echo its divine arrangements.

Yet the importance of imagination goes far beyond its role in human creativity. In a letter of 16 October 1797, Coleridge credits imaginative elements of his childhood education with preparing him for understanding the vastness of the universe. He describes how his grasp of astronomy—and its sublime scale—was supported by fantastical literary tales.

> I remember, that at eight years old I walked with my father one winter evening from a farmer's house ... & he told me the names of the stars—and how Jupiter was a thousand times larger than our world—and that the other twinkling stars were Suns that had worlds rolling round them ... I heard him with a profound delight & admiration; but without the least mixture of wonder or incredulity. For from my early reading of Faery Tales, & Genii &c &c—my mind had been habituated *to the Vast*—& I never regarded *my senses* in any way as the criteria of my belief.

Here Coleridge credits his readiness for the cosmological expansion of his mind to literature. Even fantastical tales have their place as an antidote to strict empiricism, elevating the mind to entertain ideas beyond direct observation.

Without imagination, Coleridge suggests, our understanding would lack any cosmologically unifying principles. He argues that we would be able to 'contemplate nothing but *parts*' rather than the whole. Coleridge may have had in mind Giordano Bruno, a 16th-century monk who speculated about both the infinity of the universe and the coexistence of multiple worlds. Bruno's speculations anticipated the contemporary theory of the multiverse, positing that the observable universe is but one among many occupying other regions of space-time.

While rejecting narrowly empirical education, Coleridge also argues that strictly rationalist education would be insufficient. Strict rationality in the absence of imagination would lead to 'microscopic acuteness'. Such a mind would be unable to conceive of any cosmic order. Moreover, reason alone would not prepare the mind for the perception of beauty, of the sublime, or for any intuition of a higher meaning.

This view of the imagination as not merely reproductive but as an active power of the mind is echoed by William Wordsworth, for whom imagination endows our experience with transcendent meaning that exceeds direct perception. In *The Prelude* Wordsworth writes of imagination extending the eye beyond the path over the horizon as 'an invitation into space | Boundless, or guide into eternity'. For Wordsworth productive imagination allows us to go beyond the bounds of ordinary experience and access a higher reality.

Yet the imagination also opens the subject to disruption. For as Wordsworth's speaker suggests, nature may be glimpsed through imagination as 'a dim and undetermined sense | Of unknown modes of being'. Imagination may leave the subject feeling bereft. As he writes in the 1799 version of *The Prelude*:

...In my thoughts
There was a darkness—call it solitude,
Or blank desertion—no familiar shapes
Of hourly objects, images of trees,
Of sea or sky, no colours of green fields,
But huge and mighty forms that do not live
Like living men moved slowly through my mind
By day, and were the trouble of my dreams.

Despite the surrounding nature, with imagination the subject may be left in a state of isolation, of 'blank desertion'. While imagination affords an experience of nature as beautiful, it also induces thoughts of the uncanny.

The idea that the familiarity of nature can break down, and that our relation to it must be mediated by imagination, is proposed by the German poet Friedrich Hölderlin, an early Romantic who like Coleridge was profoundly influenced by Kant's aesthetic philosophy. In his two-stanza poem 'The Half of Life', for example, Hölderlin's speaker presents, in the first stanza, the warmth and glory of summer which seems to embrace the speaker, and in the second, lifeless winter which appears 'speechless and cold'. Similarly, the eponymous protagonist of Hölderlin's novel *Hyperion* (1797) oscillates between a feeling of belonging to nature and one of despairing loss, a cycle which finds no narrative resolution. Yet in a draft of a preface for the novel Hölderlin cited the experience of beauty as a potential restoration of our lost unity with nature. For a time in thrall to Kantian aesthetics, Hölderlin recognized the free play of imagination in the experience of beauty as the prospect of a restored vitality for the human subject.

As it did for Hölderlin, aesthetic theory electrified other German Romantics, who identified in imagination the key to achieving a grasp of the 'absolute'. While understood in different ways, the absolute may signify the infinite whole encompassing all of being or, more simply, intuitive and immediate access to nature as it is in itself. The absolute could never be known directly through rational means or fully expressed in conceptual thought. Yet Romantic thinkers held out the prospect that it may be glimpsed in poetic or aesthetical intuition, for which imagination would play a crucial role.

An important Romantic theorist, Friedrich Schlegel thought that imagination was requisite for grasping true reality. As he wrote in *Philosophical Fragments*: 'No poetry, no reality. Just as there is, despite all the senses, no external world without imagination.' Furthering Kant's idea that imagination may function in a state of free play, Schlegel argued for 'the creative philosophy that originates in freedom and belief in freedom, and shows how the human spirit impresses its law on all things and how the world is its work of art'. Like Coleridge, Schlegel argued that imagination, as 'man's faculty for perceiving divinity', was required for any religious sense.

Further Romantic elaborations of the productive imagination attribute to it new powers. For Novalis (the pen name of the German poet Georg Philipp Friedrich Freiherr von Hardenberg), the human imagination, rather than merely allowing us to escape the constraints of nature, offered access to its inner secrets. His novel *Heinrich von Ofterdingen* (1802) is a psychological reflection on the inner life of its protagonist and defends the importance of imagination and its visions. In an opening scene, Heinrich discusses with his parents a dream from which he has just awoken. Heinrich recounts seeing a blue flower which bore the face of his beloved. This recurring image of the blue flower would be widely recognized among Romantics as a symbol of longing and of the unification for which we ultimately long, becoming a symbol of Romanticism in works by E. T. A. Hoffmann, Walter Benjamin, and C. S. Lewis. While Heinrich's father dismisses Heinrich's dream, Heinrich argues that it may allow a glimpse of the inner self otherwise veiled to us. The blue flower can also be read as representing the power of the imagination itself. For the dream vision stimulates, along with intense yearning, explicit reflection on the place of imagination in human life and knowledge.

Novalis planned in his notebooks to create a Romantic encyclopaedia that would gather diverse human knowledge in a single text. Such a project would not only collect but synthesize science, philosophy, religion, poetics, and aesthetics. Imagination is central to Novalis's attempt to unify not only these diverse areas of human knowledge, but also the human self with nature. For imagination promised to unite what he considered the inner and outer sensibilities, or the inner life of the human mind with its perception of the world. Through imagination, the Romantics argued, our sense of the phenomenal and the transcendent, the natural and the divine, the scientific and the artistic will no longer be fragmented but will come together in the true intuition of life.

Tragedy and the primal imagination

A harsh critic of Romantic thinkers and writers, Nietzsche thought their incessant yearning for the absolute nursed an unhealthy dissatisfaction with the world of our ordinary experience. Yet Nietzsche affirmed the deep interest in the imagination expressed by the Romantics, and considered the topic in several works. In an early essay, 'On Truth and Lies in an Extra-Moral Sense', Nietzsche defended the human imagination as a primal grasp of nature and condemned its subordination to conceptual knowledge. In *The Birth of Tragedy* (1872), Nietzsche put forth a naturalized aesthetic theory, in which tragic art is the expression of nature's creative imagination.

Nietzsche speculated on the origins of tragic poetry among the ancient Greeks, identifying what he calls the Apollonian and Dionysian drives. These—perhaps like imagination itself—are conceived as tendencies of nature expressed through the art 'without the mediation of the human artist'. Nietzsche invokes

Apollo as the god of the sun and light, order, beauty, and knowledge, as one who personifies reason, moderation, and moral virtue. The Apollonian would see reality as defined by stable, eternal, forms, epitomized by the idealizations of ancient Greek sculpture. Since Apollo is also the god of dreams—or oracular prophecy and visions—Nietzsche argues that the Apollonian vision is an illusion that hides the suffering and chaos underlying nature.

In contrast, the ancient Greeks associated Dionysus with music, intoxication, and sensuality. Nietzsche recounts the legends of the followers of Dionysus who revelled, in their rituals to the god, in drunken erotic dances and sometimes violent sacrifice. As such the Dionysian impulse represents chaotic mingling and fusion of beings, irrationality, and the boundlessness of chaos and constant change within nature. While the Apollonian art instinct produces beautiful appearances, the Dionysian unveils a violent, chaotic vitality.

Both drives, Nietzsche claims, are necessary for art. As an artform that involves spectacle or visual illusion (actors in masks on the stage), and musical poetry (the chorus was sung), tragic drama emerges from the agonistic tension between them. In a tragic age, and in great tragedies, the Dionysian impulse is fully manifest. In Nietzsche's account, the death of tragedy—and the suppression of the Dionysian insight—results from the advance of rationalist philosophy in ancient Greek society. Just as the tragic poets would be silenced by the Socrates of Plato's *Republic*, the play of imagination is suppressed by the oppressive domination of reason.

Nietzsche's essay 'On Truth and Lies in a Nonmoral Sense' (1873) challenges Plato's association of imagination with illusions and lies. The essay offers an account of the emergence of language and of the abstract structures of conceptual thought which in his view suppresses the more primal intuitions of imagination. In the essay Nietzsche argues that the repeated association of words and objects, and the generalizations necessary to construct concepts, diminish originally vivid and diverse perceptions that feed imaginative thought. In the emergence of conceptual ideas, the more original, imaginative experience of reality is diminished. Turning Plato's theory on its head, Nietzsche argues that rational thought constructs a false representation of reality at the expense of a more original, and more imaginative, experience.

The vital diversity within experience falls away when we communicate about it in words, in Nietzsche's view, just as the imprint from an ancient coin rubs off with repeated use. The word and concept for 'leaf', for example, necessarily abstract from the experiential diversity of leaves as experienced in nature. The necessary generalizations of the linguistic process lead us to think of the abstract idea of things as their essential truth, and their diverse manifestations are disregarded. While such a process of representation is necessary for higher cognition, the generalization involved, Nietzsche argues, eliminates the individuality and diversity of pre-conceptual experience.

Nietzsche may not have intended his essay to propose a serious theory of linguistic cognition, but rather concern that our evolved cognitive habits suppress the 'primal faculty of human imagination'. Some uses of language—such as poetry or lyrical music—will recover and promote imaginative thought. In referring to a 'stammering language' that might preserve our imaginative vivacity, Nietzsche seems to hold out the possibility that novel and creative uses of language may break with ordinary modes of conceptualization. Such would be the contribution of the artist or poet in restoring a more primal relation to the experienced world. This would involve what Nietzsche described as 'the return of language to the nature of imagery', recovering imagination in its interconnections with earthly life.

Modern thought might also become more imaginative, Nietzsche argued, by taking cues from philosophers who came before Plato.

In *Philosophy in the Tragic Age of the Greeks* Nietzsche described pre-Socratic philosophical thought as the expression of profound creative thinking. Ancient philosophers such as Thales identified primal elements, such as water, as the originating principles of all of being. Nietzsche describes the procedures of such thinking as 'propelled by an alien, illogical power—the power of creative imagination' as it leaps from possibility to possibility. In such thinking:

> Creative premonition will show the place; imagination guesses from afar that here it will find a demonstrable resting place. But the special strength of imagination is its lightning-quick seizure and illumination of analogies.

Here Nietzsche describes imaginative thinking as an intuitive prospecting for possibilities, through which process the mind may recognize and illuminate analogies, nurturing the eruption of new thoughts. In this analysis of cognition and in his tragic aesthetics, Nietzsche counts imagination as a vital human power and anticipates contemporary theories of creative cognition discussed in more detail in the final chapter of this book.

Imagination is involved in constituting our very experience of the world. It nurtures aesthetic experiences such as of beauty and the sublime. Yet we may also deliberately engage this capacity, in its free spontaneous play, to transform what is directly given in our experience. Productive imagination makes human creativity, and therefore human culture, possible.

Kant's acknowledgement of the productive imagination operating both in the constitution of experience and its aesthetic amplification provoked a radical affirmation of imagination by Romantic thinkers and writers. Imagination came to be understood as allowing the human mind to grasp what transcends direct experience, and to reconcile the mind with nature. Coleridge's attempt to understand imagination as both receptive and directed by our consciousness initiated a theory of creativity that will be influential in the following centuries. The Romantic view of imagination as unifying the inner life of the subject with the world is echoed, if radically transformed, in Nietzsche's affirmation of art and his call to an imaginative faculty more primal and vital than our conceptual representations of things.

In the next chapter we will explore the fascinating implications of the 'productive turn' as explored in 20th-century theories of imagination.

Chapter 5
The augmentation of reality

While imagination may contribute to the formation of experience, it also augments reality by endowing it with distinctly human meaning. The productive imagination celebrated by aesthetic philosophies of the 19th century and discussed in the previous chapter came to be explored in important philosophical movements in the 20th. In this chapter we will discuss how perception is inflected with and transformed by imagination through 'seeing-as', or interpretive perception. We will consider that imagination, though free from the constraints of reality, may also possibilize the real, or endow our sense of reality with possibility. We will turn to the means, including metaphor, narrative, political ideals, and scientific models, through which imagination is thought to generate new fictional meanings as well as new frameworks for understanding reality itself.

While hardly a divine creative power, seeing-as, first described by Wittgenstein, makes possible a human perspective on the world, and fosters imaginative expression. An important development in philosophy of imagination is its study by phenomenology, which attends to the structure of appearances to consciousness. While Sartre generally demarcated imagination strictly from perception—regarding perception as entirely separate from acts of imagination in the mind—he also acknowledged concrete imagining through which reality is imaginatively perceived and recognized in its latent possibilities. In Merleau-Ponty's studies of modern painting, this latency is regarded as an imaginative correlate of our embodied experience of the world. That is, through our experience of being an embodied subject moving in time and space among other things, we build up a repertoire of orientations and expectations which while not always fully given in direct perception are filled in and supplemented by imagination. Ricoeur shifted the philosophy of imagination from its focus on quasi-perceptual imaging to linguistic imagination, thus expanding the notion of productive imagination to account for the human ability to create new meaning. These 20th-century theories acknowledge the wide-ranging significance of imagination for the augmentation of reality in human perception, including the human encounter with a world perceived as meaningful.

Seeing-as and aspect perception

In his *Philosophical Investigations* (1953), Wittgenstein described the ability to view something in one of multiple ways as seeing-as, or 'noticing an aspect', sometimes referred to as aspect perception. In this experience perception involves imagination as a presentational power (the word Wittgenstein often uses for imagination is *Vorstellung*). Wittgenstein's recognition of the involvement of imagination in perception owes much to the idea that the imagination may work productively. 'Seeing-as' expresses both the productivity and the spontaneity of the human mind and allows us to view the world around us as latent with significance. Unlike reproductive imagination, which only presents an object that was once experienced but is now absent to perception, seeing-as interprets or embellishes the perceptual presence of an object while and as it is seen.

In order to explain seeing-as, Wittgenstein states that we have to describe 'seeing' in two different ways. There is straightforward perceptual seeing, or taking in visual data, and a further kind of perceptual recognition through resemblance. He writes:

> Two uses of the word 'see'.
>
> The one: 'What do you see there?'—I see *this*' (and then a description, a drawing, a copy). The other: 'I see a likeness in these two faces'...What is important is the categorical difference between the two 'objects' of sight. I observe a face, and then suddenly notice its likeness to another. I see that it has not changed; and yet I see it differently. I call this experience 'noticing an aspect.'

The first kind of seeing is something like primary perception. The second kind of seeing, aspect perception or seeing-as, visually registers the same object in light of its resemblance to or association with another.

In the *Investigations*, Wittgenstein offers his now-famous example of an ambiguous puzzle picture: lines on a page make out the figure of a rabbit, or alternatively that of a duck (Figure 4). Without any other changes in the perceptual object or the conditions of its viewing, the viewer notices a shift in the aspect. The same lines on the page appear in one moment as the rabbit, in another as the duck, and the imaginative embellishment of perception, or its interpretive nature, becomes evident. The English philosopher P. F. Strawson pointed out that this change in aspect 'merely dramatizes for us a feature (namely seeing as) which is present in perception in general'. The implications of this capacity are profound, particularly when we consider the range of its manifestations.

Wittgenstein identified a variety of related phenomena as seeing-as. We see a human shape where there were previously branches. We see a horse in an unmoving picture as galloping. We see a triangle 'as a mountain, as a wedge, as an arrow or pointer'. In seeing-as, one thing is not only taken for something else.

4. Ludwig Wittgenstein's 'Duck-Rabbit' in *Philosophical Investigations*.

In pretence, children designate and treat the log *as if* it were a pirate ship. Yet in seeing-as, one thing is *seen as* something other through a particular quality. One thing is perceived in light of another.

In Chapter 2 the phenomenon of seeing star clusters as constellations was discussed. This involves a dual experience of perception and figuration: a group of stars may be seen both as points of light in the sky and, for example, as the hunter Orion. In such seeing-as, the visual perception is augmented by the simultaneous eliciting of a figurative potential. I can see stars straightforwardly as points of light among others, and also recognize them as making out the likeness, figure, image of another object. The perceptual object is not itself changed in the shift from bare seeing to seeing-as, but the experienced perception is altered. Since seeing-as is enabled by imagination, we might describe it as imaginatively endowed perception.

Yet seeing-as also accounts for our ability, further, to understand representations or make out visual reference. Looking at a sketch, we can 'see' the object it makes out—a human figure, for example—rather than first and foremost the lines and physical markings which construct the representation. Wittgenstein describes this phenomenon such that 'we regard the photograph, the picture on our wall, as the object itself (the man, landscape, and so on) depicted there'. Such perceptual interpretation generates a surplus beyond mere sense-perception in the form of an identification with or recognition of what is not strictly empirically given. Wittgenstein clarifies that such cases are not merely a matter of referential knowledge, but of a form of perception. The vehicle for meaning (the branches as human figure or the picture as the landscape) is experienced perceptually *as* that which it conveys. The phenomenological philosopher Husserl called this 'picture-consciousness', and it was analysed, alongside other forms of imaginative experience, in Sartre's study *The Imaginary*.

Seeing-as allows that, beyond grasping physical facts before us, we can view things as endowed with significance or meaning. We grasp not literal connections between things, but rather what Wittgenstein called their 'internal relations', such that our perception of the facts is transformed in a lived experience. These experiences of interpretive seeing are widespread across human perception, and are necessary for the perception of art and symbolic thinking, and can also lead to creative expression. Yet seeing-as remains in tension with the freedom from reality imagination is thought to endow.

Phenomenology of mental imaging

If imagination can amplify or augment the perception of reality, it also works in sharp distinction from the real. In his major work of existentialist philosophy *Being and Nothingness* (1943), Sartre proposed that human consciousness is free because it is fundamentally distinct from the material world and can, in a sense, 'negate' it or its power over the mind. While everything else in reality has 'being', Sartre argues, consciousness is, rather, 'nothing', though it 'exists' as aware of itself and of whatever it is conscious of at any given moment. Imagination enables consciousness to distance itself from, and present alternatives to, reality. According to Sartre's philosophy, while physically I may be confined to a particular place and condition, in my mind I am free. This freedom reflects the fact that I can imagine the world differently from its actual existence and can imagine, too, elsewhere and otherwise than I directly experience.

This existential viewpoint also inflects Sartre's study *The Imaginary* (1940), which engages the practice of phenomenology, the first-person form of description mentioned in the first chapter of this book. Phenomenology allowed Sartre to defeat what he regarded as a crucial mistake in traditional accounts of imagination, namely the 'illusion of immanence', or the treatment of the mental image as if it were a thing or object in the mind. Sartre argues that the image is not an object, but a *way* of intending something not directly present to consciousness.

When we imagine something that is not present, this non-presence can take a number of forms. We can imagine something as elsewhere (to use Sartre's example, my friend Pierre in Berlin). We can imagine something as non-existent (e.g. a unicorn). We can imagine something as simply absent (a lion, wherever one may be). We can also imagine something without positing its existence or whereabouts at all (imagining something irrespective of its ontological or locational status). In terms of Sartre's own existentialism, imagination is at once constituting and negating, since it presents its object, but as a 'nothingness'. Images do not take up space in reality as do objects of perception, but inhabit what Sartre describes as an irreality—a phenomenal, experiential mode of presence to consciousness independent of reality itself. Because imagination allows us to consider any object as 'irreal', or in the mode of an image, it frees consciousness from the determinations of reality.

While rejecting the idea that the image is a thing in the mind, Sartre offers a phenomenological account of the process of inner visual imagining. The image is a way of being conscious of something, in a certain mode. When I am imagining something, he points out, the image is given or presented all at once, and therefore is not easily manipulatable: we cannot divide an image, seamlessly connect it with another, or render an already static image mobile. When imagining the Pantheon, I cannot easily count its columns, while perceiving the Pantheon I can accumulate detailed knowledge by inspecting it more closely, turning this way or that to accumulate a view of the whole. If I have an image of Pierre's head, I cannot add a top hat to it without its being merely pasted on—I can't invoke the 'look' Pierre would have wearing a top hat unless I replaced one image with another. I cannot make an imagined standing figure walk towards me except in a jerky, awkward way. Images are incomplete and ephemeral, and in this way, they are distinct from perceptions. When I supply further detail or transform an image, I have to in fact supply a new image to take its place. Contemporary theorists have taken up Sartre's interest in the manipulation of mental imagery in their defence of the relevance of mental imagery for studies of imagination. In *Image and Mind* (1980), Kosslyn pointed to such manipulation as support for the relevance of the mental image, which he continued to defend in later empirical studies, and it has served as the basis for Casey's phenomenological elaboration *Imagining* (2000).

While Sartre's description of inner envisioning is based largely on his own reflective experience, the human mind's imaging capacity is known to be variable. This variation was first proposed in 1880 by Francis Galton, who had conducted an informal survey of people asked to consider the nature of their experiences of imagining. Galton's study was recognized by William James in *Principles of Psychology* (1890), who appreciated that while some people have a remarkable facility to inwardly envision, others have poorer facilities. Failing to appreciate this difference, James argued, may lead to a 'false' view of imagination.

It is worth pausing here to consider this variation. There are, at one end of the spectrum, individuals who have extraordinary facilities of inner envisioning—what psychologists now call *hyperphantasia*, an exceptional capacity for complex visual detail. For example, the Serbian-American Nikola Tesla, inventor of the induction motor, invented in his mind before taking pen to paper. Tesla could mentally envision an invention down to the last measurements and all its moving parts, a process which enabled him to become extraordinarily prolific, with around 300 patents to his name. We can also point to novelist Vladimir Nabokov, who in his *Lectures on Russian Literature* (1981) advised his students to envision literary scenes in precise detail. When reading *Anna Karenina*, we ought to be able to see in which corner of the train carriage Anna is sitting, which direction she is facing, and what she can view from her seat—for which task Nabokov provided a diagram. On Kafka's *Metamorphosis* Nabokov supplied a drawing of the insect-like Gregor Samsa, despite the text itself leaving many details (such as how many legs Gregor has) indeterminate (Figure 5). For Nabokov it is the writer's 'vision' which the reader must enliven. At the other end of the spectrum, people with a condition called *aphantasia* cannot invoke visual images at all. James himself admitted to poor facility in visualization. Even highly literary minds may not engage inner envisioning. In *Fiction and the Figures of Life* (1970), William Gass, himself a novelist who had briefly studied with Wittgenstein, argued that fiction was not made from descriptions, but rather ideas.

In addition to wholly envisioned images, Sartre's phenomenology also takes up several different kinds of referential images—an 'image family'—of a photograph of a person, a portrait of a person, a schematic sketch of a person. While Wittgenstein included such images as instances of seeing-as, Sartre argues that in such cases we *perceive* the physical object—the photograph, the canvas and

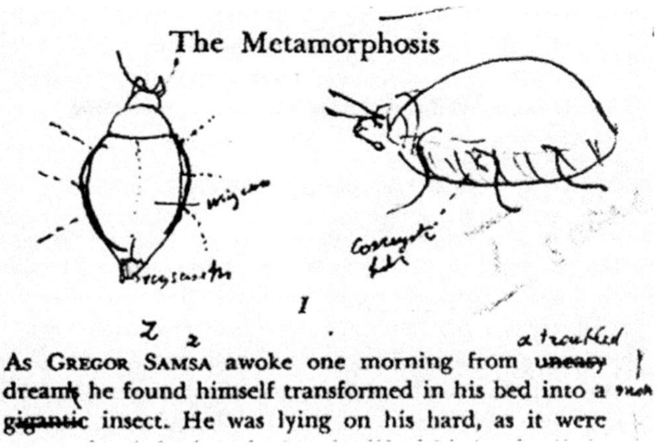

5. Vladimir Nabokov's sketch of Gregor Samsa from Kafka's *The Metamorphosis*.

paint, or the lines on a page—but we *imagine* the object it refers to. What we imagine is not the actual figure in the photograph (Pierre in the exact second it was taken) but the person it evokes. Sartre claims that a physical object serves as an 'analogon' for imagining. There is an implicit reliance here on the notion of resemblance, and thus on reproductive imagination—the photograph can serve as analogon for imagining since it resembles the person so imagined.

Sartre concedes that when, without a physical prompt such as a photograph or sketch, I simply imagine a person not present, the mind must have an 'analogon' too, but Sartre admits it is difficult to pin down what that may be. He suggests the motion of consciousness paying attention to the image, or the kinaesthetic sensations involved in the constitution of the image, and the affectivity wound up with it. Neuroscience has demonstrated that our visual imaging occurs in the same neuronal regions as does vision itself. Sartre's theory of the analogon may be difficult to square entirely with his thesis of the image as nothingness, if the analogon ends up positing something like a virtual schema in the mind produced by neurons. In other words, the image may not be strictly speaking 'nothing' but have a physical neurological correlate produced through imaginative acts of the mind.

Revealing and 'possibilizing' reality

Sartre's theory, like that of Wittgenstein, does allow for a kind of interpretive perception. When we see, for example, a spot on the tablecloth as a particular figure, faces in the fire, or rocks seeming to make out a human form, Sartre posits that we pass into an imaginative attitude. I can perceive it as a spot and that is all, or I can 'pretend to "see" the image', or survey it in a certain way. While Sartre relies on pretence to maintain his distinction between imagining and perceiving, it may be that, when seeing lines on a page which are representative (as in an illustration or schematic drawing), this potentiality is incorporated in interpretive perception of the lines themselves.

This would be supported by Sartre's recognition of imagination's involvement in 'revealing' how the world appears to us. In this Sartre owed something to the work of the German philosopher Martin Heidegger, who in his work *Being and Time* had argued that the human being is involved in 'revealing' the world. Heidegger termed the human being 'Dasein', which means 'being-there' or 'being-here', in the sense of existing, thus emphasizing how concern for our own being defines us. The activities of imagination for Heidegger would be enactive, since we as Dasein reveal the world not because we put a picture of the world together in the mind, but because we interact with it according to our projects and concerns, in light of our attunements to it and of our own relation to possibilities.

On this view, the experienced world is not merely a totality synthesized by the mind, or a collection of material stuff, but a rich and vital realm of potentiality. Experiencing the world as latent with possibilities requires our being able to transcend or go beyond what is merely there and reveal it *as* something or in certain ways. Sartre takes up Heidegger's idea that we 'reveal' reality in these ways, but while Heidegger emphasizes practical concerns, for Sartre such revealing is explicitly imaginative. For Sartre it is through imagination that we lend our emotional and aesthetic values to what we see.

The idea that imagination reveals reality from a living point of view is also explored in the work of Merleau-Ponty, who emphasized embodied interaction as the basis from which we relate to and reveal possibilities. Through our embodied, interactive engagement of things, we relate to the prospects for action and perception we can undertake with them, a relationality which unfolds in time. In 'Eye and Mind' and other essays devoted to aesthetics, Merleau-Ponty interpreted the painting of Paul Cézanne as emblematic of embodied seeing. In Cézanne's paintings objects are rendered in modulations of colour and in trembling, overlapping outlines, and their distortions, more than any photographic likeness, capture the sense of living perception (Figure 6). Such painting, according to Merleau-Ponty, shows the world not merely as a set of brute facts, but as inviting our interaction through the potentialities we register. The potentiality that surrounds things is (Merleau-Ponty claims in his work *The Visible and the Invisible*) like a halo around the visible, 'a presence of the immanent, the latent, or the hidden' in the world before us that makes it rich with implicit meaning.

Sartre also wrote extensively about works of art and literature, and sometimes in this context associated imagination with what he called the 'possibilization' of reality. Since the function of imagination is to render whatever is to be imagined 'irreal', what is imagined can be varied in the mind towards other possible configurations. While Sartre emphasized the difference between the imagined and the perceived, he also thought that our sense of the world was enriched by this difference. We can augment our

6. Paul Cézanne, *Still Life with Apples* (1890), The Hermitage, St Petersburg.

understanding of the world as it is with possibilities afforded through imagination, and generate prospective alternatives.

While philosophers had recognized that our involvement with the world is necessary for our coherent or meaningful experience of it, Sartre adds that such involvement is also necessary for the experience of irreality, which he also termed the 'imaginary'. In order to recognize an image or imagined object as 'irreal'—or ontologically distinct from reality—the world that it surpasses must too be posited. We must be able to imagine the bounds of reality in order to be able to surpass them imaginatively. Sartre argues that:

> For consciousness to be able to imagine, it must be able to escape from the world by its very nature, it must be able to stand back from the world by its own efforts. In a word, it must be free.

Standing back from the world is likened by Sartre to taking an artistic perspective. Sartre compares this to the distance an impressionist painter would take from the canvas in order to 'bring out the whole "forest" or "white water lilies" from the multitude of little strokes they have placed on the canvas'. Even recognizing reality as reality implies an irreality from which it can be distinguished. Thus our very sense of reality as real 'implies a hidden reaching beyond towards the imaginary'.

Despite his segregation of imagination and reality, Sartre recognized that imagination can also offer to perception means to its aesthetic or other symbolic realization, a revealing of reality that at once augments it. Aesthetic, affective, or symbolic meaning may not change the bare perceptual features of the reality perceived, but inflects their interpretation, how they are experienced. A mountain may appear beautiful or sublime as well as lonely or majestic, a sunset can appear glorious. In her study of Sartre, the British philosopher Mary Warnock identified examples of such 'concrete' imagining in Sartre's own descriptions of experience. When the protagonist of Sartre's novel *Nausea* looks at the gnarled dark root of the tree and sees it as existence laid bare, he is concretely imagining, for in such moments the perception itself is laden with existential value. In *Being and Nothingness* Sartre also describes moments of perception where reality is revealed in light of values informed by a given project. For a subject intending to climb the mountain, the 'brute given' of its difficult slope is 'revealed as scalable or unscalable'. To the artist, in contrast, that valuation of scalability is irrelevant, and the mountain instead 'is manifested as beautiful or ugly'. In both cases of concrete imagining, a surplus of meaning, whether of practical or aesthetic value, is provided by imagination. Sartre seems to admit that this imaginative revealing of reality is a latent possibility across the whole life of perception. The amplification of experience by imagination is poignantly suggested at the end of *The Imaginary*. Sartre writes:

Imagination is not an empirical power added to the mind, it is the mind itself in so far as it is free; *every concrete situation of the mind in the world is pregnant with the imaginary*, in that it is always present as a way of going beyond the real.

Metaphor and the generation of meaning

In order to fully appreciate the productive imagination, we must consider not only the envisioned mental image and the experiences of concrete imagining, but the imaginative work of language. Ricoeur's major writings, including *The Rule of Metaphor* (1975) and *Time and Narrative* (1983–5), along with unpublished lectures on imagination, present metaphor and narrative structure as manifesting productive imagination. These are thought to create new meanings and (virtual) worlds that go beyond and transcend reality.

A tragic drama, for example, presents a situation of life and action through narrative structure. This structure is informed, as Aristotle argued of tragedy, by knowledge not of events already occurred but of what could happen. Ricoeur brings Aristotle's insight further to argue that a literary work presents a new world, one which may provoke viewers or readers to consider anew their ordinary world. In contrast to classical treatments of literature, Ricoeur argues that this presentation exceeds mimesis or representation. Fictions are not the result wholly of reproductive imagination, but produce experiential worlds and ideas that did not exist before.

Ricoeur argues that while some imaginings may be described in reproductive terms, fictional objects cannot be wholly understood by reference to an original. There is no real Hamlet of which Shakespeare's character is a copy—no matter that several aspects of the character may be derived from what Shakespeare previously experienced or knew. The fictional Hamlet is a dual reference both to the real world of familiar things—princes, sons—and to a fictional world which supersedes that reality, since we are not to take Hamlet as a real person but as a character. Ricoeur describes the creative effect of imagination as 'productive reference', highlighting the original ontological status of creative imaginings.

In order to promote the productive imagination against a merely reproductive view, Ricoeur reorients the philosophical understanding of fiction in two ways. Firstly, Ricoeur turns to the image conjured in language rather than that evoking perception. Plato, we recall, compares the images conjured by the poet to what he regards as the visual copies of things made by the painter; the painter and poet both 'copy' what they perceive. Ricoeur aims to demonstrate the insufficiency of conceiving the imagination as making a copy from perception. Such theories regard physically or linguistically created images, as well as those of inner fantasizing, as resemblances of the thing represented. For example, in Hume's view, images derive from and are copies of perceptions, or, in Sartre's view, they resemble absent objects of perception. Either way, Ricoeur thinks, images are treated as derivative. Yet according to Ricoeur, the image is not only a faded perception or resemblance but an emerging, original meaning.

Ricoeur, secondly, shifts the discussion from describing the isolated image to the elaboration across images of imaginative experience. This happens, for example, in metaphor, when two or more things are compared. Such elaboration also occurs in the narrative shaping of fictional works that produces a world or nexus of interrelated meanings through imaginatively unfolding action. Both according to Ricoeur involve the creation of new meaning.

According to Ricoeur, metaphor enables semantic innovation. In metaphor one thing is not merely named as another, but is given predicates or qualities normally reserved for something different. With 'all the world's a stage', Shakespeare compared life to a dramatic performance. The American poet Robert Frost compared life to making one's way in the woods. In his poem 'Birches', for example, Frost's speaker complains of a moment when 'life is too much like a pathless wood' and dreams of leaving it just for a while to begin anew. In 'The Road Less Travelled' Frost's speaker tells of taking the less-worn of two paths 'and that has made all the difference'. In such examples, metaphor synthesizes two different meanings and yet maintains the old pertinence along with the new. Life is not strictly speaking a stage or a path through the woods, but again the resonances within these couplings make us think of life in new ways. In metaphoric coupling likeness is perceived across the unlikeness, and a new spark of meaning originates. Rather than merely a tarnished and faded percept of reality, the metaphoric image, Ricoeur suggests, emerges as a nascent signification.

While drawing on Aristotle and Kant in his elaboration of the productive imagination, Ricoeur also finds inspiration in the French philosopher Gaston Bachelard's phenomenological study of poetic imagery, *The Poetics of Space*. In this work, Bachelard treats poetic images as generators of meaning that draw from early embodied experiences of life. Bachelard's study focuses on spatial images, for example spaces of shelter, or open expanses of exploration. The image of a path through woods from Frost's poem would resonate with early experiences of making one's way home from the wide world. Such images do not merely mimic or represent spaces in the world, but also resonate with the reader's embodied memory. Adapting a term to his phenomenology of poetic imagery, Bachelard argues that such images 'reverberate' in the imagination, as evoked memory and new meaning are together awakened in the reader's mind.

Beyond metaphor, language also generates new meaning through narrative. In reading literary fiction, images are formed through the metaphoric evocation and display of relations. As readers of a novel, we are provoked to evoke an experiential world. As we do so, dormant memories may be awakened, similar experiences reanimated, but imagination radiates further and gives shape to a new experience in a free play of possibilities mediated by language. In contrast to Nabokov's descriptions of literary reading, literary imagining for Ricoeur is not strictly speaking a form of seeing something in the mind, but rather of apprehending a meaning alluded to in a play of related images through which emerges a fictional world.

The idea that the productive imagination augments our sense of reality can be illustrated with reference to artistic expression. Whether in writing or painting, imagination does not only represent elements of reality but performs what Ricoeur calls an 'iconic augmentation' of them. An artistic presentation can transform what it presents, for example through abridging and condensing its subject matter, and through this a surplus meaning arises. A landscape—for example, Vincent van Gogh's *Starry Night*—frames a particular point of view, and intensifies through colour, line, brushstroke, and composition the relations among the elements presented there. Such framing and intensification may occur in a poem through the play of verbal imagery. What is thereby imagined in each case is more than what is merely there.

Such surplus meaning also illuminates the ordinary world in a new way. Wallace Stevens described in similar terms the creative augmentation of our sense of things. He described a poem as:

> a particular of life thought of for so long that one's thought has become an inseparable part of it or a particular of life so intensely felt that the feeling has entered into it.

This kind of mental poetry can and does become the stuff of life experience. When we see or even merely think of a blue sky, for example, it is not merely visual or quasi-visual data but evokes a sense of the warmth of sunshine, an absence of troubling storms, new chances, limitless prospects, or even happiness. In this way the geography of the world is informed by the 'non-geography' of our imagination. Stevens expands:

> when, by way of illustration, we cite, say, the blue sky, we can be sure that the feeling has become a part of our vital experience of life, even though we are not aware of it.

Related to Wittgenstein's sense of seeing-as and to Sartre's notion of concrete imaging, this effect of productive imagination is an augmentation of our sense of things, of the reality we live. It is an expansion of our being-in-the-world, as existentialist philosophers refer to the lived world with which we meaningfully interact and through which our existence is elaborated.

Imagination is productive not only in literature and art but in many domains of human thought and life. Ricoeur describes political utopias, for example, as productive fictions, since they project ideal states which do not yet exist. Benedict Anderson argued in *Imagined Communities* (1983) that nationalistic sensibilities are constructed imaginatively across a society as individuals imagine themselves as a part of a distinct social group. Such constructions can be dangerous if unrestrained. For as the German-Jewish philosopher Hannah Arendt argued in *The Origins of Totalitarianism* (1951), the subject of totalitarianism has lost the distinctions between fiction and fact, truth and falsity. At the same time moral freedom, she noted, also requires imagination—by creating reflective distance from immediate experience, such that we can consider potential actions.

The imagination's use in the attainment of scientific knowledge also bears some comparison with its generation of meaning in other contexts. Through the generation of theoretical models, Ricoeur argues, scientists jettison old descriptions of reality in order to redescribe it with heuristic metaphor. Some examples of such scientific modelling include Thomas Young's representation of light as waves rather than particles, or James Clerk Maxwell's understanding of an electrical field in terms of fluidity. While such models aim to capture the nature of reality, they are ways of redescribing it. According to François Jacob, such models are in some ways comparable to innovative artworks. He argues that it is by undoing a perceived reality 'in order to remake it differently that the painter, the poet, or the scientist builds up a vision of the universe'.

The elaboration of the productive imagination transformed the philosophy of imagination and preoccupied philosophers throughout the 20th century. From Wittgenstein's study of seeing-as we can recognize imagination at work in symbolic and interpretive perception and expression. While describing the negating power of imagining in distinction from reality, Sartre nevertheless recognized its productive contribution to experience, and highlighted the freedom of imagination to reveal reality. Just as Sartre describes imagination's possibilization of the real, Ricoeur described its augmentation through metaphor. Merleau-Ponty's studies of painting and Bachelard's of poetic imagery both engage phenomenology to illuminate how imagination augments our reception of reality. Whether in service to knowledge, rendering landscapes, or generating fictional worlds, amplifications of productive imagination are found across many modes of human thought and action. The productive imagination and its role in human thinking will be central to understanding creativity, on which we will focus in the next chapter.

Chapter 6
Creativity from invention to wonder

Nowhere is productive imagination more visible than in creativity, where multiple modes of imagination may be put to work to generate novel, meaningful, and useful ideas. Through creativity we integrate imagination with the world around us, taking up material objects, sounds, language, or existing ideas to forge something new. Though the skills of ordinary thinking may be involved, creativity does not follow its habitual grooves, but leaps unpredictably. Creativity is essential (not only in the arts but also in science) for solving problems and enhancing our everyday lives.

While philosophers have long considered creativity as part of aesthetics, in recent decades it has been studied as a more fundamental aspect of cognition. At the same time, interest in creativity has exploded in the human sciences. Yet neither philosophers nor scientists have fully explained creativity, which eludes logical or mechanistic explanation and may be difficult to fully replicate in a laboratory. To better understand creativity, it may help to consider its flourishing in the context of our being-in-the-world, the way in which we engage with our surrounding world by transforming it, and in light of the interconnections between reality and possibility.

In this chapter we will take a closer look at creativity as a means of negotiating reality through imagination, finding insight in sources from ancient philosophy to contemporary cognitive theory. We will consider creativity's relation to imagination: its striving to overcome limitations and invest reality with possibilities. We will address inspiration and the role of cognitive play in creative thinking, and consider the roles of 'negative capability'—or the ability to proceed in uncertainty—curiosity, and wonder in nurturing creative life.

From flights of fancy to creative invention

Creativity has long been associated with metaphors of flight and ascension, and with this we can consider creativity's relation to the human imagination. In his poem 'I Wandered Lonely as a Cloud' (1807) Wordsworth described his poetic imagination as viewing the world from above, able to take in a few of 10,000 daffodils in a 'never ending line' along a bay. The Irish poet William Butler Yeats referred to 'the balloon of the mind'. If imagination soars in flights of fancy, with creativity we may strive to make that real.

An ancient Greek myth recounted in Ovid's *Metamorphoses* (8 CE) illustrates this striving. Ovid tells of the master craftsman Daedalus imprisoned with his son Icarus in a labyrinth of his own design by the king of Crete. As their means of escape Daedalus created pairs of wings from wax and feathers. Ovid's account refers to onlookers—a ploughman, an angler, and a shepherd—who 'stood there amazed, believing them to be gods able to travel the sky'. Yet Icarus ignored his father's advice not to fly too close to the sun, fell into the sea, and drowned as the wax melted and the water weighed down his wings. The myth warns against hubris. But it also illustrates the human creative drive to surpass limitations, to transform reality or our perspective on it.

Icarus' fate was depicted with tragic if playful irony by the Dutch painter Pieter Brueghel (the Elder). His *Landscape with the Fall of Icarus* (*c.*1560) shows a glorious seascape with ships floating peacefully, with the ploughman and angler going about their

7. Pieter Brueghel the Elder, *Landscape with the Fall of Icarus* (*c.*1560), Royal Museums of Fine Arts of Belgium, Brussels.

work, the shepherd staring up at the sky, no one taking any notice of a pair of legs splashing in the water (Figure 7). Only Brueghel's viewers notice Icarus, for to make sense of the painting's title, they must fill in the narrative, create their own image of the fateful plunge. They are invited to imagine Icarus and his view on the world from above, the irresistible if ultimately fatal thrill of his ascension. Brueghel's painting about the perils of ambitious creativity speaks back to and stimulates the viewer's own imagination.

Just around the time Brueghel made his Icarus painting, the explorer Pedro Ceza de León published his *Chronicle of Peru* (1553), noting on the coastal plains peculiar trail markings that were later taken to be the remains of ancient roads. We now know them as the Nazca lines or geoglyphs, monumental works carved between 200 BCE and 500 CE. The lines make out hundreds of massive figures, including a hummingbird, monkey, lizard, spider, whale, llama, and tree, a pelican spanning 285 feet, and geometric designs as large as 1,200 feet. These were first seen from above in

8. The spider, one of the geoglyphs made in the Nazca Desert in Southern Peru between 200 BCE and 500 CE by the Nazca people.

1927 when rediscovered by Peruvian pilots. What is most striking about them is that their giant figures can be viewed fully only from the sky (Figure 8).

The Nazca geoglyphs may have served a practical purpose, such as outlining walking routes for the collection of water or constructing work areas for making rope or nets. The works may have been meant as religious communication to the gods of their creators. The works materially manifest creative imagining, for without airborne vessels to view them from above, the creators of these works would have had to imagine an aerial perspective of the figures the lines would make out. The Nazca figurations would have had to be mentally projected as they were worked onto the earth, illustrating creativity as a dynamic exchange between human consciousness and the physical world.

Early in the sixteenth century Leonardo da Vinci composed his notebooks, consisting of many thousands of pages of drawings that record among other things ideas for inventions and plans to make them into reality. With apparently tireless fascination, Leonardo studied, among many other things, the flight of birds, bats, and insects, alongside human anatomy, and combined his findings in designs for flying machines, such as the ornithopter and helicopter. While among these only his parachute and hang-glider designs have been built successfully, Leonardo's ideas were centuries ahead of his time, and are now seen to anticipate contemporary biomimetic design. They instigate what would become the history of human flight, advanced by the Montgolfier brothers' hot-air balloon transport (1783), the Wright Brothers' first human-occupied powered flight (1903), and travel to the moon in Apollo 11 by Neil Armstrong and Buzz Aldrin (1969).

While these inventions may all align with pragmatic aims, creativity may be wholly free of practical purpose, pursued solely for its own exercise. In 1974 Philippe Petit famously walked unaided between the towers of the World Trade Center on a tightrope 1,350 feet (411 metres) above the ground. The high-wire performance artist described feeling overpowered by the sky, venturing into a voluptuous unknown. With this singular event, the subject of many films and books, Petit accomplished what had theretofore seemed impossible and inspired a proliferation of creative reflections. His performance reflects our human drive to explore possibilities for their own sake and to integrate them into reality.

These examples may all illustrate an ancient human dream. The desire to transcend limitations, to rise above the world, and view it as we imagine a god might see it may have been first stirred for early humans recording the positions of stars on a cave wall. These feats also demonstrate creativity as facilitating a shift in our human perspective, enabling what Sartre called the 'possibilization' of the world we experience. It may be said that in each act of creation, a new and meaningful idea is generated by combining previous ideas—wax and feathers, figurative shapes and monumental geography, birds' flight and human anatomy, a walking human and the height of skyscrapers. Yet well beyond mere combination, these creative works integrate possibility into a lived human experience, to transform a given state of reality and expand our sense of what is possible.

Inspiration and genius

How is such creativity inspired? Creative inspiration has long puzzled the artists, scientists, and inventors who depend on it and the philosophers who have attempted to explain it. For several thousand years inspiration was attributed to mystical sources received by the creative subject. Ancient Hindu texts include prayers for inspiration to Saraswati, the goddess of knowledge, music, and the arts. The ancient Greeks referred to the nine Muses as sources of human creativity, thought to inspire not only poets but also scientists and mathematicians. Their influence may be thought to involve a kind of possession. In Plato's dialogue *Ion*, Socrates describes the poet as 'unable to create until he [*sic*] becomes inspired and frenzied, his mind no longer in him'. Socrates argued that no one 'can compose or chant or prophesy' if they are not so possessed.

While eschewing much of its religious connotations, today's popular conception of creativity still echoes the ancient view of inspiration as a sudden flash of insight, a 'eureka' moment. That description of the creative moment comes from the legend surrounding Archimedes, a 3rd-century Syracusan, discovering a key to the principle of buoyant force. As author of many inventions such as the hydraulic screw, Archimedes had been asked by King Hiero to determine whether a crown was made with an admixture of inferior metals. Sitting in the baths, a solution suddenly dawned on Archimedes: that he could compare the density of objects through their respective displacement of water. He leapt from the baths shouting 'eureka!' or 'I have found [it]!' It is hard to know whether this legend recorded by the architect Vitruvius two centuries after Archimedes' death bears any historical truth. Yet it is reasonable to surmise that such solutions as Archimedes sought emerged in recognition of an analogy between distinct ideas simultaneously considered.

We might better understand creativity by acknowledging the lived context in which it emerges, or creativity as 'situated transcendence' as I termed it in *The Life of Imagination* (2018). For creativity emerges from and transforms a lived experiential situation that involves a whole cognitive ecology, or embodied, enactive situation in which the cognitive experience occurs. Although Vitruvius partly attributes Archimedes' inspiration to the Muses (as was conventional), he also points out that the inventor had spent many years in mathematical contemplation. The mathematician had frequently applied his expertise to the surrounding world—from figuring out how to best strengthen the city walls against invasion to attempting to reckon how many grains of sand might fit into the known universe. More than merely putting two ideas together, Archimedes in the eureka moment would have been stimulated by a physical context in which he considered his problem—his body submerging in water sparking an analogous recognition—along with a wide background of knowledge from different domains and a long-practised habit of problem-solving. The eureka moment, though apparently arising from nowhere, in fact arises from a whole cognitive ecology conducive to creative thought.

While the view of inspiration as a sudden flash from nowhere persisted for a long time in Western thought, by the 18th century, philosophers began to resist the convention of attributing artists' inspiration to an external source. Although in *Critique of Judgment* he described the artistic genius as the 'mouthpiece of nature', Kant also thought that the artist must attend to natural objects of beauty and attempt to create works based on their form through laborious practice.

> Hence this form is not, as it were, a matter of inspiration or of a free momentum of the mental powers; the artist is, instead, slowly and rather painstakingly touching the form up in an attempt to make it adequate to his thought while yet keeping it from interfering with the freedom in the play of these powers.

The genius is one who, giving expression to nature, can create exemplary works through gradual improvement. Kant recognized that this requires a particular exercise of cognitive faculties, balancing freedom and form through cognitive play.

It is striking that, according to Kant, genius cannot be wholly explained or consciously controlled. The genius 'cannot describe or indicate scientifically how it brings about its products', for the creator 'does not know how he [*sic*] came by the ideas for it; nor is it in his [*sic*] power to devise such products...or by following a plan, and to communicate...to others in precepts that would enable them to bring about like products'. Inspired genius, Kant thought, does not follow a formula, and cannot be taught.

Everyday and exceptional creativity

While Kant is referring to exemplary creativity, the same faculties may be at work in everyday creativity, as 20th-century theorists of cognition began to recognize. In *Art as Experience* (1934), the American philosopher John Dewey described how the human propensity to creativity shapes our perceptions and arises from ordinary everyday life. Through creativity, Dewey argued, human beings express our need to make '*an* experience' that is 'unified and total' out of the flow of experience in general. For example, through religious rituals, preparing special meals, designing gardens, planning travel adventures, giving toasts, or celebratory events, we shape experiences that stand out and are distinguished from the ordinary flow of life. This occurs through variation from ordinary habits as well as the imposition of new constraints that work to shape experiences.

The arts express a more refined channelling and curating of this everyday creativity. For example, rather than flowing unrestricted and randomly, sound is given temporal and tonal structure through music, and thereby distinguished from the background noise. Through painting, colour and shape and visual detail are made to stand out from visual perception in general. In dance, movement of the human body is cultivated. In literature, we not only communicate with words but thereby conjure imagined worlds. Such creativity enhances and curates the processes of everyday life.

The idea that creativity is not an extraordinary phenomenon but continuous with everyday thinking was further pursued by Arthur Koestler in *The Act of Creation* (1964). Examining experiences ranging from the arts and sciences to telling jokes, Koestler argued that 'bisociation is the essence of creativity', in that it brings together different frameworks of thinking, cognitive skills, or patterns of rule-governed thought or activity in a sudden fusion. Koestler described creativity as the connective association of ideas from two unrelated matrices of thought, creating a new matrix. This process could involve comparing matrices, abstracting elements from them, categorizing them, or drawing analogies and metaphors between them.

Creativity has been identified as the very core of human cognition. Building on Koestler's theory, Giles Fauconnier and Mark Turner, in *The Way We Think* (2002), proposed to explain creativity through the notion of 'conceptual blending'. According to this theory the mind comes up with new ideas by blending two disparate concepts together in a third mental space of application. On this view, Archimedes would have integrated distinct concepts (themselves results of conceptual blends): displacement of water by the body and the relation of one metal to the mass of the whole, projected onto the new mental 'space' of the crown to be assessed. Yet the theory holds that conceptual blending or integration occurs not only in the conscious efforts of heightened creativity, but as an unconscious process underlying all human thinking.

Other theorists have argued that human thinking is intrinsically creative because it relies upon resources that go beyond logical or empirical comparison. As discussed in the previous chapter, metaphor allows for the creation of meanings irreducible to the elements of comparison. For Ricoeur, metaphor expresses the productive imagination and operates not only in literary and artistic works, but in scientific models and political theory. Yet metaphor may form a dimension of everyday thinking as well. In their works *Metaphors We Live By* (1980) and *Philosophy in the Flesh* (1999), George Lakoff and Mark Johnson argue that metaphor arises in transference from primal bodily experiences (such as feeling 'up' or 'down', 'warm' or 'cold', 'balanced' or 'imbalanced'), and that such primal metaphors give rise to conceptual thinking. In *Surfaces and Essences: Analogy as the Fuel and Fire of Thinking* (2013), the cognitive theorist Douglas Hofstadter and the psychologist Emmanuel Sander argue for the ubiquity of analogy-making within human thought, rejecting the relegation of this skill to relatively rare creative moments. Competing if also resonating with conceptual blending and metaphor-based cognitive theories, Hofstadter and Sander propose analogy as the origin of creativity.

Such theories are valuable in helping to demonstrate how our capacity for innovation expresses an intrinsic feature of the human mind. They suggest that creativity, rather than arriving from a mysterious external source, draws upon facilities that characterize human thinking in general. Yet taken alone such theories may leave important aspects of creative experience unexplained. The recognition of creativity as fundamental to human consciousness does not explain, for example, the proliferation of prospective conceptual blends, metaphors, or analogies in exceptional creativity, or illuminate how this facility comes to be elaborated and directed by some imagining minds but not by others. It remains to be understood how particularly meaningful or innovative new combinations or analogies are distinguished from the potentially random flow of blends, metaphors, or analogies. Such theories also leave unexplained how creativity may direct thought against the grain of cognitive habit. Creativity even in the sciences requires deviation from standard ways of thinking, involving acceptance of risk and potential failure. These go beyond combinational or even metaphorical mechanics and entail attitudes and dispositions that may be emotive and existential in nature.

While creative inspiration appears to evade direct analysis, psychological research has revealed some of the conditions that may nurture creativity. The creativity of young children appears to thrive in relative naivety, declining in adolescence with the refinement of higher reasoning and the acquisition of knowledge. Among adults, in contrast, a wide basis of knowledge is beneficial for creativity, since it supplies ideas from which to make new and meaningful combinations. Further, cross-training or input of ideas from different fields is recognized as a promoter of creativity, enhancing the generation of new useful or meaningful combinations. The fields from which creativity draws may be very far apart. Einstein, for example, claimed that the 'combinatory play' that led to new scientific insights was stimulated when he played the violin. While Kant's view that practice and its 'process of improvement' assist creative production has been substantiated, studies show that over-practice, or an excess of repetition, may stifle it.

One aspect of creativity that has puzzled researchers is its relation to freedom and constraint. Despite his respect for disciplined practice on the part of the genius, the free play of the imagination in aesthetic experience is an important part of Kant's aesthetic theory. The association of imagination with freedom appears to be echoed in Kant's view that the genius can neither explain nor conduct the process of inspiration. Sartre emphasized the imagination's freedom from all worldly circumstances. As free and unformulaic, creativity is spontaneous. One might imagine the creator beginning with a blank page, with no constraints at all on a given project. At the same time, creative thinkers themselves have testified that constraint tends to encourage creativity rather than diminish it.

For example, while modernist avant-garde artists broke with accepted tradition, throwing out many accepted conventions, they also praised the virtues of some formal limitations for creating new works. The French poet Charles Baudelaire revolutionized poetry by rejecting romantic descriptions of beautiful nature and instead turning to the outcasts and refuse of modern urban Paris for his themes. In his revolutionary collection *Les Fleurs du mal* (*Flowers of Evil*) (1857), he described the creative yearning in a poem as a kind of voyage to plumb 'the bottom of the Unknown in order to find something new'. Yet in his essay 'The Salon of 1859', Baudelaire also advised artists not to venture haphazardly away from traditional form. Rules for the production of art, he claimed, 'have assisted the birth of originality', as they respect the human need for some sense of order. Baudelaire thought that the restrictiveness of the formal sonnet, for example, could intensify the bursting forth of an idea.

Similarly, Robert Frost warned of the modern poet's tendency to follow arbitrary associations, leading to mere abstraction from life and inconsequential associations. In 'The Figure a Poem Makes', Frost warned of 'giving way to undirected associations and kicking ourselves from one chance suggestion to another in all directions' like a grasshopper on a hot afternoon. On Frost's view, poetry is most fulfilling when it offers 'a momentary stay against confusion' and this may be aided by aspects of form which are not only restrictive but generative. Of poetic metre, for example, Frost advises that: 'The possibilities for tune from the dramatic tones of meaning struck across the rigidity of a limited metre are endless.'

The Russian composer Igor Stravinsky also praised constraint as necessary for art, despite his own radical contributions to avant-garde music. In his *Poetics of Music* (1942), Stravinsky claimed that:

> The more that art is controlled, limited, worked over, the more it is free... In art as in everything else, one can build only upon a resisting foundation: whatever constantly gives way to pressure, constantly renders movement impossible... My freedom thus consists in my moving about within the narrow frame that I have assigned to myself for each one of my undertakings...

Stravinsky's respect for creative constraint is all the more striking when we consider the intensity of his innovations in modern music. His ballet *The Rite of Spring* provoked a riot at its 1913 premiere in Paris. The audience was scandalized not only by the jerky, awkward, or erotic movements of the dancers of Diaghilev's Ballets Russes but by the harsh primitivist sounds and the intense dissonance of the score. T. S. Eliot wrote of Stravinsky's work that he had made music from the 'barbaric cries of modern life' and its 'despairing noises'.

Jazz music, based on unscripted improvisation, perhaps best epitomizes the play between freedom and constraint in creative thinking. Jazz, traditionally dispensing with reliance on written scores, historically emerged from an early 20th-century black American culture striving for freedom from societal oppression, and is thus culturally as well as artistically associated with freedom. In discussing jazz, which served as the motif for her novel of that title, Toni Morrison wrote that 'imagination fosters real possibilities'. Yet despite its innovative freedom, the improvisation fundamental to jazz relies upon established practice, mastery of techniques, and deviation from standards long familiar. Improvisational performance is enabled by its characteristic call and response among musicians, who inspire one another by generating an ongoing collaborative framework for innovative nuance, unfolding in real time.

Advances within the jazz genre can also illuminate the relationship between freedom and the constraints of artistic foundations. With his album *Kind of Blue* (1959), Miles Davis advanced a new musical direction, that of modal jazz. Working with the music theorist George Russell, Davis shifted the basis for improvisation from chord changes to scales or modes. Combinations were almost limitless, allowing for extraordinarily inventive expression. Yet the expansive freedom invoked by modal jazz was enabled by the new parameters—playing 'in the sound' of a given set of scales, as the album's pianist Bill Evans formulated it. *Kind of Blue* catalysed the evolution of jazz music and is regularly cited as the most successful jazz album ever recorded.

Cognitive play

The collaboration of freedom and form, standard practice and innovation that characterizes jazz music is captured in the notion of cognitive play, about which we can find some insight from aesthetic theory. Like much insight into imagination, the notion of cognitive play first came to prominence with Kant's aesthetics. We have seen that for Kant, artistic creativity along with receptive aesthetic experience involves the free play of cognitive powers. This idea was expanded by the German writer Friedrich Schiller towards a theory of the creative impulse of the human mind, or a theory of play. In his work *On the Aesthetic Education of Man in a Series of Letters* (1795), Schiller adapts Kant's ideas towards a social aesthetic of play.

Schiller suggests that human activity is directed by three interrelated instincts or 'drives', those of sense, form, and play. Schiller understands the modern human spirit as suffering an opposition between sense and form—or between intuition of the material, changing temporal world, and the formal measure associated with timeless laws. Schiller argues that the specialized rationality of modern life has fractured the 'inner unity of human nature', thus alienating these orientations from each other. Unchecked, the intuitive and free imagination squanders the fruits of rational thinking, while the abstract tendencies of understanding stifle imaginative vitality.

In play, however, these impulses come together in dynamic and productive activity. What Schiller calls the 'play drive' allows for a unification of these diverging orientations. Play generates 'living form' as we may find expressed in dynamic aesthetic experiences. As examples we might now think of the open choreography of modern dance, the improvisational play of jazz, interactive theatre, or imaginative children's play with surrounding objects as examples of reconciling sensuous or material spontaneity with the need for form. In *Aesthetic Education*, Schiller claims that it is 'precisely play and play alone, which in every human condition makes human beings whole and unfolds both sides of their nature at once'. Anticipating Winnicott's thesis on the necessity of play for a true sense of oneself, Schiller argued that play is the basis for a unified self, and makes us fully human.

The concept of play was further developed by the German philosopher Hans-Georg Gadamer. In his *Truth and Method* (1960), Gadamer conceives play as a relation between an activity and its participants (a game and its players, for instance), that is undertaken for its own sake, and manifests as a phenomenon that can be shared. In this sense, play is not simply a subjective enjoyment but a communicative activity. Since it takes shape through a manifest or objective event, play in this sense is equivalent to expressive creativity.

While creative play makes us most human, it also connects us with nature. In creative play we freely take up the stuff and experience of the material world and give it shape or form. Gadamer likens human play, including the play of words in literature, to the appearance of play in nature, such as the play of light, of waves, or of wind in the trees. Both human and elemental play are conceived as primal movements of energy. Human play is neither merely subjective (taking place wholly in the mind of the individual) nor wholly objective, but a living worldly exchange. Echoing Dewey's theory of art as the demarcation of *an* experience from its general flow, play as such becomes *a* play when its energy is shaped by form to create a representation for others.

Like play more generally, cognitive play entails both freedom and constraint, spontaneity and work, fluidity and form, while exposing new prospective directions for creative thought. The idea of cognitive play is important for understanding why neither knowledge nor practice, while important, are sufficient in themselves to ensure the generation of creative ideas. It also indicates why creativity is not only a matter of combining old ideas, but requires shifting the grooves of ordinary ways of thinking. When contemporary cognitive theorists try to explain creativity as a combinatory process, they tend to acknowledge randomness or chance as an element in the emergence of fruitful ideas. Yet it may be that cognitive play encourages the occasion of new prospects, for which the mind must be both open to and able to elaborate valuable, unexpected potentialities.

Negative capability, defamiliarization, curiosity, and wonder

Creativity consists not only of combinatory cognitive skill, but also requires a disposition of openness to possibility and an elaborative engagement of a given context. Through cognitive play, creativity invites new ideas that may, in turn, also shift our perspective on what we know. This entails that, in order to be creative, we must be tolerant of, or even invite, the cognitive or aesthetic discord new ideas introduce, which may expose existing knowledge or practices as incomplete, limited, or in need of revision. While creativity can benefit from wide or deep knowledge and from formal or material constraints, it also requires tolerance for unknowing, for that which lies beyond expectation or the grasp of established knowledge or practice.

This crucial aspect of creativity was famously addressed in the English poet John Keats's notion of 'negative capability', which he defined as the ability, necessary for creative genius, to abide in 'uncertainties, mysteries, and doubts'. Keats found a model of negative capability in Shakespeare, in that the writer's expansive examination of human experience was undertaken with explorative depth and in acceptance of ambiguities not fully understood. In contrast, Keats chided the more established poet Coleridge for looking too much to philosophy for a universal certainty. Keats charged that one could not be open to discovery if one were 'incapable of remaining content with half-knowledge'. Too-fixed ideas were, he thought, incompatible with aesthetic experience. The wonder one might take in beauty, for example, did not demand explanation, for it 'overcomes every other consideration, or rather obliterates all consideration'.

For Keats negative capability meant, further, suspending the need for rationalization or factual verification, ceasing to appropriate the world to one's own established idea of truth, in favour of an intensely empathetic and varied perception. This may mean upsetting habitual perception and its assumptions, and an openness to surprising influences. We might find a visual illustration in van Gogh's *Starry Night* (1889), in which the artist depicted the summer skyscape above a Provençal town. In the previous chapter we referred to how a painting of a landscape might enable 'iconic augmentation' of its subject matter, a generation of meaning achieved through abridgement, or selection of the boundaries of the frame, and condensation, or intensification of the relations within it. We can see this in how van Gogh's work, with visionary empathy, depicts the stars in vital

9. Vincent van Gogh, *The Starry Night* (1889), Museum of Modern Art, New York.

and explosive movement, the moon in riotous glow (Figure 9). The sky appears as if communing with a human habitation almost swallowed up by nature in the form of undulating fields and cypress trees curling upward like dark flames. Merleau-Ponty thought that van Gogh's work showed how life is 'not shut up in the depths of the mute individual but diffused through all he sees'. At the time of its composition, the painting was a radical departure from conventional artistic representation of nature, and its first viewers found it unsettling.

The large morning star depicted in the painting represents what van Gogh could see from his asylum window where he temporarily resided towards the end of his life. Yet with its wave-like cloud currents and rolling fields, the painting may have also been inspired by the Japanese artist Katsushika Hokusai, in whose book of colour prints—including the famous *The Great Wave Off*

10. Katsushika Hokusai, *The Great Wave off Kanagawa*, woodblock print from *Thirty-Six Views of Mount Fuji* (1831).

Kanagawa (c.1829–33)—van Gogh had taken a keen interest. Van Gogh shaped his vision of the sky cresting over the hills with the same intense motility as Hokusai's magnificently curving wave, which threatens to overwhelm boats in the Sagami Bay and dwarfs Mount Fuji (Figure 10). Among many aspects of van Gogh's accomplishment was his recognition in the skies above not of a cold and distant otherworldly space or a distance as would be measured by astronomers, but of fluid nature with momentum and vitality, suggesting an intuition of an interconnected and dynamic universe.

For van Gogh's contemporaries, *Starry Night* was distressing for the unnatural liberties it took with its subject matter and for the intense emotion it expressed. Van Gogh's brother Theo was anxious about Vincent's poor mental health, and therefore praised (in his correspondence) van Gogh's more conventionally naturalist landscapes while passing over the more strikingly innovative work in silence. Even the painter himself worried that in the kind of abstraction in *Starry Night*—'stars too big, &c'—he had trodden on 'enchanted ground', taking a risk after a 'life of searching, of fighting hand-to-hand with reality'. Van Gogh died a year after painting *Starry Night*, having sold only a single painting in his lifetime. Yet after 71 of his paintings were exhibited at a retrospective in Paris in 1901, van Gogh would be recognized as the father of Expressionist painting and a key founder of modern art. Van Gogh's negative capability consisted in pursuing an original vision of the world and a radically new form of painting beyond the bounds of established sense and artistic practice.

Related to negative capability expressed in van Gogh's radical depiction of the night sky is the idea of defamiliarization. The Russian art theorist Viktor Shklovsky wrote of the 'defamiliarization' of the everyday in modern art, which it effected by diverging from expectations and prolonging the process of perception as the viewer faced an unfamiliar rendering of the world. Instigated by van Gogh among other innovators, modernist artists suspended what had been accepted as realist depiction. Expressionist painting highlighted a more intense and intuitive form of perception—with bold movement and explosive, sometimes incongruous, colour. Cubist painting sought not merely to fragment the look of the ordinary world but to reveal its availability to multiple perspectives. Surrealism challenged everyday appearances by blending depictions of recognizable things with illogical images to provoke raw feeling and dream-like associations.

Looking at things in an unfamiliar way may call our ordinary understanding of them—our cognitive habits—into question. Merleau-Ponty wrote that in modern painting it is towards a truer revelation of the world 'that its ordinary ties are broken'. But this departure from expectation is not merely a matter for art history or aesthetics. For with modern physics too the human intellect came to understand reality not as absolutely measurable in fixed terms but as defined by our ways of interacting with it. From a cultural perspective, the breakdown of appearances in modernist painting bears some analogy to a modern vision of reality itself.

In her acceptance speech for the Nobel Prize, the Polish poet laureate Wisława Szymborska paid tribute to the ideas of negative capability and defamiliarization in calling for an appreciation of astonishment. She argued that the task for the creative thinker is not merely to defeat the unknown, but to allow it to upset our usual expectations. Szymborska described how astonishment challenges the self-evident appearance of the ordinary world:

> What astonishment really exposes is that for all our acquisition of knowledge, all the comfortable familiarity we may have achieved, the world itself is anything but obvious.

Despite its divergence from a path of reasoning and fact, astonishment may be important for paradigm-shifting discovery even in the sciences. Szymborska cited Marie Curie and Isaac Newton as examples of scientists open to astonishment. In *The World as I See It* (1934), Einstein affirmed tolerance of the unknown or as he puts it, 'the mysterious'. For Einstein wonder at the mysterious 'is the fundamental emotion which stands at the cradle of true art and true science'. It befits a scientific outlook, he thought, to consider the highest achievements of the human mind as but 'an inkling of the marvelous structure of reality'.

Yet if the negative capability, defamiliarization, and astonishment associated with creative thinking suspend a need for rationalization, such dispositions may be in tension with curiosity, or the desire for knowledge. In their defence of rationality, some philosophers have regarded wonder with ambivalence, as did Descartes in his treatise *On the Passions of the Soul* (1649). He defined wonder as an effect of surprise on the soul that arises suddenly, provoked by novel and extraordinary phenomena. In a state of wonder we experience an interruption of previous expectation and a pause for inquisitive reflection. Descartes warned that excessive wonder may neutralize curiosity, or even 'entirely block or pervert the use of reason'. Yet wonder can motivate the pursuit of knowledge and so stimulate scientific study, as Descartes himself did in studying rainbows. Descartes exercised imaginative as well as rational cognition in demonstrating that the rainbow could be analysed through the principles of mathematics.

Wonder may initiate creativity, since it strikes us with difference from what we already know, our horizons of expectation thereby exposed, our cognitive habits for a moment suspended, our sense of possibilities awakened. As I discussed in *The Ecstatic Quotidian* (2007), artists and writers have noticed how the world as we experience it is vulnerable to such transformation. Rilke's poem 'Archaic Torso of Apollo' from his *New Poems* (1907) illustrates this kind of provocation. The poem describes an ancient Greek sculpture the poet came upon in the Louvre during a stay in Paris. Rilke's speaker feels existentially confronted by the fragmentary statue of the god Apollo, as it touches him with extraordinary power.

As the poem tells us, there is much the speaker cannot know about the original statue or the god it once represented. For it is but a fragment: 'we cannot know his legendary head', the poem begins. Yet, gazing at the artwork, the speaker is astonished by its sensuality, perfection, and vitality, and comes to feel gazed at in turn. In Rilke's famous final lines, the speaker feels to be directly addressed in the encounter: 'There is no place that does not see you. | You must change your life.' This unmistakably existential directive issues from the statue as if it opened a window to another world, a world that, gazing back upon the speaker, awaited a creative response. Rilke's poem of course does not tell the speaker, or the reader for that matter, what to do in changing a life, how to make the change, or even why. The provocation invites imagination in the contemplation of possibilities with which readers must engage if they are to answer the demand of the poem. The viewer of the Apollo statue and implicitly the reader of the poem are provoked not only to experience astonishment, but to creatively elaborate it.

While in Rilke's 'Archaic Torso of Apollo' this directive appears exceptional, a glance at some of the other experiences described in the *New Poems* suggests the latent wonder available to ordinary moments of life. We find the speaker of these poems fascinated by the rose window in a cathedral, a black cat, a blind woman making her way through a café, a panther at the Jardins du Luxembourg, an apple orchard viewed just after sunset, the glance of a dog from the perspective of which the speaker imagines its world taking shape. Just as creativity relies upon the mechanisms of everyday cognition, so too are we in everyday moments potentially vulnerable to wonder which may provoke a creative response.

Creativity not only contributes to human innovation but also has existential significance, and is an important ingredient in human happiness. Despite the stereotype of creative thinkers as suffering artists, contemporary psychological research shows that undertaking creative activities enhances feelings of well-being. This may be because through creativity we can stimulate what philosophers have called the 'feeling of life' in imagination's free play. Creativity reminds us of our own possibilities, and with its contribution to shaping our experience, promotes human flourishing.

We began this chapter by considering examples of creative expression that concretely manifest the metaphor of imaginative flight. We have seen that while inspiration sets creative moments apart from everyday experience, creativity draws from the same resources that subtend everyday thinking. Cognitive play describes diversion from habitual paths of thinking, connecting freedom and constraint, knowledge and openness to the not yet known. Negative capability and defamiliarization foster tolerance for the not yet fully understood, and wonder may stimulate shifts in ordinary thinking and spark our creative response. Creativity makes manifest and expressive the imagination that enlivens and liberates human thinking and supports our apprehension of a meaningful world.

References

Chapter 1: What is imagination?

Blaise Pascal, *Pensées* (New York: Dutton, 1958 [1669]), p. 82.

Samuel Johnson, *The History of Rasselas, Prince of Abissinia* (London: Cassell & Co., 1889 [1759]), p. 167.

Wallace Stevens, *The Necessary Angel: Essays on Reality and the Imagination* (New York: Alfred A. Knopf, 1951), p. 13.

Seamus Heaney, *The Redress of Poetry* (New York: Farrar, Straus and Giroux, 1995), pp. 3, 2.

Albert Einstein, 'What Life Means to Einstein', Interview with George Sylvester Vierack, *Saturday Evening Post* (October 1929), p. 117.

Albert Einstein and Leopold Infeld, *The Evolution of Physics* (London: The Scientific Book Club, 1938), p. 95.

Elizabeth Blackburn, 'Why Beauty is So Important to Us', *The New York Times*, Turning Points 2020: <https://www.nytimes.com/interactive/2019/12/07/opinion/elizabeth-blackburn-why-is-beauty-important.html>.

David Hume, *A Treatise of Human Nature*, ed. L. A. Selby-Bigge (Oxford: Clarendon, 1896 [1739]), p. 24.

Immanuel Kant, *Critique of Pure Reason*, trans. Paul Guyer and Alan W. Wood (Cambridge: Cambridge University Press, 1998 [1781]), A141:B180–1.

Gilbert Ryle, *The Concept of Mind* (New York: Routledge, 2009 [1949]), pp. 224–5.

Jean-Paul Sartre, *The Imaginary: A Phenomenological Psychology of Imagination*, trans. Jonathan Webber (London and New York: Routledge, 2004 [1940]).

Chapter 2: Imagination in human evolution

For background on human cognitive evolution see Steven Mithen, 'The Evolution of Imagination: An Archeological Perspective', *Substance*, issue 94/95 vol. 30 nos 1–2 (2001), 28–54; Robin Dunbar, *The Human Story: A New History of Mankind's Evolution* (London: Faber and Faber, 2005); Peter Gärdenfors, *How Homo Became Sapiens: On the Evolution of Thinking* (Oxford: Oxford University Press, 2003); R. Dale Guthrie, *The Nature of Paleolithic Art* (Chicago: University of Chicago Press, 2005); Christopher Collins, *Paleopoetics: The Evolution of the Preliterate Imagination* (New York: Columbia University Press, 2013); and chapter 2 of Jennifer Gosetti-Ferencei, *The Life of Imagination: Revealing and Making the World* (New York: Columbia University Press, 2018).

D. W. Winnicott, *Playing and Reality* (London: Tavistock, 1971), p. 67.

Paul L. Harris, *The Work of Imagination* (Oxford: Blackwell, 2000).

Maurice Merleau-Ponty, *The World of Perception*, trans. Oliver Davis (London and New York: Routledge, 2004), p. 74.

For background on animal imagining see Anthony D. Pellegrini and Peter K. Smith, eds, *The Nature of Play: Great Apes and Humans* (New York: Guilford Press, 2005); and Robert W. Mitchell, *Pretending and Imagination in Animals and Children* (Cambridge: Cambridge University Press, 2011).

Chapter 3: From divine madness to cognitive power

Plato, *Republic, vols. I and II*, trans. Paul Shorey, Loeb Classical Library (Cambridge, Mass. and London: Harvard University Press and William Heinemann, 1942). Citations are from 598b, 601b–c, 603a.

Plato, *Statesman, Philebus, Ion*, trans. Harold North Fowler, Loeb Classical Library (Cambridge, Mass. and London: Harvard University Press and William Heinemann, 1925). Citations are from *Philebus*, 39b, 39e.

Aristotle, *On the Soul, Parva Naturalia, On Breath*, trans. W. S. Hett, Loeb Classical Library (Cambridge, Mass.: Harvard University Press, 2000). Citations are from *On the Soul*, 428a2–3, 428a16, 427b20, 429a4, 431a17–18, 431b 4–5, 431b6–9.

Miguel de Montaigne, *Essays in Ten Volumes*, trans. Charles Colton, ed. William C. Hazlett (New York: Edwin C. Hill, 1910 [1580]), citation vol. 1 p. 214.

William Shakespeare, *The Complete Works*, 2nd edition, ed. John Jowett et al. (Oxford: Oxford University Press, 2005). Citations are from *A Midsummer Night's Dream*, Act I Scene 5, and *Richard II*, Act I Scene 3.

René Descartes, *Discourse on Method and Meditations on First Philosophy*, trans. Donald A. Cress (Indianapolis: Hackett, 1998 [1637/1641]), pp. 19, 22, 28, 22.

David Hume, *Enquiries Concerning Human Understanding*, ed. Tom L. Beauchamp (Oxford: Oxford University Press, 1999 [1748]), p. 124.

Hume, *A Treatise of Human Nature*, p. 259.

Chapter 4: The productive and aesthetic imagination

Immanuel Kant, *Anthropology from a Pragmatic Point of View*, ed. Robert B. Louden (Cambridge: Cambridge University Press, 2006 [1798]), p. 7:153.

Kant, *Critique of Pure Reason*, p. A120.

Immanuel Kant, *Critique of Judgment*, trans. Werner S. Pluhar (Indianapolis: Hackett, 1987 [1790]), pp. 242, 314, 315.

Edmund Burke, *A Philosophical Enquiry into the Origin of Our Ideas of the Sublime and the Beautiful*, ed. J. T. Boulton (London: Routledge and Kegan Paul, 1958 [1757]), p. 57.

Kant, *Critique of Judgment*, pp. 255, 259, 262.

Jean-François Lyotard, *Lessons on the Analytic of the Sublime*, trans. Elizabeth Rottenberg (Stanford, Calif.: Stanford University Press, 1994).

Samuel Taylor Coleridge, *Biographia Literaria, The Collected Works of Samuel Taylor Coleridge vol. 7*, ed. James Engell and W. Jackson Bate (Princeton: Princeton University Press 1985 [1817]), p. 295.

Samuel Taylor Coleridge, *Letters vol. I*, ed. Earl Leslie Griggs (Oxford: Clarendon, 1959), p. 354.

William Wordsworth, *The Prelude, 1799, 1805, 1850: Authoritative Texts, Context and Reception, Recent Critical Essays*, ed. Jonathan Wordsworth, M. H. Abrams, and Stephen Gill (London and New York: Norton, 1979). Citation is from the 1799 version, lines 121–9.

Friedrich Hölderlin, *Hyperion and Selected Poems*, ed. Eric L. Santer (New York: Continuum, 1990), p. 189.

Friedrich Schlegel, *Philosophical Fragments*, trans. Peter Firchow (Minneapolis and London: University of Minnesota Press, 1991), pp. 70–1, 39, 95.

Friedrich Nietzsche, *The Birth of Tragedy: Out of the Spirit of Music*, trans. Shaun Whiteside (London and New York: Penguin Classics, 1993), p. 18.

Friedrich Nietzsche, 'On Truth and Lies in a Nonmoral Sense', in *Philosophy and Truth: Selections from Nietzsche's Notebooks of the Early 1870s*, ed. and trans. Daniel Breazeale (Amherst, NY: Humanity Books, 1999), p. 86.

Friedrich Nietzsche, *Philosophy in the Tragic Age of the Greeks*, trans. Marianne Cowan (Washington, DC: Regnery, 1962), p. 40.

Chapter 5: The augmentation of reality

Ludwig Wittgenstein, *Philosophical Investigations*, trans. P. M. S. Hacker and Joachim Schulte (Oxford: Blackwell, 2009 [1953]), p. 193.

P. F. Strawson, 'Imagination and Perception', in *Freedom and Resentment and Other Essays* (New York: Routledge, 2008 [1974]), p. 58.

Wittgenstein, *Philosophical Investigations*, pp. 200, 205.

Stephen. M. Kosslyn, *Image and Mind* (Cambridge, Mass.: Harvard University Press, 1980).

Edward S. Casey, *Imagining: A Phenomenological Study*, 2nd edition (Bloomington: Indiana University Press, 2000).

William James, *Principles of Psychology* (New York: Henry Holt and Company, 1890/1950), p. 58.

Vladimir Nabokov, *Lectures on Russian Literature* (New York: Harcourt, 1981).

William H. Gass, *Fiction and the Figures of Life* (New York: Albert Knopf, 1970).

Maurice Merleau-Ponty, 'Eye and Mind', in *The Merleau-Ponty Aesthetics Reader*, ed. Galen A. Johnson (Evanston, Ill.: Northwestern University Press, 1993).

Maurice Merleau-Ponty, *The Visible and the Invisible, Followed by Working Notes*, trans. Alphonso Lingus (Evanston, Ill.: Northwestern University Press, 1968).

Jean-Paul Sartre, *Being and Nothingness*, trans. Hazel Barnes (New York: Washington Square, 1992 [1943]), p. 488.

Sartre, *The Imaginary*, pp. 183, 236.

Paul Ricoeur, 'The Narrative Function', in John B. Thompson, ed., *Paul Ricoeur: Hermeneutics and the Human Sciences* (Cambridge: Cambridge University Press, 1979), p. 292.

Stevens, *The Necessary Angel*, p. 65.

Benedict Anderson, *Imagined Communities* (New York: Verso Books, 2006 [1983]).
Hannah Arendt, *The Origins of Totalitarianism* (New York: Harcourt Brace, 1951).
François Jacob, 'Imagination in Art and in Science', trans. Tracy Ryan, *The Kenyon Review* New Series 23:2 (Spring 2001), 113–21, p. 120.

Chapter 6: Creativity from invention to wonder

Plato, from *Ion* in *Statesman, Philebus, Ion*, p. 534b.
Gosetti-Ferencei, *The Life of Imagination*, p. 218.
Kant, *Critique of Judgment*, pp. 312–13, 308.
John Dewey, *Art as Experience* (New York: Capricorn Books, 1934), p. 15.
Arthur Koestler, *The Act of Creation*, p. 231.
Gilles Fauconnier and Mark Turner, *The Way We Think: Conceptual Blending and the Mind's Hidden Complexities* (New York: Basic Books, 2002), p. 18.
Charles Baudelaire, *Les Fleurs du mal/Flowers of Evil*, revised, edited, trans. John E. Tidball (Bishopston Editions, 2016), p. 429.
Charles Baudelaire, from 'The Salon of 1859', in *The Mirror of Art: Critical Studies*, trans. and ed. Jonathan Mayne (New York: Doubleday 1956), p. 241.
Robert Frost, *Collected Prose of Robert Frost*, ed. Mark Richardson (Cambridge: Belknap, 2007), pp. 131, 132, 131.
Igor Stravinsky, *The Poetics of Music in the Form of Six Lessons*, trans. Arthur Knodel and Ingolf Dahl (Cambridge, Mass.: Harvard University Press, 1947 [1942]), pp. 63, 64–5.
Toni Morrison, *The Source of Self-Regard: Selected Essays, Speeches, and Meditations* (New York: Knopf, 2019), p. 320.
Friedrich Schiller, *On the Aesthetic Education of Man in a Series of Letters*, ed. and trans. Elizabeth M. Wilkinson and L. A. Willoughby (Oxford: Clarendon Press, 1967 [1774–75]), p. 107.
Hans-Georg Gadamer, *Truth and Method*, trans. Joel Weisenheimer and Donald G. Marshall (London: Bloomsbury Academic, 2013).
John Keats, in a letter to his brothers of 1817, in *The Complete Poetical Works and Letters of John Keats, Cambridge Edition* (New York: Houghton, Mifflin and Company, 1899), p. 277.
Maurice Merleau-Ponty, *Signs*, trans. Richard McCleary (Evanston, Ill.: Northwestern University Press, 1964), pp. 53, 56.

Vincent van Gogh 'Letter to Emile Bernard', 26 November 1889, in *Painted with Words: Letters to Emile Bernard*, ed. Leo Jansen, Hans Luijten, and Nienke Bakker (New York: The Morgan Library and Amsterdam: Van Gogh Museum, 2007), pp. 339–40.

Viktor Shklovsky, 'Art as Technique', in *Russian Formalist Criticism: Four Essays*, ed. Lee T. Lemon and Marion J. Reiss (Lincoln: University of Nebraska Press, 1965), pp. 3–24.

Wisława Szymborska, Nobel Lecture. NobelPrize.org. Nobel Prize Outreach AB 2022. Tue. 19 July 2022. <https://www.nobelprize.org/prizes/literature/1996/szymborska/lecture/>.

Albert Einstein, *The World as I See It*, trans. Alan Harris (London: John Lane, 1935), pp. 4–5.

René Descartes, *The Passions of the Soul*, trans. Stephen H. Voss (Indianapolis/Cambridge: Hackett Publishing, 1989), p. 59.

Rainer Maria Rilke, 'Archaic Torso of Apollo', in *New Poems, Bilingual Edition*, trans. Stephen Mitchell (New York: Knopf Doubleday, 2013).

Further reading

Brann, Eva T. H., *The World of the Imagination: Sum and Substance* (Savage, Md: Rowman & Littlefield, 1991).

Casey, Edward S., *Imagining: A Phenomenological Study*, 2nd edition (Bloomington: Indiana University Press, 2000).

Collins, Christopher, *Neopoetics: Evolution of the Literate Imagination* (New York: Columbia University Press, 2016).

Currie, Gregory, and Ian Ravenscroft, *Recreative Minds: Imagination in Philosophy and Psychology* (Oxford: Oxford University Press, 2002).

Edelman, Gerald, and G. Tononi, *A Universe of Consciousness: How Matter Becomes Imagination* (New York: Basic Books, 2000).

Fauconnier, Gilles, and Mark Turner, *The Way We Think: Conceptual Blending and the Mind's Hidden Complexities* (New York: Basic Books, 2002).

Gosetti-Ferencei, Jennifer Anna, *The Ecstatic Quotidian: Phenomenological Sightings in Modern Art and Literature* (University Park, Pa: The Pennsylvania State University Press, 2007).

Gosetti-Ferencei, Jennifer Anna, *The Life of Imagination: Revealing and Making the World* (New York: Columbia University Press, 2018).

Hannay, Alastair, *Mental Images: A Defence* (Abingdon and New York: Routledge, 2002).

Hofstadter, Douglas, and Emmanuel Sander, *Surfaces and Essences: Analogy as the Fuel and Fire of Thinking* (New York: Basic Books, 2013).

Husserl, Edmund, *Phantasy, Image Consciousness, and Memory (1898–1925)*, trans. John Brough (Dordrecht: Springer Academic Publishers, 2005).
Iser, Wolfgang, *The Fictive and the Imaginary: Charting Literary Anthropology* (Baltimore: The Johns Hopkins University Press, 1993).
Johnson, Mark, *The Body in the Mind: The Bodily Basis of Meaning, Imagination, and Reason* (Chicago: University of Chicago Press, 1990).
Kandel, Eric, *Reductionism in Art and Brain Science: Bridging the Two Cultures* (New York: Columbia University Press, 2016).
Kearney, Richard, *Poetics of Imagining: Modern to Post-Modern* (New York: Fordham University Press, 1998).
Kind, Amy, and Peter Kung, eds, *Knowledge through Imagination* (Oxford: Oxford University Press, 2016).
Kind, Amy, ed., *The Routledge Handbook of Philosophy of Imagination* (London and New York: Routledge, 2016).
Koestler, Arthur, *The Act of Creation* (London and New York: Penguin, 1964).
Kosslyn, Stephen M., William L. Thompson, and Giorgio Ganis, *The Case for Mental Imagery* (Oxford: Oxford University Press, 2006).
Lakoff, George, and Mark Johnson, *Metaphors We Live By* (Chicago: University of Chicago Press, 1980).
Lakoff, George, and Mark Johnson, *Philosophy in the Flesh: The Embodied Mind and Its Challenge to Western Thought* (New York: Basic Books, 1999).
Lennon, Kathleen, *Imagination and the Imaginary* (New York: Routledge, 2015).
Lewis-Williams, D., *The Mind in the Cave: Consciousness and the Origin of Art* (London: Thames & Hudson, 2002).
Lyons, John D., *Before Imagination: Embodied Thought from Montaigne to Rousseau* (Stanford, Calif.: Stanford University Press, 2005).
Merleau-Ponty, Maurice, *The Merleau-Ponty Aesthetics Reader*, ed. Galen A. Johnson (Evanston, Ill.: Northwestern University Press, 1993).
Modell, Arnold H., *Imagination and the Meaningful Brain* (Cambridge, Mass.: MIT Press, 2003).
Nichols, Shaun, ed., *The Architecture of Imagination: New Essays on Pretence, Possibility, and Fiction* (Oxford: Oxford University Press, 2006).

Paul, Elliot Samuel, and Scott Barry Kaufman, eds, *The Philosophy of Creativity: New Essays* (Oxford: Oxford University Press, 2014).
Ricoeur, Paul, *The Rule of Metaphor* (Chicago: Chicago University Press, 1977).
Ricoeur, Paul, *A Ricoeur Reader: Reflection and Imagination*, ed. Mario J. Valdés (Toronto: University of Toronto Press, 1991, reprinted 2012).
Sartre, Jean-Paul, *The Imagination: A Psychological Critique*, trans. Forrest Williams (Ann Arbor: University of Michigan, 1962).
Sartre, Jean-Paul, *What is Literature? and Other Essays* (Cambridge, Mass.: Harvard University Press, 1988).
Sartre, Jean-Paul, *The Imaginary: A Phenomenological Psychology of Imagination*, trans. Jonathan Webber (London and New York: Routledge, 2004). First published 1940.
Scarry, Elaine, *Dreaming by the Book: On Literary Imagining* (Princeton: Princeton University Press, 1999).
Schultz, Alexander M., *Mind's World: Imagination and Subjectivity from Descartes to Romanticism* (Seattle: University of Washington Press, 2009).
Scruton, Roger, *Art and Imagination* (London: Methuen, 1970).
Sepper, Dennis L., *Descartes's Imagination: Proportion, Images, and the Activity of Thinking* (Berkeley and Los Angeles: University of California Press, 1996).
Sternberg, Robert J., *Handbook of Creativity* (Cambridge: Cambridge University Press, 2008).
Taylor, Marjorie, ed., *Oxford Handbook of the Development of Imagination* (Oxford: Oxford University Press, 2013).
Turner, Mark, *The Literary Mind* (Oxford: Oxford University Press, 1997).
Turner, Mark, ed., *The Artful Mind: Cognitive Science and the Riddle of Human Creativity* (New York: Oxford University Press, 2006).
Turner, Mark, and Gilles Fauconnier, 'A Mechanism of Creativity', *Poetics Today* 20:3 (1999).
Warnock, Mary, 'Imagination in Sartre', *British Journal of Aesthetics* 10:4 (1970), 323–36.
Warnock, Mary, *Imagination* (Berkeley and Los Angeles: University of California Press, 1976).
Weisburg, Robert W., *Creativity: Beyond the Myth of Genius* (Hoboken, NJ: Wiley, 2006).
White, Alan R., *The Language of Imagination* (Oxford: Blackwell, 1990).

Index

For the benefit of digital users, indexed terms that span two pages (e.g., 52–53) may, on occasion, appear on only one of those pages.

D

E

F

G

H

I

DREAMING

A Very Short Introduction

J. Allan Hobson

What is dreaming and what causes it? Why are dreams so strange and often hard to remember?

In this *Very Short Introduction*, J. Allan Hobson provides a new and increasingly complete picture of how dreaming is created by the brain. Hobson offers possible answers to long-held questions on activation, function, and the interpretation of dreams, and reveals how dreaming maintains and develops the mind. As well as investigating the relationship between dreaming, learning, memory, and consciousness, Hobson investigates his own dreams to illustrate and explain some of the fascinating discoveries of modern sleep science.

www.oup.com/vsi

MEMORY

A Very Short Introduction

Michael J. Benton

Why do we remember events from our childhood as if they happened yesterday, but not what we did last week? Why does our memory seem to work well sometimes and not others? What happens when it goes wrong? Can memory be improved or manipulated, by psychological techniques or even 'brain implants'? How does memory grow and change as we age? And what of so-called 'recovered' memories? This book brings together the latest research in neuroscience and psychology, and weaves in case-studies, anecdotes, and even literature and philosophy, to address these and many other important questions about the science of memory - how it works, and why we can't live without it.

www.oup.com/vsi

BEAUTY

A Very Short Introduction

Roger Scruton

In this *Very Short Introduction* the renowned philosopher Roger Scruton explores the concept of beauty, asking what makes an object - either in art, in nature, or the human form - beautiful, and examining how we can compare differing judgements of beauty when it is evident all around us that our tastes vary so widely. Is there a right judgement to be made about beauty? Is it right to say there is more beauty in a classical temple than a concrete office block, more in a Rembrandt than in last year's Turner Prize winner? Forthright and thought-provoking, and as accessible as it is intellectually rigorous, this introduction to the philosophy of beauty draws conclusions that some may find controversial, but, as Scruton shows, help us to find greater sense of meaning in the beautiful objects that fill our lives.

A fascinating book, which I heartily recommend.

Brya Wilson, Readers Digest

www.oup.com/vsi

FAIRY TALE

A Very Short Introduction

Marina Warner

From wicked queens to goblins and giants, glass slippers to poisoned apples, the characters and images of fairy tales have cast a spell over readers for centuries. Few forms of literature have greater power to enchant us and rekindle our imagination than a fairy tale.

In this *Very Short Introduction*, Marina Warner digs into a rich hoard of fairy tales in all their brilliant and fantastical variations, in order to define a genre and evaluate a literary form that keeps shifting through time and history. Drawing on a glittering array of examples, from classics such as Red Riding Hood, Cinderella, and The Sleeping Beauty, to modern-day realizations including Walt Disney's *Snow White*, Warner forms a persuasive case for fairy tale as a crucial repository of human understanding and culture.

www.oup.com/vsi

Chaos
A Very Short Introduction
Leonard Smith

Our growing understanding of Chaos Theory is having fascinating applications in the real world - from technology to global warming, politics, human behaviour, and even gambling on the stock market. Leonard Smith shows that we all have an intuitive understanding of chaotic systems. He uses accessible maths and physics (replacing complex equations with simple examples like pendulums, railway lines, and tossing coins) to explain the theory, and points to numerous examples in philosophy and literature (Edgar Allen Poe, Chang-Tzu, Arthur Conan Doyle) that illuminate the problems. The beauty of fractal patterns and their relation to chaos, as well as the history of chaos, and its uses in the real world and implications for the philosophy of science are all discussed in this *Very Short Introduction.*

> '. . . Chaos . . . will give you the clearest (but not too painful idea) of the maths involved . . . There's a lot packed into this little book, and for such a technical exploration it's surprisingly readable and enjoyable - I really wanted to keep turning the pages. Smith also has some excellent words of wisdom about common misunderstandings of chaos theory . . .'
>
> popularscience.co.uk

www.oup.com/vsi

COMEDY

A Very Short Introduction

Matthew Bevis

What is humour, and how may it be used (or abused)? When do we laugh, and why? What is it that writers and speakers enjoy—or risk—when they tell a joke, indulge in bathos, talk nonsense, or encourage irony?

This *Very Short Introduction* considers comedy not only as a literary genre, but also as a broader impulse at work in many other historical and contemporary forms of satire, parody, and play. Matthew Bevis takes us through the history of comedy, from the work of John Gay and Richard Sheridan in the eighteenth century to twentieth-century dramatists like Ionesco, Brecht and Cocteau, up to present day interpretations of comedy, such as Charlie Kaufman's *Being John Malkovich* and Channel 4's *Peep Show*.

www.oup.com/vsi

CONSCIENCE

A Very Short Introduction

Paul Strohm

In the West conscience has been relied upon for two thousand years as a judgement that distinguishes right from wrong. It has effortlessly moved through every period division and timeline between the ancient, medieval, and modern. The Romans identified it, the early Christians appropriated it, and Reformation Protestants and loyal Catholics relied upon its advice and admonition. Today it is embraced with equal conviction by non-religious and religious alike. Considering its deep historical roots and exploring what it has meant to successive generations, Paul Strohm highlights why this particularly European concept deserves its reputation as 'one of the prouder Western contributions to human rights and human dignity throughout the world.

www.oup.com/vsi

FASHION
A Very Short Introduction
Rebecca Arnold

Fashion is a dynamic global industry that plays an important role in the economic, political, cultural, and social lives of an international audience. It spans high art and popular culture, and plays a significant role in material and visual culture. This book introduces fashion's myriad influences and manifestations. Fashion is explored as a creative force, a business, and a means of communication. From Karl Lagerfeld's creative reinventions of Chanel's iconic style to the multicultural reference points of Indian designer Manish Arora, from the spectacular fashion shows held in nineteenth century department stores to the mix-and-match styles of Japanese youth, the book examines the ways that fashion both reflects and shapes contemporary culture.

'Her fascinating little book makes a good framework for independent study and has a very useful bibliography.'

Philippa Stockley, Times Literary Supplement

www.oup.com/vsi

GENIUS

A Very Short Introduction

Andrew Robinson

Genius is highly individual and unique, of course, yet it shares a compelling, inevitable quality for professionals and the general public alike. Darwin's ideas are still required reading for every working biologist; they continue to generate fresh thinking and experiments around the world. So do Einstein's theories among physicists. Shakespeare's plays and Mozart's melodies and harmonies continue to move people in languages and cultures far removed from their native England and Austria. Contemporary 'geniuses' may come and go, but the idea of genius will not let go of us. Genius is the name we give to a quality of work that transcends fashion, celebrity, fame, and reputation: the opposite of a period piece. Somehow, genius abolishes both the time and the place of its origin.

www.oup.com/vsi

LOVE

A Very Short Introduction

Ronald de Sousa

Erotic love has been celebrated in art and poetry as life's most rewarding and exalting experience, worth living and dying for and bringing out the best in ourselves. *And yet it has excused, and even been thought to justify, the most reprehensible crimes. Why should this be?*

This *Very Short Introduction* explores this and other puzzling questions. Ronald de Sousa considers some of the many paradoxes created by love, looking at the different kinds of love (affections, affiliation, *philia*, *storage*, and *agape*) with a focus on *eros*, or romantic love. He considers whether our conventional beliefs about love and sex are deeply irrational and argues that alternative conceptions of love and sex, although hard to formulate and live by, may be worth striving for.

www.oup.com/vsi